DATE DUE

DEC 27 '66			
APR 18 1978			
MAY 2 1978			
APR 26 1979			
FEB 1 4 1990			
SEP 1 1998			
DEC 1 8 2000			
OCT 0 8 2001			
GAYLORD			PRINTED IN U.S.A.

HARVARD STUDIES IN EDUCATION

PUBLISHED UNDER THE DIRECTION OF
THE GRADUATE SCHOOL OF EDUCATION

VOLUME 16

"THE OLD SACHEM"

A portrait of Jefferson painted by Bass Otis in 1816 at the time he was planning the organization of Central College. In 1816, Jefferson wrote to Dr. William Thornton *(Coolidge Collection, M. H. S.)* with one of his rare touches of humor: "With respect to the merit of Otis's painting I am not qualified to say anything; for this is a case where the precept of 'Know thyself' does not apply. The ladies from the studies of their looking glasses may be good judges of their own faces; but we see ours only under a mass of soap-suds and the scrapings of the razor".

THE EDUCATIONAL WORK
OF THOMAS JEFFERSON

BY

ROY J. HONEYWELL

NEW YORK
RUSSELL & RUSSELL · INC
1964

PRINTED IN THE UNITED STATES OF AMERICA

CONTENTS

x   CONTENTS

LIST OF TABLES

LIST OF CHARTS

LIST OF ILLUSTRATIONS

CHRONOLOGY

1818, August 1–4   Commissioners met at Rockfish Gap
1819, January 25   Central College became the University of Virginia
1819, February 13   Visitor of the University
1819, March 29   Rector of the University
1819, March 29   Committee of Superintendence
1824, January 27   University freed from debt
1825, March 7   University opened
1826, July 4   Died at Monticello, Virginia

INTRODUCTION

THERE are at least three reasons for a study of the educational work and views of Thomas Jefferson. Doubtless the mere interest we all take in the opinions of any prominent man on any subject of common interest is reason enough. But, in the case of Jefferson we have not only a man who gained prominence of the first order in the field of politics, but one who set in motion political and social tendencies which have vitally influenced American life ever since. His educational plans were a very necessary part of his political and social reforms, and his educational ideas were as vital as were his political theories. Add to this the facts that his political opinions were widely disseminated through the South by many agencies but especially through the great university which he established, and that they came to be the guiding principles of that section during the critical years after his death, and we have a larger interest in what he expected to result from the spread among the common people of those principles which he regarded as the fundamentals of Americanism. He was among the foremost advocates of appropriate and progressive education for all, and of that cornerstone of democracy, the American public school. It is unfortunate that his prominence in other fields has tended to obscure the value not only of what he did but of what he proposed for universal education.

In this study quotations have been used frequently. This was primarily because when Jefferson stated an idea it usually was stated well. Moreover, shades of meaning and touches of personality often are conveyed by a man's own words but are lost when another attempts to rephrase his thoughts. When quotations are taken from secondary sources, such as the published writings of Jefferson, they are reproduced as they appear in the source. Some of these writings have suffered from mistakes of editors in reading the original or from attempts to correct real or supposed errors. In another sense they have suffered from the modernizing of the spelling and form of composition. Jefferson, especially in his old age, made mistakes of fact.   In one place he alludes to ten collegiate districts being provided for by his bill of 1779 and in another place to twenty-four.   The real number was twenty.   At times he wrote absent-mindedly, as when he proposed annual elections on February 29. He used a few older forms of spellings, such as "antient," which give his writings a pleasing touch of quaintness.   A few other peculiarities of spelling appear.   The word *knowledge* he spelled in at least three ways, all different from the modern usage, but *knolege* was the usual form.   In one letter he spelled *Priestley* three times with and three times without the second "e."   Among other idiosyncrasies of composition are his habit of beginning sentences without capitals and his erratic use of periods and commas.   In his old age when writing became increasingly painful he used many abbreviations and elisions.   All of these circumstances have interest for the reader who is studying not only the ideas but the personality of Jefferson.   For this reason, when passages are quoted directly from the manuscript they appear exactly as Jefferson wrote them.

It is a pleasure to acknowledge valuable assistance from many sources.   Professor A. O. Norton of Harvard and Welles-ley gave invaluable advice on the formulation and treatment of the subject.   Professor A. M. Schlesinger of Harvard read the manuscript, making many helpful criticisms.   Professor Charles Swain Thomas of Harvard, Professor Malone, Mr. Clemons, Librarian, and Dr. Bruce, Historian, of the University of Virginia, Mr. Jordan of Independence Hall, Philadelphia, Mr. Bayley of the Copley Gallaries, Boston, Mr. Tuttle of the Massachusetts Historical Society, Mr. Tufts of Harvard Library, and Miss Locke of the library of Boston University all have shown a kindness worthy of a more adequate acknowledgment.   Every courtesy has been shown by the libraries of Congress, Harvard and Boston Universities, the University of Virginia, the Massachusetts Historical Society, the American Antiquarian Society, and the City of Boston.   The manuscript was prepared chiefly by the Misses Geraldine Roberts, Ruth Bluestone, and Elsie Pentleton.

R. J. H.

BOSTON
June 20, 1930

THE EDUCATIONAL WORK OF
THOMAS JEFFERSON

CHAPTER I

THE EDUCATION OF THOMAS JEFFERSON

SHADWELL on the banks of the Rivanna was in the midst of a country scarcely touched by the hand of man in 1743 when Thomas Jefferson was born in this frontier home.[1] * Eight years earlier his father, Peter Jefferson, had taken up one thousand acres of land on both sides of the river, and, when he built his house at Shadwell about 1737, was the third or fourth settler in that part of the country.[2] Shadwell was almost at the foot of Monticello, so this part of Virginia had for Thomas Jefferson a lifelong association. In these surroundings the boy lived for two years and again from the age of nine until well into his fifteenth year, so it is not strange that he became fond of hunting and of nature and came later to be a recognized authority on the animals, birds, insects, and flowers of Virginia.[3] As Colonel of Albemarle County, Peter Jefferson had important relations with the Indians, and his hospitality and kindness often brought the red men to Shadwell. Conspicuous among these was Ontassere, the great warrior and orator of the Cherokees. The youthful Jefferson never forgot the awe and admiration roused in him by Ontassere's farewell oration to his people before his departure for England.[4] However, it would be a mistake to suppose that he had contact only with savages and frontiersmen. His mother, a daughter of Isham Randolph, belonged to a noted Virginia family with a long history,[5] and early in the settlement of Albemarle the principal citizens were those who had brought to their new homes all the refinement of manners and high civic spirit that had distinguished eastern Virginia.[6]

In 1745 Peter Jefferson removed to Tuckahoe to become the guardian of the estate and son of his friend William Randolph, and did not return to Shadwell until 1752.[7] At the age of five

* The small superior numbers appearing at frequent intervals in the text refer to books and pamphlets listed in Chapter XII, "Authorities and Sources."

Thomas was sent to the English school and at nine to the Latin school of the Reverend William Douglas of St. James, Northern Parish, Goochland. This Scotch clergyman he describes as a "superficial Latinist, less instructed in Greek,"[8] but from him he learned the rudiments of these languages and of French, and he remained in this school until the death of his father in 1757. Peter Jefferson's education had been neglected, but he was eager for information and improved himself by reading.[9] His library contained the *Spectator,* and the works of Shakespeare, Swift, and Doddridge. Doubtless home reading from such masters of English contributed to what John Adams twenty years later was to characterize as "Mr. Jefferson's incisive style of writing."

Resolved that his son should have better opportunities than he had enjoyed, Peter Jefferson left instructions for his further education; and, after the father's death in 1757, Thomas went to the school of the Reverend James Maury, formerly rector of Fredericksville Parish, Louisa County, who conducted the most famous school in the vicinity of Shadwell.[10] This clergyman was "a correct classical scholar," educated at William and Mary, a Whig of Huguenot ancestry and of broad views.[11]

Jefferson's earliest known letter has a peculiar interest as showing at the same time some notable views on educational values and the stirrings of that zest for learning which was to lure him into so many fields of scholarship. It was written to his guardian during his seventeenth year:

To John Harvey at Bellemont.

Shadwell, January 14, 1760.

Sir:—I was at Colo. Peter Randolph's about a Fortnight ago, and my schooling falling into Discourse, he said he thought it would be to my Advantage to go to the College, and was desirous I should go, as indeed I am myself for several Reasons. In the first place, as long as I stay at the Mountain, the loss of one-fourth of my Time is inevitable, by Company's coming here and detaining me from School. And likewise my Absence will in a great measure, put a Stop to so much Company, and by that Means lessen the Expenses of the Estate in Housekeeping. And on the other Hand by going to the College, I shall get a more universal Acquaintance, which may hereafter be serviceable to me; and I suppose I can pursue my Studies in the Greek and Latin as well there as here, and likewise learn something of the Mathematics. I shall be glad of your opinion, And remain, Sir, Your most humble servant,

Thomas Jefferson.[12]

Ten weeks later he entered the College of William and Mary.[13]

During the two years of his college career Jefferson came into close contact with two men who exercised a far-reaching influence upon his life. One was Dr. William Small of Scotland, Professor of Mathematics and Acting Professor of Philosophy. He made the youth his daily companion and kindled in him that love for learning which endured to the end of his life.[14] Through him Jefferson became intimate with George Wythe, a prominent lawyer, and with Governor Fauquier, an able, refined, and cultured gentleman. From the conversation of these men, who habitually made him the fourth member of their circle, the youthful Jefferson learned much of lasting worth. In particular, from Dr. Small he gained a conception of the scope of philosophy, from Mr. Wythe of the great principles of politics, and from Governor Fauquier of the refinements of society and of music.[15] Through Dr. Small's influence Jefferson, after his graduation in 1762, was admitted to the law office of George Wythe and for five years he continued the study of law. In 1767 he began practice before the general court, still under the guidance of his eminent friend.[16]

Of Jefferson's interests as a student reliable records are few. Before his college days he had excelled in swimming and riding [17] and at the end of his first year in college he felt remorse for spending too much on dress and horses.[18] He was a member of a fraternity, founded in 1750, and known as the "Flat Hat Club." [19] When he entered college the students were rowdy, and he seems for a time to have entered into the spirit of his associations. Doubtless this reflects the inexperience of youth and the deference with which the back-country boy regarded the social usages of the eastern counties. He gives the credit for his rescue from this bad living to Dr. Small, Mr. Wythe, and Peyton Randolph, whom he carried constantly in his mind as models of integrity and judgment.[20] In his old age Jefferson said that Dr. Small was to him as a father to whom he was indebted for everything, and that, when he returned to Europe in 1762, he "filled up the measure of his goodness to me by procuring for me from his most intimate friend, George Wythe, a reception as a student of law under his direction. . . . Mr. Wythe continued to be my faithful and beloved Mentor in youth and my most affectionate friend through life." [21] *   This strong and affectionate language indicates more than the gratitude of an apt pupil for faithful instruction in philosophy and law. The penetrating Scotchman saw in the undeveloped youth an intellectual power worth cultivating and a moral value worth saving.   While he was leading him into the greatness of science and philosophy he was bringing him under the unnoticed influence of his own urbanity and sturdy character.   Before he left the country he arranged for a continued association of the immature student with his most intimate and trusted friend which should continue through Jefferson's most formative years.   His success in this greatest of a teacher's purposes we see in the picture of Jefferson during the latter part of his college career, studying fifteen hours a day, with only the diversion of a swift evening run into the country and back to his books,[22] and in his lasting respect for these two great friends and their ideals.

Extensive reading in a large and well-chosen library and association or correspondence with eminent men of Europe and America helped to make Jefferson a recognized master of subjects as diverse in nature as Anglo-Saxon and architecture or politics and plows.   His first library was lost with the burning of his Shadwell home in 1770.   He estimated the cost of these books at £200 sterling, and especially regretted the loss of his books on the Common Law and of all his papers.[23]   For the next forty-five years he was building up a choice collection of rare and valuable works on every subject, but especially of those relating to America.   His residence in France gave him the opportunity to select many books which could not have been found at home.[24]   The manuscript catalogue of this library is dated March 6, 1783.   It contains a large number of classified titles, indicating those which he then possessed and those he intended to procure.   Different ink indicates many additions after the first draft of this catalogue, and partial erasures seem to show that in some way he disposed of a considerable number of books which he at some time had possessed.   A total of 2640 volumes is entered where a previous notation had been erased.   Many of these works were in French or Latin.   Some were in Greek

* Wythe was a signer of the Declaration of Independence and was established at William and Mary as the first professor of law in America by Jefferson in 1779. Heatwole, *Education in Virginia*, 91.

or Spanish, and a few were in other languages.[25] This library was sold to Congress in 1815. At that time it contained 6487 volumes, many of them folios, for which he was paid $23,950.[26] While it contained works on virtually every subject, those on history and philosophy are especially prominent.[27] At his death he left nearly one thousand volumes which were sold by his executor. Among them were the standard histories in which he long had found delight.[28] Many of these works were bought for him in Europe by George Ticknor from 1816 to 1819.[29] *

Jefferson's religious views seem to have been influenced by reading the works of Bolingbroke some time after 1764, and his attitude toward primogeniture and entail can be traced, through his commonplace Book, to Sir John Dalrymple's *Essay Toward a General History of Feudal Property*, to Francis Stoughton Sullivan's *An Historical Treatise of the Feudal Laws and the Constitution of the Laws of England*, and to Lord Kames' *Historical Law Tracts*.[30] In his seventeenth year Jefferson met Patrick Henry. During the years that followed he awoke in Jefferson a revolt against ecclesiastical oppression which led to the Bill for Religious Freedom and the spirit of resistance to all oppression which culminated in the Declaration of Independence.[31] These seem to have been among the most conspicuous influences in shaping the character or views of Thomas Jefferson during his most formative years.

He was repeatedly honored by the learned societies and colleges. In 1790 he was elected a member of the American Academy of Arts and Sciences. From 1797 to 1815 he was president of the American Philosophical Society,[32] and he was one of the first members of the American Antiquarian Society.[33] He advocated the affiliation of local societies with a central academy at the national capital to aid in the publication of information and to promote useful emulation.[34] William and Mary conferred upon him the honorary degree of Doctor of Laws in 1782, and he received the same degree from Yale in 1786, from Harvard †
and Brown in 1787, and from Princeton in 1791.[35] He accepted

---

* Some of these books were bought from a New York dealer. Jefferson ordered them sent "one volume at a time and a week apart so as not to load our weekly mail." Manuscript letters to J. L. F. Gelone, May 6 and July 21, 1817, *Coolidge Collection, M. H. S.*
† In the chronology accompanying his edition of Jefferson's *Autobiography* Paul Leicester Ford states that this degree was conferred on June 20, 1788, but the records of the Harvard Corporation show that it was voted "at a meeting of the President and Fellows of Harvard College, April 10, 1787."

the honor from Yale with courteous expressions of appreciation.[36]   The title became him as much as it did Dr. Franklin or
others who have borne it most worthily.   In spite of his later
antipathy to honorary degrees as empty forms of social or political adulation there is a peculiar fitness, after his retirement from
politics, in the designation—"Dr. Jefferson."

CHAPTER II

A SYSTEM OF PUBLIC EDUCATION

THE revolution in Virginia, launched by back countrymen under such leaders as Patrick Henry, was as much a revolt against the political and social system which made a privileged class of the Tidewater aristocrats as it was against the oppression of Lord Dunmore and his royal master. Since the days of Nathaniel Bacon the small farmers and frontiersmen of the back country had felt themselves wronged by the wealthy plantation owners of the eastern counties. Maintained by slave labor and intrenched in the legal system of the colony, this aristocracy long had dominated both church and state. Nearness to the seat of government, leisure for politics, and disproportionate representation in the colonial assembly accomplished the latter, while a law establishing the Church of England, compelling contributions from Anglicans and dissenters alike, and permitting severe penalties for heresy, stifled religious freedom. A law of primogeniture caused the great estates to descend unimpaired to the eldest sons, and entails often so restricted them that they could not be alienated nor attached for debt. A complex body of laws prescribed the death penalty for felony and imposed severe and cruel punishments for the lesser offenses. These were the more conspicuous of the evils which Patrick Henry and his associates felt must be reformed in order that the Revolution might bring democracy to Virginia.[1]

The triumph of the radical party in Virginia, the Declaration of Independence, and the adoption of a state constitution with broad guarantees of private rights paved the way for a further reform movement. The author of the great Declaration with his broad legal training and studious habits naturally superseded the poorly educated Henry as the radical leader in legal reform. Against this movement there soon arose a powerful

7

opposition, friendly to the Revolution but attached to some part of the old order such as slavery or the established church. These conservatives were led by strong men like Edmund Pendleton and Robert Carter Nicholas.[2]

Early in the autumn of 1776 Jefferson retired from Congress and took up the struggle in the Virginia legislature.   In October he introduced a bill abolishing entail, and in nine days it was the law of the state.[3]   At the same time he introduced bills for the naturalization of foreigners on easy terms, for the establishment of civil courts, for the removal of the capital from Williamsburg to Richmond, thus making it more accessible to people in the western counties, and for a general revision of the laws.[4] The latter passed late in October, and the legislature promptly chose Jefferson, Pendleton, Wythe, Mason, and Lee as a committee to draft the revision.   Mason and Lee, not being lawyers, declined to serve, so Jefferson and his two associates apportioned the work among them.   Early in 1779 they met and together went over what each had done, making such changes that all could agree upon the proposals to be reported to the legislature.[5] In June the committee presented their recommendations in the form of 126 bills.   Among them were bills to establish religious freedom, to abolish primogeniture, to humanize the criminal code, to establish elementary and intermediate schools, and to reorganize William and Mary College.   The bill on slavery was to be amended to provide for the gradual emancipation of the slaves, their colonization, and the importation of free laborers to take their places.[6]   These were Jefferson's especial projects. The bill for religious freedom and that abolishing primogeniture soon were enacted.   The *Bill for the More General Diffusion of Knowledge* which was to provide primary and secondary schools for all the people was long delayed, but Jefferson always regarded it as an essential part of these reforms, without which they would be neither permanent nor effective.   In 1813 he explained the interdependence of his principal reform projects in a letter to John Adams:

> At the first session of our legislature after the Declaration of Independence, we passed a law abolishing entails.   And this was followed by one abolishing the privilege of primogeniture, and dividing the lands of intestates equally among all their children, or other representatives.   These

laws, drawn by myself, laid the axe to the root of pseudo-aristocracy. And had another, which I proposed, been adopted by the legislature, our work would have been complete. It was a bill for the more general diffusion of learning. This proposed to divide every county into wards of five or six miles square, like your townships, to establish in each ward a free school for reading, writing, and common arithmetic, to provide for the annual selection of the best subjects from these schools, who might receive at the public expense a higher degree of education at a district school, and from these district schools to select a certain number of the most promising subjects, to be completed at a university where all the useful sciences should be taught. Worth and genius would thus have been sought out from every condition of life, and completely prepared by education for defeating the competition of wealth and birth for public trusts.[7]

He added that the law of religious freedom had put down the aristocracy of clergy and restored freedom of mind, the abolition of entail had nurtured an equality among men, and the school system would have raised the mass of the people to the moral status necessary to good government and security. He held that no nation can be ignorant and free in a state of civilization and that the only safe guardians of liberty are a free press and an intelligent and reading people.[8]

Before the Revolution there were a few "old field" schools in Virginia. For the most part these were as unproductive as the abandoned lands on which they commonly were built. Teachers were licensed by the Bishop of London, whose diocese included Virginia, or by the governor on recommendation of the county courts. The only support came from fees arranged between teachers and parents, and the only supervision was the trifling attention given by the county justices.[9] A few grammar schools, like that of Mr. Maury, and the services of private tutors, offered meagre and often temporary opportunity to the sons of well-to-do Virginians to gain a grounding in Latin and in a few other subjects. William and Mary College, limited in faculty and curriculum, offered equally meagre opportunities for higher education.[10] There was virtually no coördination between the elementary schools and the grammar schools and very little between these and the college. The elementary school did not prepare for the grammar school, nor did this prepare for the college as well as did private tutors. The college graduate was not prepared for any profession, unless the ministry of the Church of England, nor was he well prepared for the learning of a profession nor for the usual career of a Virginia planter.[11]   Moreover, the cost of this education placed it beyond the reach of the poor.   The parents of children in the elementary schools paid all costs.[12]   When Jefferson attended Mr. Maury's school in 1757 tuition and board were £20 per year.[13]   In 1779 a student at William and Mary could attend the classes of two professors for 1000 pounds of tobacco or three for 1500.[14]   Under the Two Penny Act this would have been worth £8, 6s., 8d. and £12, 10s. respectively, Virginia money.[15]   Lotteries had been employed to raise school funds, but these were forbidden in 1779 unless authorized by a special act of the legislature.[16]

In June, 1779, a few days after his election as governor by that body, Jefferson submitted to the legislature of Virginia his *Bill for the More General Diffusion of Knowledge.**   It had been drafted by him alone, but was a part of the revised code reported with the full approval of Pendleton and Wythe.[17] Under this notable plan the state was to be divided into districts five or six miles square, called wards or hundreds.   In each ward was to be established a free elementary school to teach reading, writing, and arithmetic.   The reading books were to be such as would acquaint the students with the main facts of Greek, Roman, English, and American history, and any general plan of reading and instruction recommended by the visitors of William and Mary should be followed.   This was intended to bring the fundamentals within the reach of every boy and girl in Virginia.   Every September the boy of greatest promise in each school among those whose parents could not afford to give them further education was to be selected by the local visitor and sent to the grammar school for one or more years of free instruction.

These grammar schools, academies, or colleges, as they were variously called, were to be established one in each of twenty great districts into which the state was to be divided.   The boys sent up from the ward schools were to remain for one year.   At the end of that time one third of their number who showed least ability after careful examination should be discontinued as public foundationers.   At the end of the second year all should be discontinued except the one of greatest ability, who might

* The full text of this bill will be found in Appendix A.

remain for four more years at public cost and should be known as a senior. "By this means twenty of the best geniuses will be raked from the rubbish annually," wrote Jefferson.[18] In alternate years half the districts of the state were to select each its senior of best ability who should go to William and Mary to be educated, boarded, and clothed for three years at public expense. In this manner half of the "best geniuses" would be discontinued at the end of six years with the training appropriate for grammar school masters. The other half, chosen for their superiority, should go forward to additional training for still higher forms of service. The ultimate result, as Jefferson saw it, would be to teach all children reading, writing, and arithmetic; to select annually ten boys of superior genius, well taught in Greek, Latin, geography, and higher arithmetic; to select ten of still higher ability who should add to these branches such sciences as their genius might lead them to, and to furnish schools, where the children of the wealthy might be educated at their own expense, thus providing educational opportunities adapted to every one's needs. The quest of genius among the poor was "to avail the state of those talents which Nature has sown as liberally among the poor as the rich, but which perish without use if not sought for and cultivated." [19]

In order that those seeking the higher education might have greater freedom to follow their scholarly interests and to fit themselves for other learned professions than that of divinity, a separate bill to amend the charter of William and Mary was offered.[20] * This provided for a much smaller board of visitors, free from all control by English church or laws, for a larger faculty, a broader curriculum, and a more certain financial support. Another brief bill made provision for a public library, not as an adjunct to the college, but to be located in Richmond for the free use of all comers.[21] *

Thus broadly did Jefferson plan, in the midst of the struggle for independence, for the education of all the people in his great state, which at that time included West Virginia, Kentucky, western Pennsylvania, and a great wilderness beyond the Ohio. The plan as a whole was intended to meet the present need and to be easily adapted to changing conditions. The academy dis-

* Appendix A.

tricts in the thickly settled eastern counties approached uniformity in size and population.   They were laid out with careful consideration both of the hindrances and the helps to travel and were intended to be permanent.   Beyond the Blue Ridge these districts were larger, consisting in most cases of two or three Valley counties, already well advanced in population, and a large but sparsely settled area to the west.   This made possible higher education for the youth of a frontier region which could not maintain academies for itself.   With the growth of population these eastern counties would naturally separate from the West, forming districts of normal size, in many cases with an academy already centrally located.   The western counties would be grouped into districts of appropriate size by such successive reorganizations as the increase of population should warrant.   These great western districts with their academies and the bulk of their population far to the east resembled the state as a whole, extending from the Atlantic to the Mississippi, but with its reorganized college in the midst of the Tidewater counties.   When Jefferson proposed to locate the state library in Richmond he may already have foreseen the day when the center of higher education for Virginia should move west from Williamsburg.

Jefferson never lost his enthusiasm for a general education for all the people.   In his old age his anxiety to see a progressive university firmly established led him temporarily to cease his exertions for the common schools and to oppose for the time being the creation of district academies, but this was because others had taken up the advocacy of common schools, and because private academies were in a measure meeting the need for intermediate schools at the time.   He felt that any plan which could then be adopted would waste the scanty educational funds of the state, leaving little to aid the University, then in a very critical position.   Moreover, the other schools had other advocates, but the university movement would probably have failed had he not worked until he saw it securely established.[22]

In 1786 he wrote from Paris to George Wythe, his colleague on the committee of revision:

I think by far the most important bill in our whole code is that for the diffusion of knowledge among the people.   No other sure foundation can be devised for the preservation of freedom and happiness.   Preach, my dear

Sir, a crusade against ignorance. Establish and improve the law for educating the common people. . . . The tax which will be paid for this purpose is not more than the thousandth part of what will be paid to kings, priests, and nobles who will rise up among us if we leave the people in ignorance.[23]

Earlier in the same year he had written to General Washington:

It is an axiom in my mind that our liberty can never be safe but in the hands of the people themselves, and that, too, of the people with a certain degree of instruction. This is the business of the state to effect, and on a general plan.[24]

I do most anxiously wish to see the highest degree of education given to the higher degrees of genius [he wrote in 1795] nd to all degrees of it, so much as may enable them to read and understand what is going on in the world and keep their part of it going on right.[25]

Fifteen years later he wrote to the governor of Virginia (after stating that he was through with politics):

I have indeed two great measures at heart without which no republic can maintain itself in strength. 1. That of general education to enable every man to judge for himself what will secure or endanger his freedom. 2. To divide every county into hundreds of such size that all the children of each will be within reach of a central school in it.[26]

About the time that Jefferson drew his great bill to establish elementary schools (September, 1817), enlarged the next month to provide also for higher education, his writings are full of his enthusiasm for general education—"Enlighten the people generally, and tyranny and oppression of body and mind will vanish like evil spirits at the dawn of day";[27] "If the condition of man is to be progressively ameliorated, as we fondly hope and believe, education is to be the chief instrument in effecting it." [28]

After three years of struggle for a university during which Jefferson's opponents had accused him of seeking to provide privileges for the few at the expense of the many, he wrote that he had suggested the first plan for general education in the state more than forty years before and never had proposed to sacrifice the primary schools to higher institutions.[29] At the height of the legislative struggle for the University he urged his friends to work for the primary schools as well as for a university, declaring that of the two he would rather abandon the latter because it is safer to have all the people moderately enlightened than a few highly educated and the many in ignorance.[30] Within a few days, however, he was convinced that it would be better for the friends of the University to avail themselves of the temporary discredit brought upon the public-school movement by the extravagant proposals of some of its supporters until the University should be secure, then to come forward heartily as patrons of the primary schools.[31]

Jefferson's plan for a system of schools remained before the Virginia legislature for many years. Even when modified by others, acting without his express approval, it was still regarded as his plan. Near the end of 1786 Madison wrote to Jefferson, then in Paris, that the bill on education had undergone an indulgent consideration, that the chief objection to it had been the inability of the country to bear the expense, and that it seemed well to let it lie until a plan could be devised to lessen this objection.[32] Earlier in the same year Jefferson had written to Washington the suggestion that the passage of the bill for the more general diffusion of knowledge would make unnecessary the charity schools which Washington was thinking of founding by the gift of shares in the Potomac and James river companies.[33] He hoped that these shares might help establish a good seminary if public education could be otherwise provided for.[34] At the next session of the legislature the bill passed two readings by small majorities but was not pushed to a third. All felt the necessity of a systematic provision for general education, but this plan was opposed because it was expected to incur an expense beyond the ability of the people to pay, to be difficult of execution in the sparsely settled parts of the state, and because of the inequality of the academy districts in the west.[35] In 1796 that part of the bill which provided for elementary schools became a law, but left the county courts power to determine whether it should be put in operation or not. Jefferson believed that this provision defeated it because, as the schools were to be supported by a general tax, the wealthy justices would be unwilling to incur this expense for the education of the poor.[36] Norfolk seems to have been the only county in which schools were started.

Free schools maintained by private charity for the benefit of the poor had long been common in Virginia. As early as 1780 "certain escheated lands" in Kentucky County were given by the state for schools in that county. On January 12, 1802, the glebe lands were taken from the churches and, with the plate of deserted churches, forfeited, unclaimed, and deserted lands, could be sold by the county for the benefit of "free" schools. As free schools were for the poor, these funds were to be administered by the county overseers of the poor.[37]   In October, 1809, Jefferson was the guest of Governor Tyler, a zealous supporter of his educational bill thirty years before. In December the Governor sent to the legislature a message urging some provision for public education. The result was the establishment of the Literary Fund on February 8, 1810. All funds accruing to the state from forfeitures, escheats, and similar sources were to be devoted to public education. Dr. Bruce suggests that Jefferson's visit to Governor Tyler was the cause of his message to the legislature.[38]   This gains color from Jefferson's letter to the Governor seven months later in which he discusses his educational plans as a familiar subject between them.[39]   It is significant that Joseph C. Cabell, for many years Jefferson's faithful supporter in the legislature, was a member of the committee which prepared the bill establishing the Literary Fund.[40]   Jefferson later pronounced the Literary Fund "a solid provision," but advocated an additional tax to maintain the primary schools.[41]

Happenings of an apparently accidental character gave new life to Jefferson's interest in schools and started him upon a project for the active promotion of general education which quickly became his all-absorbing interest and was terminated only by his death.

One day in the spring of 1814 while riding through Charlottesville he was called into the meeting of the trustees of Albemarle Academy and asked to advise them. His interest and knowledge of educational questions led to his immediate election as a member of this board and the request of his associates that he prepare a plan for the actual establishment and organization of their long-projected school. This he did, and set forth his ideas in his famous letter to his nephew Peter Carr, president of the board, dated September 7, 1814.[42] *   As this is primarily a plan for intermediate and higher education, he discusses elementary schools only in an incidental way, but he opens that discussion with this characteristic sentence: "It is highly interesting to our country and it is the duty of its functionaries to provide that every citizen in it should receive an education proportioned to the condition and pursuits of his life."

He adds that there are two classes of citizens—the laboring and the learned. The former need elementary education for life and the latter as a foundation for more advanced work. He refers to his plan of ward schools with confidence, and alludes to the law of 1796 as "an ineffectual expedient." With this letter he sent a petition of the trustees of Albemarle Academy to the legislature, asking certain appropriations and the reorganization of the institution as Central College, and the draft of a bill to make these changes. He did not lose the opportunity to include an amendment to the law of 1796 transferring from the Court of Albemarle to the trustees or visitors of Central College authority to establish elementary schools in the county:[43]

The reason is obvious: The members of the court are the wealthy members of the counties; and as the expenses of the schools are to be defrayed by a contribution proportioned to the aggregate of other taxes which every one pays, they consider it as a plan to educate the poor at the expense of the rich. It proceeded, too, from a hope that the example and good effects being exhibited in one county, they would spread from county to county, and become general.[44]

This provision was stricken out of the bill reorganizing Albemarle Academy,[45] and Jefferson failed in this attempt to institute in his home county and largely under his supervision and control the plan of primary schools in which he had such confidence but which he saw slight opportunity to establish throughout the state.

Three years were occupied in obtaining funds for Albemarle Academy and having it transformed into Central College. Jefferson's school plan was before the legislature during this period, but it was opposed largely on the ground that it would entail a heavy expense. To meet this objection and to adapt the plan to the changes of forty years, he drew a new bill for elementary

* Appendix E.

schools in 1817.   This he sent to Cabell on September 9 with a letter stating his plans for a system of schools and his views on legal style with a delightful humor:

I promised you that I would put into the form of a bill my plan of establishing the elementary schools, without taking a cent from the literary fund. I now send you the result. If twelve or fifteen hundred schools are to be placed under one general administration, an attention so divided will amount to a dereliction of them to themselves. It is surely better, then, to place each school at once under the care of those most interested in its conduct. In this way the literary fund is left untouched to complete at once the whole system of education, by establishing a college in every district of about eighty miles square, for the second grade of education, to wit: languages, ancient and modern, and for the third grade a single university, in which the sciences shall be taught in their highest degree.

I should apologise, perhaps, for the style of this bill. I dislike the verbose and intricate style of the modern English statutes, and in our Revised Code I endeavored to restore it to the simple one of the ancient statutes, in such original bills as I drew in that work. I suppose the reformation has not been acceptable, as it has been little followed. You, however, can easily correct this bill to the taste of my brother lawyers, by making every other word a "said" or "aforesaid", and saying everything two or three times over, so as that nobody but we of the craft can untwist the diction, and find out what it means; and that, too, not so plainly but that we may conscientiously divide, one half on each side. Mend it, therefore, in form and substance to the orthodox taste, and make it what it should be; or, if you think it radically wrong, try something else, and let us make a beginning in some way, no matter how wrong; experience will amend it as we go along, and make it effectual in the end.[46]

He advised that this bill should not be known as coming from him lest any opposition which it might arouse should react to the injury of Central College.[47]   With only slight modifications it was included in the *Bill for Establishing a System of Public Education** which he sent to Cabell on October 24 to aid in the opposition to a plan urged by Charles Fenton Mercer of Loudoun County which proposed to establish one university, four colleges (besides the three then in existence), twenty-five academies, and primary schools throughout the state.   These were to be supported by the Literary Fund, but Jefferson declared the funds in hand would not meet the requirements of Mercer's bill in a century.[48]   Mercer proposed to augment the fund with the profits of a system of twenty-three Literary Fund

* Appendix H.

banks to be capitalized about one third from the Literary Fund and two thirds from the sale of stock.[49]   Two years earlier Mercer had brought about a great increase in the Literary Fund by obtaining the appropriation to the fund of a large sum owed to Virginia by the federal government.   At the same time he obtained a resolution calling for a plan for "an university, colleges, academies, and such schools as will diffuse the benefits of education throughout the commonwealth." [50]   At that time Cabell reported that Mercer was much pleased with Jefferson's views on education as embodied in his letter to Peter Carr and that he intended to coöperate with Mercer, making this plan the basis of their measures.[51]   The governor, as president of the directors of the Literary Fund, asked advice of Jefferson in the preparation of the plan required by Mercer's resolution.   As the governor was none other than his old friend Wilson C. Nicholas, Jefferson gave this advice the more freely.   In his letter of April 2, 1816,* he called attention to his plan of 1779 and his letter to Peter Carr.[52]   The report was presented on December 10, 1816, and seems to have been very little influenced by Jefferson, for it stated that existing plans for primary schools had failed because "no revenue was set aside; schools were made to depend on funds to be extracted directly from the people." [53]

The bill embodying Mercer's plan passed the House of Delegates, January 7, 1817, by a ten to one vote but was defeated in the Senate by Jefferson's friends.   On February 15 Mercer offered a substitute which was opposed by Cabell and his associates because it would locate the university in the Valley and would give the western counties a disproportionate influence in the state Board of Public Instruction.   This bill included a modification of some of Jefferson's principles, for it divided the state into townships and gave free instruction to white children whose parents were not able to pay.   It passed the House, but, after Cabell had failed to amend it to name Charlottesville as the site of the university, it was defeated in the Senate by a tie vote.[54]   By 1817 Mercer was recognized as the champion of the West, advocating centralized control and indirect support, while Jefferson, through his supporters in the legislature, was equally

* Appendix G.

recognized as the foremost advocate of local control and support.

That part of Jefferson's bill of 1817 which applied to primary schools did not differ radically from that of 1779. It made less detailed provision for the location of schoolhouses and the breaking of tie votes and omitted the opening discussion of the value of popular education. It provided much more carefully for the collection of labor or money taxes for the erection or repair of schoolhouses and of contributions of money or provisions for the support of teachers. The earlier plan had authorized the voters of the county to elect three aldermen who should supervise the erection or repair of schoolhouses. The aldermen were to appoint an overseer for every ten schools and he should choose the teachers and superintend their work. In 1817 it was proposed that the judge of the Superior Court should appoint three visitors for the county who should choose and supervise the teachers, subject to an appeal to the judge. The voters of the ward should elect a warden who should have charge of the erection and repair of schoolhouses and of the collection of taxes for school purposes.[55] The later bill also provided that no minister of the gospel could serve as a visitor, that citizenship be withheld from the illiterate, and that any ward unduly burdened for the education of poor children might receive aid from the county.[56]

In his letter of October 24 accompanying his *Bill for Establishing a System of Public Education* Jefferson had written:

However, take it, and make of it what you can, if worth anything. Communicate it also to Mr. Rives, if you please. I meddle no more with it. There is a time to retire from labor, and that time is come with me. It is a duty as well as the strongest of my desires to relinquish to younger hands the government of our bark, and resign myself, as I do willingly, to their care.[57]

Nevertheless, the great legislative battle of the following winter, led by his faithful lieutenant, Joseph C. Cabell, was rightly recognized as the last as it was the greatest of his efforts to establish his whole system of education in his native state. Though he received constant reports of the doings of the legislature from Cabell and wrote several letters in the interest of Central College, only once was he induced to take up again the discussion of the primary schools. This was in answer to the objection that his plan of ward schools would be unpopular because it laid a direct tax upon the people.[58] In a long letter to Cabell he showed that by his plan the primary schools ought not to cost more than one fifth of the general tax at that time being paid to the state by property owners and less than one tenth what parents then had to pay to give their children the same grade of education.[59] *

In December, 1817, Cabell had sent to Mr. Scott of Richmond, chairman of the Committee of Schools and Colleges, copies of the bills recently received from Jefferson, with the omission of some passages which might arouse hostility.[60] † It was his hope that this would influence the school bill to be prepared by the committee.[61] When the bill appeared it was very disappointing to the advocates of Jefferson's plan.[62] On February 5, at Cabell's instance,[63] Samuel Taylor, of Chesterfield, offered Jefferson's bill in the House of Delegates as a substitute for the committee's bill and had it printed for distribution.[64] On February 11 the House rejected Jefferson's bill but adopted a substitute offered by Mr. Hill of King William which provided only for the education of the poor.[65] Jefferson's attitude is shown in his letter of February 15 to Albert Gallatin. He described his general plan, and added:

> But it has to encounter ignorance, malice, egoism, fanaticism, religious, political, and local perversities.[66]

The next day he wrote to Cabell:

> I believe I have erred in meddling with it at all, and that it has done more harm than good. A strong interest felt in the subject, and through my whole life, ought to excuse me with those who differ from me in opinion, and should protect me against unfriendly feelings. Nobody more strongly than myself, advocates the right of every generation to legislate for itself, and the advantages which each succeeding generation has over the preceding one, from the constant progress of science and the arts.[67]

The reply to this letter brought unexpected news:

> The school bill came up in the Senate in the form of Mr. Hill's amendment. We engrafted upon it a provision for an university. In that shape it passed here by a majority of fourteen to three. This important vote took place yesterday. The bill has gone back to the House of Delegates,

* See Appendix I.   † See Appendix H.

an attempt has been made to postpone it, and lost by an immense majority. . . . I tremble with anxiety for the great result I anticipate.[68]

These anticipations were justified, and the bill became a law on February 21. It appropriated $45,000 annually from the Literary Fund for the education of poor children and $15,000 for the University, and it directed that from five to fifteen commissioners, appointed by the court, should have charge of the schools in each county.[69]

The enactment of this law can be said to be a triumph for Jefferson's plan for primary schools only in the particular that it took from the courts the discretion left them by the law of 1796 and made the appointment of commissioners compulsory. His friends accepted a system of schools for the poor in which they did not believe in order to get the University established. He always believed it to be both inefficient and wasteful, and more than once urged an attempt to remedy its defects. In 1820 he wrote:

Would it not have a good effect for the friends of the University to take the lead in proposing and effecting a practicable scheme of elementary schools? To assume the character of friends, rather than the opponents, of that object? The present plan has appropriated to the primary schools $45,000 for three years, making $135,000. I should be glad to know if this sum has educated one hundred and thirty-five poor children? I doubt it much. And if it has, they have cost us $1,000 a piece, for what might have been done with $30. Supposing the literary revenue $60,000, I think it demonstrable that this sum equally divided between the two objects would amply suffice for both. One hundred counties divided into about twelve wards each, on an average, and a school in each ward, of perhaps ten children, would be 1,200 schools, distributed proportionably over the surface of the State. The inhabitants of each ward, meeting together, (as when they work on the roads,) building good log houses for their school and teacher, and contributing for his provisions, rations of pork, beef, and corn in the proportion, each of his other taxes, would thus lodge and feed him without feeling it, and those of them who are able, paying for the tuition of their own children, would leave no call on the public fund, but for the tuition fee of here and there an incidental pauper who would still be fed and lodged with his parents. Suppose this fee $10, and $300 apportioned to a county on an average, (more or less duly proportioned) would there be thirty such paupers for every county? I think not. The truth is that the want of common education with us is not from our poverty, but from the want of an orderly system. More money is now paid for the education of a part, than would be paid for that of the whole if systematically arranged. . . . Do then, dear sir, think of this and engage our friends to take in hand the whole subject. It will reconcile the friends of the elementary schools, (and none is more warmly so than myself,) lighten the difficulties of the University, and promote in every order of men the degree of instruction proportioned to their condition and to their views in life. It will combine with the mass of our force a wise direction of it, which will insure to our country its future prosperity and safety.[70]

Three months later he wrote urging the suspension of the primary schools for a year or two while a remedy for their defects was being devised, in a letter intended to be shown to members of the legislature, for the purpose of obtaining the primary school funds for the University.[71] * The next year he expressed himself still more incisively:

> An act of our legislature will inform you of our plan of primary schools, and the annual reports show that it is becoming completely abortive and must be abandoned very shortly, after costing us to this day $180,000 and yet to cost us $45,000 a year more until it shall be discontinued, and if a single boy has received the elements of common education, it must be in some part of the country not known to me. Experience has but too fully confirmed the early predictions of its fate.[72]

Three years later he wrote to Cabell, urging the need for more detailed reports on the operation of the primary school law in order that the public might know the quantum of education provided in each county each year. He suggested one month of schooling for each pupil as the unit for this report, and sent a sample of the tabular form to be required and a resolution to be introduced into one branch of the legislature "to be moved by some member in nowise connected with us; for the less we appear before the House, the less we shall excite dissatisfaction." [73] A year later, within five months of his death, we find him again writing to his faithful lieutenant: "I hope you have not lost sight of the annual tabular report of the primary schools, necessary as a preliminary to perfect that branch of the general system of education." [74]

Although Jefferson did not intend the university or academies of his plan to be open to girls, he did recognize the need of their education. This he intended to go beyond the purely elementary stage, but he had no theories about it which were signifi-

* Appendix A.

cantly different from the generally accepted ideas of his time. His plan for ward schools always provided that girls should attend on the same terms as boys.   His first proposal, in 1779, was ten years before Boston allowed girls in the public schools.[75] To his daughter Martha in her twelfth year, while under the instruction of Mrs. Hopkinson, he suggested the following division of time:

> From 8 to 10 practise music.
> From 10 to 1 dance one day and draw another.
> From 1 to 2 draw the day you dance, and write a letter next day.
> From 3 to 4 read French.
> From 4 to 5 exercise in music.
> From 5 till bedtime read English, write, etc.

He further advised her to be careful of spelling and neatness of clothing and to learn to draw.   Answering a troubled question from the little girl, he assured her that the best preparation for death would be never to do a bad thing and faithfully to obey her conscience.[76]   Many years later he answered a request for advice on education and books for girls [77] by explaining that he had given little consideration to female education except that of his own daughters with a view to their educating their own daughters, or even sons if necessary.   To this he added:

> A great obstacle to good education is the inordinate passion prevalent for novels and the time lost in that reading which should be instructively employed.   When this poison infects the mind, it destroys its tone and revolts it against wholesome reading.   Reason and fact, plain and unadorned, are rejected.   Nothing can engage attention unless dressed in all the figments of fancy, and nothing so bedecked comes amiss.   The result is a bloated imagination, sickly judgment, and disgust toward all the real business of life.   This mass of trash, however, is not without some distinction; some few modelling their narratives, although fictitious, on the incidents of real life, have been able to make them interesting and useful vehicles of a sound morality. . . .   For a like reason, too, much poetry should not be indulged.   Some is useful for forming style and taste.   Pope, Dryden, Thompson, Shakespeare, and of the French, Molière, Racine, the Corneilles, may be read with pleasure and improvement.

He further recommended French, because it was the language of the general intercourse of nations and because extraordinary advances had made it the depository of all science.   The ornaments and amusements he considered proper—for a girl, dancing, drawing, and music.   He approved the French rule that no lady dance after marriage, because of the physical risks of motherhood, and denominated drawing as an innocent amusement, sometimes useful.[78]

Even the negro had a place in Jefferson's plan.   The report of the revisers in 1779 contemplated the manumission and education of slaves.[79]   In 1791 Banneker, the colored astronomer, sent the manuscript of his first almanac * to Jefferson, who wrote in reply:

> Nobody wishes more than I do to see such proofs as you exhibit that Nature has given to our black brethren talents equal to those of the other colors of men, and that the appearance of a want of them is owing only to the degraded condition of their existence both in Africa and America — I have taken the liberty of sending your almanac to Monsieur de Condorcet, Secretary of the Academy of Sciences at Paris, and member of the Philanthropic Society, because I consider it a document to which your whole color has a right for their justification against the doubts which have been entertained of them.[80]

The public library came to have a place in Jefferson's plan as a means of civic and general education for those lacking better opportunities.   In answer to a letter asking his advice regarding a newly founded library, he wrote:

> The people of every country, are the only safe guardians of their own rights, and are the only instruments which can be used for their destruction. And certainly they would never consent to be so used were they not deceived.   To avoid this they should be instructed to a certain degree.   I have often thought that nothing would do more extensive good at small expense than the establishment of a small circulating library in every county, to consist of a few well-chosen books, to be lent to the people of the country under such regulations as would secure their safe return in due time.   These should be such as would give them a general view of other history, and particular view of that of their own country, a tolerable knowledge of geography, the elements of Nature, Philosophy, of Agriculture, and Mechanics.[81]

Later in the year he was asked to recommend books for this library, giving information about prices, best editions, and comparative usefulness of works on history, natural philosophy, and agriculture.[82]

---

* This almanac was widely circulated in the middle and southern states. It won the admiration of scientific men in Europe, and was produced in the British Parliament by Pitt, Fox, and Wilberforce as an argument for the abolition of slavery.

This system of public education was intended to make it easy for the parents in every community in Virginia to establish schools where their children could learn the rudiments which every person needs for daily business and to understand current happenings. It was equally intended to provide higher schools and a university so coördinated that each would prepare the student for the next. As free instruction in the primary school was intended to make intelligent citizens of the poorest children, without any stigma of pauperism, so the selection of the most promising among these for free higher education was to open the doors of opportunity so that exceptional ability might be developed and brought into the public service in spite of poverty. As it was intended to create the intelligent and self-reliant citizenship necessary in any democracy and to free the state from dependence upon wealth and aristocracy for the leadership, equally necessary in a democracy, it was an essential part of the revolutionary program, intended to perpetuate and complete the reforms already begun.

CHAPTER III

PRIMARY EDUCATION

As THE system of public education was the "keystone of the arch" of revolutionary reform, so the primary school for the benefit of all the people was the foundation of the whole design for educational reform. Jefferson had very definite plans for organizing the system and putting it in operation as well as equally definite ideas of what these schools would cost and of how the people would respond to the proposal, though he overlooked some facts of geography and the distribution of population.

The counties of the state were to be divided into wards or hundreds to serve as school districts as well as for other civic purposes. These were to be five or six miles square, so that a school could be built within walking distance of every home.[1] The division into wards and the calling of the first ward meetings were to be compulsory. This was to be accomplished by declaring the existing militia captaincies to be wards and by having someone attend the regular militia muster to explain the purpose of the law to the company, to have them determine where their school should be located and have them come together and build it.[2] The wards would be subject to change, but Jefferson assumed that the population that would maintain a company of militia would be the smallest number who could well support a school.[3]

Experience has justified one contemporary criticism of this plan. There were many sections of Virginia where the population was so sparse that a militia captaincy extended over distances far too great to be traversed daily by school children. This objection was urged in the legislative sessions of 1786 [4] and 1817,[5] and when the plan finally was tried in the reconstruction period it quickly showed that these objections were well founded.[6] While Jefferson intended the wards or hundreds to be much more than school districts, the sparseness of population in parts of the state which made them impracticable as civic divisions was a still more serious objection to them as school districts.

Jefferson's plan of organization and administration was more detailed and democratic in 1779 than in 1817. By the former plan the voters of each county were annually to elect three aldermen. These should, in the first instance, divide the county into wards or hundreds and call meetings of the voters in each ward to determine the location of the school. The aldermen should have the schoolhouse built and kept in repair and should appoint annually an overseer for every group of approximately ten schools in the county. The overseers should appoint teachers for the several schools and should superintend their work. The overseers of the several counties of the district should locate their grammar school, procure the site, and have the necessary buildings erected. The overseers of each county should appoint a visitor annually. The visitors of the district should employ a master and should supervise his work. The master should employ a steward to provide for the material necessities of master and pupils and for the care of the buildings. Each overseer should select one boy of especial promise, the son of poor parents, to go to the grammar school at public expense. The visitors of the district should select one of these to go to William and Mary at public expense.[7]

In his provision for overseers Jefferson manifested a surprising short-sightedness. Each overseer was to have charge of ten schools, or the number nearest to ten into which the schools of the county could be divided. There was no provision for any overseer having charge of schools in more than one county, and several provisions of the bill so plainly assume the opposite as to constitute a tacit prohibition.[8] Repeatedly Jefferson stated that the wards or hundreds should be about six miles square.[9] Assuming this as the normal area of a ward, there would be twenty-eight counties east of the Blue Ridge which would have fewer than ten wards and only four of the others would be large enough to employ more than one overseer. Undoubtedly he expected that each county would have at least one overseer, but he probably overlooked the fact that in some of the smaller counties he would have very few schools to supervise. By this principle of division the following counties would have had the number of wards shown. By Jefferson's plan they might have had an equal number of schools or a smaller number, for he depended upon the enlightened self-interest of the warders to establish the school when the opportunity should offer:

TABLE I

NORMAL NUMBER OF WARDS PER COUNTY

COUNTY	AREA IN SQUARE MILES	NORMAL NUMBER OF WARDS
Elizabeth City	54	1
Warwick	69	2
Lancaster	130	3
Middlesex	146	4
York	136	4
James City	164	4
New Kent	191	5
Charles City	188	5
King George	180	5
Northumberland	205	6
Richmond	204	6

By the plan of 1817 the judges of each county court should appoint three visitors for the elementary schools who should divide the county into wards and hold ward meetings which should elect a warden and provide for the location and construction of the school buildings. The warden should have charge of the erection and repair of the buildings. Wardens were to be elected annually, but visitors were appointed for four years. The visitors should employ the teachers and supervise their work. Their decisions should be subject to appeal to the Superior Court of the county. Visitors for the district colleges should be appointed by the state Board of Public Instruction for four years. The visitors were to recommend a location for the district college, to be determined by the Board of Public Instruction, and should obtain a site and provide for the erection and preservation of the buildings. The visitors should employ the instructors and should have general control of the college.[10]

The most conspicuous changes in the administrative features of these two plans are the appointment of visitors for four years instead of one, selection by the county court and the state board instead of by the voters and the overseers of the county, and the limitation of popular control to the choice of a warden and to matters concerning the local school. The number of schools in a single county was immaterial under the later plan, because no overseers were provided for. The earlier plan was inconsistent in one particular. The overseer, chosen as an expert to supervise the local school, had only the relation to the grammar school which the voters of the ward had to the ward school—that of determining its location and providing for its buildings. Expert supervision of the higher institution was left to visitors to be chosen by the overseers—though the bill did permit the selection of one of their number by the visitors. As has been pointed out, this would have permitted the solitary overseer in nearly every county east of the Blue Ridge to appoint himself the county's visitor to the grammar school. The increase in state control may have been due to the establishment of the Literary Fund between the dates of these two bills.

The plan for selecting the most promising among the sons of poor parents in the ward schools for free instruction at the college and university embodied in the bill of 1817 was distinctly simpler than that of 1779. Section 42 of the *Bill to Establish a System of Public Education* provided that the visitors of the ward school should meet at the courthouse of the county and select the one of greatest promise among those who had been in the ward school for three years. From among these boys of the various counties two should be selected by the visitors of each collegiate district to attend the college for five years at public expense. At the end of that time the visitors should select the one of greater promise for three years of free instruction at the university. In this way eighteen would be selected from about one hundred for instruction in ancient and modern languages, geography, and mathematics. Nine would be dismissed with enough training to become grammar-school masters or private tutors, and nine would have the opportunity to obtain a broad scientific or professional education. The plan of 1779 was much more complex and would have given some free education to a much larger number. Every overseer should annually appoint one boy from the schools under his care to go to the district college, so eighty or more boys would have received at least one year at the grammar schools.   There would have been from two to seven of these boys at each of the twenty grammar schools —in most cases either three or four.   At the end of a year one third of those at each school would have been discontinued,* but the rest would have remained for an additional year.   This would have given the second year of free schooling to fifty or sixty poor boys.   At the end of the second year the one of greatest promise would have been selected.   This would have given four more years of free education to twenty boys.   Every alternate year the visitors of the district should select the one of greatest ability for three years of free education at William and Mary.   This would virtually be limited to a choice between the one who was in his fourth year and the one in his third year as a senior.   Ten boys would have been selected annually for this higher instruction at public expense.   The following tabulation shows by the exact method which Jefferson specified for public-school reports the quantity of free education which he proposed in 1779 and in 1817 for poor but promising boys:

TABLE II

JEFFERSON'S RECOMMENDATIONS FOR FREE EDUCATION TO BE PROVIDED BY THE STATE

	ALLOTMENT	PUPILS	AGGREGATE YEARS
	Grammar school, one year only...	about 80	80
	Grammar school, two years only..	about 53	106
	Grammar school, six years.......	about 20	120
1779	Total in Grammar schools.......	about 153	306
	College, three years............	10	30
1817	District college for five years.....	18	90
	University for three years.......	9	27
	Total, plan of 1779.............	153	336
	Total, plan of 1817.............	18	117

* Without being entirely facetious, this may be cited as another evidence that Jefferson had not considered how many wards there would be in a county nor how many pupils appointed by the overseers to any one school.   Had he done so, this bill, drafted with excessive attention to detail and elaborate provision for every minute contingency, would have specified that one third of the two, four, five, or seven boys at any one school should be determined, like the number of schools under a single overseer, "without fractional divisions."   Section VII.

Literally the bill of 1817 provides for only one fourth of the free instruction indicated by specifying that the visitors of the ward schools should select their candidates for appointment to the district colleges on February 29. This is manifestly absurd, as the rest of the paragraph shows. Jefferson had provided for quadrennial appointment of visitors by naming February 29 as the day on which they should be named. Writing Section 42 as an afterthought, he absent-mindedly used the same date, plainly not meaning what he wrote.

Jefferson had consistently advocated what he intended to be an adequate control of the ward school by the warders, though in 1779 he thought of little more than the location and care of the buildings. He opposed every attempt to place them directly under state control. In 1816 he stated his position to Cabell:

> If it is believed that these elementary schools will be better managed by the Governor and Council, the Commissioners of the Literary Fund, or any other general authority of the Government, than by the parents within each ward, it is a belief against all experience. Try the principle one step further and amend the bill so as to commit to the Governor and Council the management of all our farms, our mills, and merchants' stores. No, my friend, the way to have good and safe government, is not to trust it all to one; but to divide it among the many, distributing to every one exactly the function he is competent to.[11] *

At the time of drafting the bill for elementary schools he wrote to Cabell:

> If twelve or fifteen hundred schools are to be placed under one general administration, an attention so divided will amount to a dereliction of them to themselves. It is surely better, then, to place each school at once under the care of those most interested in its conduct.[12]

During the next three years he became convinced that not only the erection and care of buildings but the supervision of the school should be brought more directly under local control. This view he explained in a letter written late in 1820:

> I had formerly thought that visitors for the schools might be chosen by the county, and charged to provide teachers for every ward, and to superintend them. I now think it would be better for every ward to choose its own resident visitor, whose business it would be to keep a teacher in the ward, to superintend the school, and to call meetings of the ward for

---

* A longer quotation from this letter appears in Appendix F.

all purposes relating to it; their accounts to be settled and wards laid off by the courts. I think ward elections better for many reasons, one of which is sufficient, that it will keep elementary education out of the hands of fanaticising preachers, who in county elections would be universally chosen, and the predominant sect of the county would possess itself of all its schools.[13]

When it is remembered that Jefferson always intended the wards to be important political divisions as well as school districts, it may well be questioned whether he weighed sufficiently the implications of this proposal. With the warden abolished and the visitor of the local school placed in his stead as the political head of the ward, there is grave question whether the idealism of the educational expert would be applied to ward affairs in general. The schools might perhaps be prostituted to the ends of the local politician who could get himself elected to this important position. Jefferson had high faith in the efficacy of an intelligent public opinion if given the necessary opportunity for expression,[14] but had he been better acquainted with the New England town which he held in such high esteem, he might have been more conscious of certain of its limitations. In the last months of his life we find him again urging the simplicity of public reports in order that the people might understand and intelligently direct the conduct of their schools.[15]

As a general principle Jefferson was opposed to indirect financial methods and favored the straightforwardness and reliability of a direct tax for schools. The bill of 1779 proposed that the expenses of building and repairing the ward schools and of the teachers' salaries should be met by the counties but that the living expenses of the teacher should be assessed upon the ward on the same basis as other taxes.[16] The grammar-school buildings and the expenses of the students receiving free instruction there or at the college were to be provided for by the state.[17] The salaries of masters and stewards were to be met by student fees. The same year he proposed to substitute a tax of five pounds of tobacco on every hogshead exported from the state for the duties on furs, skins, and liquors with which William and Mary had been endowed, primarily because this was expected to yield a more uniform and dependable income.[18] While he favored any reasonable move to raise money for education, he invariably regarded other expedients to be inferior to a direct tax. In 1810 the trustees of the East Tennessee College asked him to sell lottery tickets for them. In his reply he explained that he was on principle opposed to lotteries.[19] In 1816 he approved the Literary Fund but recommended a perpetual tax of a cent a head on the population of the state to set in motion and maintain his entire educational system.[20]

The bills of September and October, 1817, provided that the cost of building and repairing the ward schools and the salaries and subsistence of the teachers should be assessed to the taxpayers of the ward, with aid from the county in case the regular levy should be extremely burdensome to any ward.[21] Jefferson frankly declared it his purpose to levy the expense of the elementary schools upon the wealth of the county.[22] The same bills would have charged the expense of building the district colleges and of the students being educated at public expense, besides a basic salary for the teachers in the district colleges, to the Literary Fund.[23] To both bills he appended a note so fully explaining how he expected the ward schools to operate that it deserves to be quoted in full:

Estimating 800 militia to a county, there will be twelve captaincies or wards in a county on an average. Suppose each of these, three years in every six to have children enough for a school who have not yet had three years' schooling. Such a county will employ six teachers, each serving two wards by alternate terms. These teachers will be taken from the laboring classes as they are now, to wit: from that which furnishes mechanics, overseers, and tillers of the earth; and they will chiefly be the cripples, the weakly, and the old of that class who will have been qualified for these functions by the ward schools themselves. If put on a footing, then, for wages and subsistance with the young and the able of their class, they will be liberally compensated; say with 150 dollars wages and the usual allowance of meat and bread. The subsistance will probably be contributed in kind by the warders out of their family stock. The wages alone will be a pecuniary tax of about 900 dollars. To a county this addition would be of about one-fifth of the taxes we now pay to the state, or about one-fifth of one percent on every man's taxable property; if tax can be called that which we give to our children in the most valuable of all forms, that of instruction. Were these schools to be established on the public funds, and to be managed by the governor and council, or the commissioners of the Literary Fund, brick houses to be built for the schools and teachers, high wages and subsistance given them, they would be badly managed, depraved by abuses, and would exhaust the whole Literary Fund.

While under the eye and animadversion of the wards and the control of the wardens and visitors, economy, diligence, and correctness of conduct will be enforced, the whole Literary Fund will be spared to complete the general system of education by colleges in every district for instruction in the languages and an university for the whole of the higher sciences; and this by an addition to our contributions almost insensible, and which, in fact, will not be felt as a burden because applied immediately and visibly to the good of our children.[24]

Those members of the legislature most friendly to Jefferson's projects opposed his plan for a tax and urged that the primary schools be supported from the Literary Fund.[25] . To this he replied with a long letter on January 14,* showing that the cost of the elementary schools by his plan would be much less than was supposed, but suggesting as an alternative that two thirds of the literary fund be invested and the income given to the elementary schools.[26]

A curious inconsistency appears in Jefferson's plans for the financing of the ward schools. In his letter of November 28, 1820, he proposed that enough of his plan be adopted so that the people of the wards would build their own schoolhouses and provision the teacher with contributions in kind, but that the tuition fees be paid by the parents. The few unable to pay would be provided for from the Literary Fund. This he urged to remedy the waste of $45,000 which the state was spending annually for the education of the poor, as he believed, with very poor results.[27] Apparently Jefferson was accepting the principle of the existing law, which provided free education for the poor, in order to get schools for all established on the economical basis which he advocated. However, the bills of 1817 contained the same inconsistency. While Section 6 provided for free instruction for all, Section 10 required help from the county when "the judge of the Superior Court shall be of opinion that the contributors of any particular ward are disproportionably and oppressively overburdened with an unusual number of children of non-contributors of their ward." As stated, this seems absurd, for the cost of maintaining the school would be substantially the same, except for the trifling item of the supplies used by the pupils, whether attended by ten or twenty children and whether some were paupers or not. All was to be paid by an

* Appendix I.

assessment, not upon the parents, but upon the property owners of the ward. A ward might be burdened by the expenses of its school if it contained insufficient taxable property, but not from an excess of poor children. The same idea appears in a letter of February 2, 1816:*

> Get them to meet and build a log school-house, have a roll taken of the children who would attend it, and of those of them able to pay; these would probably be sufficient to support a common teacher, instructing, gratis, the few unable to pay.[28]

This indicates confusion of thought rather than a change of plan before 1820. At that time, though he saw no way to have his entire system adopted, he thought that a part of it could improve the existing system.

Jefferson's services to the school board of the District of Columbia during his presidency form only an interlude in his long struggle for education in his native state. The schools of Washington were started by subscription in 1804. Jefferson's contribution was $200. He was elected to the first governing board, which consisted of seven citizens appointed by the city council and six elected from among the subscribers,[29] and Jefferson was promptly chosen its chairman.[30] These schools were made free to the poor by a special tax on slaves, dogs, liquors, and public exhibitions, while the children of the well-to-do paid $5 each quarter.[31] To what extent this policy was due to the influence of the chairman is not known.

Although he believed the state to be entitled to the services of its citizens and that the value of these services would be enhanced by education, Jefferson did not wish to compel school attendance from the unwilling or the indifferent. However, he felt it to be entirely reasonable that some of the privileges of citizenship should be withheld from those who had neglected their opportunities to learn how to exercise them wisely. Section 6 of the bill for elementary schools, September, 1817, originally was written as follows:

> At this school shall be received and instructed gratis, every infant of competent age who has not already had three years' schooling. And it is declared and enacted, that no person unborn or under the age of twelve

* Appendix F.

years at the passing of this act, and who is compos mentis, shall, after the age of fifteen years, be a citizen of this commonwealth until he or she can read readily in some tongue, native or acquired.[32]

Jefferson's note to this section shows that he did not mean to be so radical as he seemed, and that all he intended was the disfranchisement of the illiterate. This note states his attitude toward compulsory school attendance:

A question of some doubt might be raised on the latter part of this section as to the rights and duties of society toward its members, infant and adult. Is it a right or a duty in society to take care of their infant members in opposition to the will of the parent? How far does this right and duty extend? — to guard the life of the infant, his property, his instruction, his morals? The Roman father was supreme in all these; we draw a line, but where? Public sentiment does not seem to have traced it precisely. Nor is it necessary in the present case. It is better to tolerate the rare instance of a parent refusing to let his child be educated, than to shock the common feelings and ideas by the forcible asportation and education of the infant against the will of the father. What is proposed here is to remove the objection of expense, by offering education gratis and to strengthen parental excitement by the disfranchisement of his child while uneducated. Society has certainly a right to disavow him whom they offer and are not permitted to qualify for the duties of a citizen. If we do not force instruction, let us at least strengthen the motives to receive it when offered.[33]

This device for stimulating the interest of parents had been in Jefferson's mind for about three years. He derived the idea directly from the new Spanish constitution. In 1814 he wrote to De Onis, who had sent him a copy of the constitution:

There is one provision which will immortalize its inventors. It is that which, after a certain epoch, disfranchises every citizen who cannot read and write. This is new, and is the fruitful germ of the improvement of everything good, and the correction of everything imperfect in the present constitution. This will give you an enlightened people, and an energetic public opinion which will control and enchain the aristocratic spirit of the government.[34]

Two years later he wrote still more enthusiastically of this idea to Dupont de Nemours in a letter containing much interesting philosophy:

In the constitution of Spain, as proposed by the late Cortes, there is a principle entirely new to me, and not noticed in yours that no person born after that day, should ever acquire the rights of citizenship until he could read and write. It is impossible sufficiently to estimate the wisdom of this provision. Of all those which have been thought of for securing fidelity in the administration of the government, constant ralliance to the principles of the constitution, and progressive amendments with the progressive advances of the human mind, or changes in human affairs, it is the most effectual. Enlighten the people generally and tyranny and oppressions of body and mind will vanish like evil spirits at the dawn of day. Although I do not, with some enthusiasts, believe that the human condition will ever advance to such a state of perfection as that there shall no longer be pain or vice in the world, yet I believe it susceptible of much improvement, and most of all in matters of government and religion; and that the diffusion of knowledge among the people is to be the instrument by which it is to be effected. The constitution of the Cortes has defects enough; but when I saw in it the amendatory provision, I was satisfied all would come right in time under its salutary operation.[35]

In these primary schools Jefferson intended that reading, writing, and arithmetic should be taught. In 1779 he proposed that the reading books should be those which would acquaint the student with ancient, English, and American history.[36] In 1817 he made no mention of history but included geography among these subjects.[37] These fundamentals were intended to equip the common people for the business of life and for the duties of citizenship. The growth of the country and the increasing importance of domestic and foreign trade may account for the addition of geography in 1817 to the subjects to be taught in the primary schools.

CHAPTER IV

SECONDARY EDUCATION

IN THE *Bill for the More General Diffusion of Knowledge* Jefferson planned for the grammar schools or academies as carefully as for the primary schools. He divided the state into twenty districts. The overseers of the primary schools in the district were to determine the location of a schoolhouse for the district,[1] were to acquire a site, by legal process if necessary,[2] and to have built a stone or brick house to accommodate a master and usher and twenty or twenty-five scholars.[3] Land and buildings were to be paid for by the state.[4] In these schools were to be taught "the Latin and Greek languages, English Grammar, Geography, and the higher parts of numerical arithmetick, to wit, vulgar and decimal fractions, and the extrication of the square and cube roots."[5] A visitor from each county should be appointed annually by the overseers of the county, and the visitors of the district should have power to employ teachers and to fix the rate of tuition. They should supervise the schools and see that any plan of instruction recommended by the visitors of William and Mary should be followed.[6] Provision was made for boarding the students and for keeping the buildings in repair.[7] Annually each overseer of primary schools should appoint, under oath, the boy whom he believed to be of best ability among those who had attended the schools under his supervision at least two years and whose parents were too poor to give them further schooling, to attend the grammar school at state expense.[8] Annually one third of the boys who had been at the grammar school for one year by the overseers' appointment —those showing least ability—should be discontinued, and all others at the end of two years except the one of greatest promise who should remain four years longer.[9] The visitors of the districts south and west of the James in odd-numbered years and those of the remaining districts in even-numbered years should

38

select the senior of greatest promise in their respective districts to attend William and Mary for three years at state expense.[10]

During the years from 1779 to 1814 Jefferson seems to have been less actively interested in the intermediate schools than in those more elementary or more advanced. In 1783 he was attracted by the movement to found a grammar school in Albe-

TABLE III

COLLEGE DISTRICTS AS PLANNED BY JEFFERSON IN 1779

NUMBERED AS LISTED IN BILL; NAMED BY COUNTY SPECIFIED FOR FIRST MEETING	AREA IN SQUARE MILES	POPULATION– 1790		STATE CENSUS 1782–5 WHITES	SECTION
		Slaves	Total		
1. Nansemond....	1431	16231	40355	15874	
2. Sussex........	1691	18996	37818	12059[f]	
12. James City....	1119	22015	39768		
13. King and Queen	1516	28584	48256		
14. Richmond.....	791	16105	29448	11020[e]	Tidewater
15. Spotsylvania...	1626	23404	52141		
11. Accomack.....	741	7506	20848		
3. Lunenburg....	1963[a]	21490	42881		
4. Chesterfield....	1360	26128	46245	19014[e]	
5. Henrico.......	1645	27457	50782		
6. Charlotte......	1666	14367	32900	10677	
7. Pittsylvania...	4331[a]	10845	45116		Piedmont
8. Albemarle.....	2718[a]	16509	39988	15825[e]	
16. Loudoun......	1459[a]	10672	36854		
17. Orange........	1583	17220	30493		
18. Frederick......	1323[b]	4762	30191		
19. Berkeley......	2936[b]	3775	34995		Valley
9. Botetourt.....	50273[bc]	15839	112940		Valley and Trans Alleghany
10. Augusta.......	15593[b]	2711	26204		Trans Alleghany
20. Monongalia....	12670[bd]	1351	75761		Trans Alleghany

[a] Approximate, possibility of a slight error.

[b] Estimated, possibility of substantial error.

[c] Kentucky County considered as having the same area as the present state of Kentucky — 40,598 square miles.

[d] Including 4210 square miles now in Pennsylvania.

[e] One county missing — estimated from 1790 figures.

[f] Two counties missing — estimated from 1790 figures.

marle, and was asked by its promoters to inquire for a teacher while on a journey through the northern states. He reported that he was unable to find any suitable person at Princeton, and added:

I enquired in Philadelphia for some literary character of the Irish nation in that city. There was none such; and in the course of my inquiries I was informed that learning is but little cultivated there and that few persons have ever been known to come from that nation as tutors. I concluded, on the whole, then, if the scheme should be carried on and fixed on so firm a basis as that we might, on its faith, venture to bring a man from his own country, it would be best for me to interest some person in Scotland to engage a good one. From that country we are surest of having sober, attentive men. However, this must await your information.[11]

More than forty years later he did "interest some person in Scotland" in finding a professor of anatomy and medicine for the new college in Albemarle.[12]

By 1814 Jefferson seems to have come to feel that the intermediate schools could be enlarged in scope to give much of the general education which he had previously reserved for the highest institutions and that the latter could be limited to truly professional schools for high specialization. Three months after his election as a trustee of Albemarle Academy he wrote a long letter to his old friend John Adams, outlining his views of contemporary education and asking advice on the scope and organization of a course of study. After expressing his contempt for the fatuity of those who treat Plato's *Republic* as a classic because it is fashionable to do so, he added in more than his usual incisive style of writing:

Our post-revolutionary youth are born under happier stars than you and I were. They acquire all learning in their mother's womb and bring it into the world ready made. The information of books is no longer necessary, and all knowledge which is not innate is in contempt, or neglect at least. Every folly must run its round; and so, I suppose, must that of self-learning and self-sufficiency; of rejecting the knowledge acquired in past ages and starting on the new ground of intuition. When sobered by experience I hope our successors will turn their attention to the advantages of education. I mean of education on the broad scale and not that of the petty academies, as they call themselves, which are starting up in every neighborhood and where one or two men, possessing Latin and sometimes Greek, a knowledge of the globes, and the first six books of Euclid, imagine and communicate this as the sum of science. They commit their pupils to the theatre of the world with just taste enough of learning to be alienated from industrious pursuits and not enough to do service in the ranks of science. We have some exceptions indeed. . . . I hope the necessity will at length be seen of establishing institutions here, as in Europe, where every branch of science, useful at this day, may be taught in its highest degree. Have you ever turned your thoughts to the plan of such an institution? I mean to a specification of the particular sciences of real use in human affairs, and how they might be so grouped as to require so many professors only as might bring them within the views of a just but enlightened economy? I should be happy in a communication of your ideas on this problem, either loose or digested.[13]

Adams replied promptly, recommending a wide range of studies and suggesting a grouping of grammar, rhetoric, logic, and ethics under one professor; mathematics, mechanics, and natural philosophy under a second; geography and astronomy under a third; law and government, history and chronology under a fourth; the classics under a fifth.[14]

While Jefferson's contempt for the "petty academies" may have been more on account of their alleged self-sufficiency than because of their limited curriculum, it will be noted that he describes them as offering substantially the same course of study that he had proposed for his academies in 1779 and the same that he was to urge again in 1817 except that he then included modern languages and some practical applications of mathematics.[15] Two months later in his letter to Peter Carr he followed Adams's suggestions with such modifications as would group the subjects recommended under four instead of five professors. In the same letter he names the same course of study for the elementary schools that he did in 1779, but for the second or general grade he suggested substantially the same studies that he had for William and Mary in the proposed reorganization of that year.[16] Of that plan he wrote in his autobiography: "A second bill proposed to amend the constitution of William and Mary College, to enlarge its sphere of science, and to make it in fact a university." [17]

When we consider that this greatly enlarged intermediate school was proposed to Peter Carr and through him to the Virginia legislature just at the time when Jefferson was asking that body to change Albemarle Academy to Central College, to reduce its board of trustees from eighteen to six, and to give them authority to institute the primary schools in the county, it seems evident that he hoped to establish near his home an institution which would realize much of his plan for higher education, and by coördinating this with the primary schools through a common authority, to bring within the scope of two grades of schools much of what he had originally included in three.   About this time he wrote to Cabell:

> I think I have it now in my power to obtain three of the ablest characters in the world to fill the higher professorships of what in the plan is called the second or general grade of education; three such characters as are not in a single university of Europe; and for those of languages and mathematics, a part of the same grade, able professors doubtless could also be readily obtained.   With these characters I should not be afraid to say that the circle of the sciences composing that second or general grade would be more profoundly taught here than in any institution in the United States, and I might go farther.   The first or elementary grade of education is not developed in this plan; an authority only being asked to its Visitors for putting in motion a former proposition for that object.[18]

Here he is carefully using the phraseology of intermediate education while proposing to employ specialists needed only for the most advanced instruction, and five of them as suggested by Adams rather than four as proposed by him to Peter Carr.   At this very time he was asking advice on plans for a university to teach "all the branches of science useful to us, and at this day— in their highest degree." [19]   In 1800 he had asked suggestions from Dr. Priestley about the university he hoped to establish on a liberal and modern plan in the upper country, and he suggested substantially the same group of studies that he did to Peter Carr in 1814.[20]   In 1803 he mentioned his plan to propose to the Virginia legislature the establishment of a university on as large a scale as circumstances would permit when a favorable opportunity should occur.[21]   Early in 1816 Cabell wrote to Jefferson that he feared opposition from Staunton "should a great state seminary be established at Charlottesville," [22] and in 1817 Jefferson wrote regarding the subscription papers for Central College:

> The difficulty, I find, is to eradicate the idea that it is a local thing, a mere Albemarle Academy.   I endeavor to convince them it is a general seminary of the sciences meant for the use of the State.   In this view all approve of the situation and rally to the object.   But time seems necessary to plant this idea firmly in their minds.[23]

It is doubtful if the letter to Peter Carr shows any material change in his general plan for intermediate schools.   He seems to have utilized the opportunity which he found in an academy already chartered to gain local financial support from lotteries, subscriptions, and the sale of glebe lands without starting any controversy over the location of a state university. His hope seems to have been that he could set in motion an institution, largely under his personal supervision and control, which would take the students as they came from the elementary and private schools and carry them through so excellent a course of instruction that the college would come to be recognized as the most progressive institution in Virginia, and because of this and of its central location would some day be adopted by the government as a state university. When it actually was so adopted he urged the establishment either of the district colleges or of a preparatory school at a safe distance from the university.[24] From this it would appear that his proposal in 1814 to extend the scope of the intermediate schools far into the field which both earlier and later he set apart for the university was intended to be both local and temporary in its application.

In the autumn of 1817 Jefferson again set forth his general plan for a system of schools on the same principles as in 1779 but with significant variations. The state, now much reduced in size by the settlement of the Pennsylvania boundary and by the erection of Kentucky and the regions beyond the Ohio as separate states, was divided into nine collegiate districts. With a fine touch of affection and respect for his old mentor, Jefferson proposed that the first district, comprising the oldest counties of tidewater Virginia, should be called the District of Wythe. The names of the other eight he left blank. The western districts were very large, though not so large as those of 1779. In the more thickly settled eastern part of the state the 1817 districts were about equal to three of those planned in 1779. They were more uniform in size and shape and less influenced by mountains and rivers. One problem appears in the arrangement of these districts.

The great central district, having Charlottesville not far from its center, was much larger than the normal eastern districts and was surpassed in area only by those containing large and sparsely inhabited mountain regions.* Its population in 1820 was no-

* See Table IV.

tably greater than that of any other district. Under these circumstances it is fair to ask why Jefferson included in this district Rockbridge and Augusta counties in which are situated Lexington and Staunton, both west of the Blue Ridge and both so situated as to be easily placed in a more logical grouping. With this area subtracted the Central District would have been

TABLE IV

COLLEGE DISTRICTS AS PLANNED BY JEFFERSON IN 1817

NUMBER AND SECTION	AREA SQUARE MILES	POPULATION	
		White–1820	Total–1820
I Eastern	3638	56,906	127,079
II Southeastern	3429	45,649	100,893
III Northeastern	4325	73,167	143,957
IV Central *	6861	89,764	188,185
V Southern	4992	58,085	142,309
VI Southwestern	7015	65,198	102,249
VII Northern	6904	84,307	106,649
VIII Northwestern	9817	58,016	61,873
IX Western	17300	71,832	82,165

* Without its abnormal remote parts the Central District would have been as follows.

Without Henrico and Richmond	6581	78,001	164,518
Without Augusta and Rockbridge	5238	67,763	159,498
Without either	4958	56,000	135,831

slightly larger than any other of the eastern districts and would still have been substantially greater in population. Similarly we may inquire why he included Henrico County and the city of Richmond, situated far to the southeast. Without them the district would still have been abnormally large, and Henrico could easily have been included either in the Eastern or the Southern district without making either abnormally great in area or population. He appears to have deliberately included Richmond, Lexington, and Staunton in the same district with Charlottesville for reasons other than those of area and population.

He repeatedly declared his principle to be to place a college within a day's ride of the homes of the people by dividing the state into areas roughly eighty miles square. The Southern District would have corresponded much more nearly to this principle if Buckingham, Cumberland, and Powhatan had been included, but this would have made the inclusion of Henrico in the Central District grotesquely inappropriate. Had Henrico been included with the counties south of the James this district would still have been considerably smaller than the Central District in area and white population. This would have placed Hampden-Sidney much nearer the center of the Southern District. Richmond was nearer the physical center of such a district than of the Central District as proposed, and was much nearer to Williamsburg than to Charlottesville. Inclusion either in the Eastern or Southern Districts would have seemed more logical than in the Central. The latter, bounded by the James and the Blue Ridge, could have included a group of counties from the mountains to the bend of the Potomac. This would have relieved an abnormality in the Northeastern District and have kept the Central within more reasonable bounds—but Charlottesville would have been far from the center of such a district, and Lexington and Staunton would have been outside. Again, the district could have included these places with, possibly, a few counties to the north, such as Rockingham, Madison, or Spotsylvania. This would have made Charlottesville more central in the district than it was by Jefferson's plan—but Richmond would have been outside. For nearly two years Jefferson and his friends had been frankly discussing the possibility of having Central College adopted as the state university.[25] Perhaps, as a means to this end, he wished it adopted as the intermediate school for the Central District. It is more probable that he wished to withhold any advantage which adoption as a district college might give to any of the rivals of the Central College in the struggle for the university. A movement to locate the state capital at Staunton was already on foot, and both the promoters of that town and the friends of Washington College at Lexington were openly bidding for the location of the state university.[26] The plan to remove William and Mary to Richmond had not yet taken definite form,[27] but the situation and urban attractions of the capital, reënforcing movements to establish a medical school and a preparatory school there, made it a competing location for the university and a factor to be separated from rather than allied to the known hostility of William and Mary.[28] *   With the three rivals included in the same district as Charlottesville, but all far from its center, no one of these could become the site of the district college.   No one of the three was less than 125 miles distant from the opposite extremes of the district, while Charlottesville was about eighty miles from the most remote point.   If the district college should be established at any of the four it must be at Charlottesville. But, whether adopted as a district college or not, Central College was expected by its friends soon to overshadow all rivals. "Should the question of location [of the university] be deferred to another session, our claims would grow stronger every day of the interval," wrote Cabell late in December, and six weeks later, believing himself beaten in the great struggle, he wrote:

> The friends of Staunton and Lexington wish to keep down the Central College.   I believe they would oppose the appropriation of a dollar to it.   Should it get even a little annuity, it would be established; and one year more would throw Staunton out of the chase altogether, and Lexington in the back-ground.   For these reasons, I believe the back country will oppose a small appropriation to the Central College with nearly as much zeal as it would the establishment of the University at that place.[29]

Jefferson strongly opposed any plan for weaving existing institutions into his system of district colleges when urged by Cabell as a means to overcome opposition.

> You ask if we should not associate with it the petty academies and colleges spread over the state, in order to engage their interest?   Why should we?   For their funds?   They have none.   Scarcely any of them have funds to keep their buildings in repair.   They depend on what they get from their students.   Aggregated to our regular system, they would make it like the image of brass and clay, substances which can never amalgamate, They would only embarrass, and render our colleges impracticable.   I have always found it best never to permit a rational plan to be marred by botching.   You would lose on the vote more honest friends than you would reconcile dishonest enemies, under which term I include those who would sacrifice the public good to a local interest.[30]

---

* "Some winters back my respect for your better judgment restrained me from active support of my medical friends at Richmond." — Cabell to Jefferson, May 5, 1824 — *Cabell*, 307.

It seems apparent that the friends of Central College were as willing to keep down Staunton and Lexington, or William and Mary should it become dangerous either at Williamsburg or at Richmond, until their institution should be securely established as the state university as the friends of Staunton and Lexington were to keep down the Central College. That Jefferson saw a means of doing this when he planned his great Central District seems entirely probable.

Another question of some interest arises when we inquire why Jefferson reduced the districts from twenty to nine in 1817, making those east of the mountains about equal to three of the districts of 1779. When we consider that he was much less influenced by mountain and river barriers, it seems reasonable to infer that the transportation improvements of forty years, such as turnpikes, canalized rivers, and steamboats, had made longer journeys to the colleges seem reasonable. In 1779 he provided for from twenty to twenty-four resident students at each of the twenty grammar schools.[31] In 1817 he thought accommodations for thirty-two at each of the nine colleges would be sufficient.[32] In 1826 he thought that these colleges would not have more than thirty pupils each.[33] Larger districts seemed necessary to provide a student body large enough to warrant the offer of a broader course of study, and at least two masters seemed necessary to teach adequately this greater variety of subjects.

There was another reason why the college districts must be decreased in number. The funds available for this purpose were only sufficient to adequately establish a small number of these schools, necessarily more expensive than those planned in 1779. In 1823 when the university was in debt and a proposal to reorganize the primary schools was pending, Jefferson even thought that no state aid should go to intermediate education until the other parts of the system were secure:

> With respect to the claims of the local academies, I will make no compromise. The second grade must not be confounded with the first, nor treated of in the same chapter. The present funds are not sufficient for all the three grades. The first and third are most important to be first brought into action. When they are properly provided for, and the funds sufficiently enlarged, the middle establishment should be taken up systematically. In the meantime, it may more conveniently than either of the

others be left to private enterprise; 1, because there is a good number of classical schools now existing; and 2, because their students are universally sons of parents who can afford to pay for their education.[34]

In 1826 Mr. Garland brought forward a project to divide the funds for intermediate education among the twenty-four senatorial districts.[35]   The state had at that time $155,000 for educational purposes.   "Twenty-four such schools, as proposed by Mr. Garland, with $5,000 each, would not have enough to do more than maintain one Connecticut teacher," was Jefferson's comment; and he proceeded to show how by his plan ten colleges could be endowed with sufficient funds to erect their buildings and maintain two tutors, with a balance of $55,000 to finish the University and make it permanently independent.[36]   It must be remembered that Jefferson expected most of the support of these schools to come from fees paid by all students except the small number of those too poor to pay who had been appointed to the academies on account of excellence in scholarship, and thus the resources of the school would be largely proportioned to the number of students.

Another question of some interest grows out of varying proposals about the subjects to be taught in the intermediate schools. Section XIII of the bill of 1779 directed that Latin, Greek, English grammar, geography, and higher numerical arithmetic should be taught in the grammar schools.   Passing by the proposals to Peter Carr in 1814 as of special application, we note that Section 21 of the bill of 1817 proposed that Greek, Latin, French, Spanish, Italian, German, English grammar, geography, higher numerical arithmetic, the mensuration of land, the use of globes, and the elements of navigation be taught in the district colleges.* | Practically, this is merely the addition of the four modern languages to the 1779 program.   A year later in the Rockfish report Jefferson proposed the same program without the modern languages.[37]   Six years later he referred to the Rockfish report but included French and the elements of astronomy and natural philosophy among the subjects which could be taught by two professors.[38]   He believed that advanced mathematics and abstruse sciences were too difficult for

* A month later he mentioned collegiate institutions for "antient & modern languages, for higher instruction in arithmetic, geography, & history".   To George Ticknor, November 25, 1817—*Ms. L. C.,* Vol. 211.

boys under fifteen years of age, and that they should largely be occupied in learning languages, which is more a matter of memory.[39] In the absence of further evidence it seems reasonable to conclude that in the renewed enthusiasm of 1817 while the establishment of the University was as uncertain as that of the district colleges, Jefferson hoped to see established in nine localities in the state, schools which would offer a thorough grounding in languages during the receptive years of youth, but that the bitter legislative struggle for the University forced upon him the practical problems of expense and led him to conclude that, now that the University was assured and would offer instruction in modern languages, it would be well to limit the intermediate schools to such subjects as could be taught by two masters. The difficulty of finding competent instructors in so many languages may have been an additional consideration. Years afterward when the University was ready to open, his thoughts turned again to the many youths who never would be able to attend, and he sought to offer a little wider field of culture in the intermediate schools without passing the limits of the ability of two competent instructors. French he included because he believed "French is the language of general intercourse among nations, and as a depository of human science, is unsurpassed by any other language, living or dead."[40] Astronomy and natural philosophy he doubtless included because they are among the most immediate and tangible of the sciences.

A new development impelled Jefferson to agree to radical changes in his plan for intermediate schools. In the spring of 1824 a project, strongly supported by various interests, was proposed to remove William and Mary to Richmond and associate with it a school of medicine.[41] Jefferson recommended no action by the friends of the University "until the old institution is loosened from its foundation, and fairly placed on its wheels,"[42] when the legislature should assert its control of the college and appropriate "the derelict capital of William and Mary and the large library they uselessly possess" to the University, which would use them much better to realize the purpose for which they originally were contributed.[43] Cabell opposed this project, and recommended that the funds of William and Mary be used in aid of certain colleges already in operation.[44]

Jefferson acquiesced in part, but seized the opportunity to urge once more his plan for intermediate schools. He argued that the establishment of William and Mary at Richmond with all its funds and a medical school would ruin the University because there would not be enough students to maintain both institutions at a high standard. He pointed out that William and Mary had acknowledged the power of the legislature to control the college by asking legislative action to effect the removal, and urged that, if the removal should actually be determined upon, the funds of the college should be used to establish district colleges throughout the state:

> You have now an happy opportunity of carrying this intermediate establishment into execution, without laying a cent of tax on the people, or taking one from the treasury. Divide the state into college districts of about eighty miles square each; there would be about eight such districts below the Alleghany, and two beyond it, which would be necessarily of larger extent, because of the sparseness of their population. The only advance these colleges would call for, would be for a dwelling house for the teacher, of about $1200 cost, and a boarding house with four or five bed rooms and a school room, for probably about twenty or thirty boys. The whole should not cost more than $5,000; but the funds of William and Mary would enable you to give them $10,000 each. The districts might be so laid off that the principal towns and the academies now existing, might form convenient sites for their colleges, as for example, Williamsburg, Richmond, Fredericksburg, Hampden Sidney, Lynchburg or Lexington, Staunton, Winchester, etc. Thus, of William and Mary, you will make ten colleges, each as useful as she ever was, leaving one in Williamsburg, itself, placing as good a one within a day's ride of every man in the State, and get our whole scheme of education completely established. I have said that no advance is necessary but for the erection of buildings for these schools, because the boys sent to them would be exclusively of a class of parents in competent circumstances to pay teachers for the education of their own children. The $10,000 given to each would afford a surplus to maintain by its interest one or two persons, duly selected, for their genius, from the primary schools, of those too poor to proceed further of their own means. . . . This occasion of completing our system of education is a God-send, which ought not to pass away neglected. Many may be startled at the first idea, but reflection on the justice and advantage of the measure will produce converts daily and hourly to it. I certainly would not propose that the University should claim a cent of these funds in competition with the district colleges.[45]

From this letter we see that Jefferson intended the division of the funds of William and Mary only as an act of self-defense on the part of the University. In proposing schools in the important towns and at the seats of established institutions he was giving up his principle that districts should be laid out with chief reference to distance from the homes to the schools. Probably at the same time he was consciously trying to make the plan attractive to the influential interests associated with each of these localities or institutions which had contributed to the defeat of his plan on earlier occasions. In the weariness of old age it seemed better to establish an imperfect plan than none, and he caught eagerly at this unexpected opportunity to make a beginning. Cabell reported that the proposal in Jefferson's letter was too bold for existing public opinion and would be brought forward only if necessary as a substitute for the motion of removal. He added:

The letter has had a considerable effect. The hostile party, apprised of this, endeavor to destroy its influence, by reporting that you have sent orders to the assembly to plunder the college, and bribe the different parts of the State. I shall hereafter show the letter to very few.[46]

Ten days later he wrote in haste, asking Jefferson to draft a bill providing for the division of the funds of William and Mary. "You alone can prepare a bill that will enable us to vanquish the host opposed to us." [47] Six days later Jefferson mailed the bill, explaining that he had not meddled with the Lexington academy because it was a private institution, founded by General Washington with private property; that he had provided a substitute for Hampden-Sidney in Nottoway, as he foresaw that that institution would not accept the increased measure of state control necessary to obtain this state aid; and that he had avoided laying off districts as unnecessary and liable to contest.[48] In this bill he named Williamsburg, Hampden-Sidney, Lynchburg, Richmond, Fredericksburg, Winchester, Staunton, Fincastle, Lewisburg, and Clarksburg as the sites for the new colleges, and directed that the funds of William and Mary should be divided equally among them for procuring grounds and erecting buildings. Seven visitors were to be appointed by the Governor for each college and were to be persons living nearer that than any other of the colleges. This arrangement would have placed one college in Tidewater, two near the Fall Line, two in the southern

Piedmont counties, three in the Valley, and two in Trans-Alleghany.   Some of these localities were less than forty miles apart; others were sixty-five, ninety, or a hundred and ten from any other.   In the West there were parts of the state at least two hundred and fifteen miles from the nearest college; in the East, nearly a hundred.   This bill was never introduced, for on February 7 Cabell wrote that the motion to remove William and Mary had been defeated and that he believed it would not be wise to move for the division of the college funds at that time.[49]

Garland's plan to found a college in each of the twenty-four senatorial districts brought Jefferson and his loyal lieutenant for the last time into the arena as champions of district colleges in the session of 1826.   On February 4 Jefferson wrote:

Whatever fund may be contemplated for the intermediate colleges, I should be sorry to see any of it diverted from the impartial and general object.   I know no principle of distribution which can be adopted for the second grade of schools, but that of placing one within a day's ride of every man — say in districts of about eighty miles square below the North Mountain, which would give them seven, and leave three for the sparse population beyond.[50]

This would have differed little from the district plan of 1817 except that the sparsely settled counties between the Shenandoah Valley and the Alleghanies would be joined with the counties farther west and three instead of two colleges provided for this region.   On the 8th Cabell wrote that he wished to oppose Garland's plan with a better one.   He proposed to bring forward again the plan of 1817 which he believed to be much superior to that of 1825 as regards location and distribution of the colleges:

In that first bill you looked only to the people of Virginia, without taking any notice of the old colleges. . . .   It is almost impossible to weave them into any good system; and they will never consent to give up their charters.   Why then should we embarrass ourselves with them?   Let us let them alone and ask them to let us alone.[51]

He asked Jefferson to revise the bill of 1817, suggesting that each district be required to contribute land and buildings, so that the only charge upon the Literary Fund would be for the support of the professors, and that reasonable restrictions be placed upon the commissioners to insure the location of the schoolhouse in a fairly central place. Ten days later Jefferson wrote that he was greatly cheered by the prospect of success for the plan for intermediate schools but was suffering too much to amend the bill. "This, however, occurs to my mind at once," he added, "that I always considered the first plan as far the best, but the second the only one which could be obtained from the local interests it enlisted." [52]

He urged Cabell to make whatever changes seemed wise, and continued: "Some, indeed, are specified in your letter, and in general I approve of all your new suggestions. Pray then do not wait a moment, but drive at once the nail which you find will go. . . . Equal rights, the principle of the first bill, is the polar star to be followed."

Before receiving this letter Cabell wrote again, discussing the cost of nine colleges distributed according to the 1817 plan, and added:

The Senator from the S.W. corner of the State is much dissatisfied with his district, as the center is in high mountains. But what is to be done? We cannot give the trans-Alleghany country three, and the Kanawha Valley must be postponed for the present. I think there is judgment in proposing now the same arrangement you did formerly. I like much the idea of having one near the University as a preparatory school.[53]

An amended bill was proposed in the House but defeated by the friends of primary schools. Cabell's estimates were said to be too low. He carefully prepared a plan to prove probable cost. It was loaned to a friend and lost, and its author did not find time to work out another. Before the next session of the legislature the directing and impelling hand was still in death. Cabell became interested in a project for inland waterways and never took up the plan for district colleges again.[54] In 1906 Virginia appropriated a substantial sum to maintain secondary schools among the congressional districts.[55]

CHAPTER V

HIGHER EDUCATION

An essential part of the great plan of 1779 was an institution in which subjects of broad human interest, both new and old, should be taught by a faculty free from ecclesiastical dictation under a simple but efficient administration. Jefferson sought to accomplish this through the bill to amend the constitution of William and Mary College.* This proposed to reduce the number of visitors from eighteen to five and to increase the chancellors from one to three, both being elected by the legislature, the visitors annually and the chancellors for an indefinite term. The visitors were to be free from the restraint "by the royal prerogative, or the laws of the kingdom of England; of the canons or the constitution of the English church," imposed by the charter.[1] As organized at that time, the College consisted of "one school of sacred theology, with two professorships therein, to wit, one for teaching the Hebrew tongue, and expounding the holy scriptures; and the other for explaining the common places of divinity, and controversies with heretics; one other school for philosophy, with two professorships therein, to wit, one for the study of rhetoric, logic, and ethics, and the other of physics, metaphysics, and mathematics; one other school for teaching the Latin and Greek tongues; and one other for teaching Indian boys reading, writing, vulgar arithmetic, the catechism and the principles of the Christian religion." [2] This bill proposed eight instead of six professors:

There shall, in like manner, be eight Professorships, to wit, one of moral philosophy, and the laws of nature and of nations, and of the fine arts; one of law and police; one of history, civil and ecclesiastical; one of mathematics; one of astronomy and medicine; one of natural philosophy and natural history; one of the ancient languages, oriental and northern; and one of modern languages. The said professors shall likewise appoint, from

* Appendix A.

54

time to time, a missionary, of approved veracity, to the several tribes of Indians, whose business shall be to investigate their laws, customs, religions, traditions, and more particularly their languages, constructing grammars thereof, as well as may be, and copious vocabularies, and, on oath to communicate, from time to time, to the said President and Professors the materials he collects, to be by them laid up and preserved in their library.[3]

Jefferson believed that this bill failed because the college was an establishment of the Church of England and the dissenters opposed anything which might give an advantage to the Anglicans.[4]

CHART I

REORGANIZATION OF WILLIAM AND MARY COLLEGE — 1779

EXISTING PROFESSORSHIPS	JEFFERSON'S PROPOSALS IN THE BILL OF 1779	CHANGES MADE BY JEFFERSON AS VISITOR
Hebrew and the Scriptures	Ancient languages — oriental and northern	
Theology and apologetics	History — civil and ecclesiastical	
Rhetoric, logic, and ethics	Moral philosophy, law of nature and nations, fine arts	Moral philosophy, law of nature and nations, fine arts
Physics, metaphysics and mathematics	Natural philosophy and natural history	Mathematics, natural philosophy and natural history
	Mathematics	
Latin and Greek	Modern languages	Modern languages
	Law and police	Law and police
	Anatomy and medicine	Anatomy, medicine, and chemistry
School for Indian boys	Missionary to the Indians	

Soon after Jefferson's election as Governor of Virginia on June 1, 1779, he was chosen a visitor of the College, and, in cooperation with President Madison, promptly set about the reorganization contemplated by the bill still awaiting action by the legislature, so far as this could be effected by executive authority. More than forty years later he summarized these changes:

When I was a visitor, in 1779, I got the two professorships of Divinity and grammar school put down, and others of law and police, of medicine, anatomy, and chemistry, and of modern languages substituted; but we did not then change the above statutes, nor do I know they have since been changed.[5]

The Latin and Greek school likewise was dropped, for the income of that professor was needed to support the more practical scientific and political studies now provided for and because the district grammar schools were expected to offer these subjects in twenty new localities in the state.[6] Moreover, Jefferson declared the Latin and Greek school to be merely a preparatory school which "filled the college with children." [7] By combining natural philosophy and natural history with mathematics and chemistry with anatomy and medicine, Jefferson succeeded in bringing within the scope of five professorships all that he had proposed for eight, except history and ancient languages, and to provide for one science not mentioned in the bill.[8] He hoped to add to these by legislative aid:

To the professorships usually established in the universities of Europe it would seem proper to add one for the ancient languages and literatures of the North on account of their connection with our own languages, laws, customs, and history.[9]

At the same time he established the lecture method of instruction, first introduced by his honored teacher, Dr. William Small. The elective system and the principles underlying the honor system had their beginnings at this time.[10]

After his residence in France Jefferson showed no interest in enlarging the curriculum of William and Mary but was more or less actively connected with several projects for new institutions of higher learning. One of these was the ambitious plan of Chevalier Quesney de Beaurepaire, grandson of Dr. Quesney, the French philosopher and economist and court physician to Louis XV. After serving in Virginia as a captain in the American army, 1777–78, Quesney suffered a long illness which led him to give up military ambitions. He conceived the plan of an academy in America, patterned after the French Academy. It was to be established at Richmond, with branches in Baltimore, Philadelphia, and New York, and was to be affiliated with the royal societies of London, Paris, and Brussels. By vigorous propaganda Quesney raised 60,000 francs. Nearly a hundred original subscribers were Virginians, and leading men in other states were interested. The foundation of the building at Richmond was laid with Masonic ceremonies on June 24, 1786, and Quesney returned to Paris to promote his project. He interested some of the most eminent men in France and England, and mentions among them *"Thomas Jefferson, Ministre Plenipotentiaire des États-Unis de l'Amerique septentrionale, à Paris."* Dr. Adams concludes that Jefferson must have favored the project to permit his name to be used in this way.[11] His letter to Quesney shows that by 1788 he had taken a very cautious attitude toward the subject:

I feared it [the plan] was too extensive for the poverty of the country. You remove the objection by observing it is to extend to several states. Whether professors itinerant from one state to another may succeed I am unable to say, having never known an experiment of it. The fear that those professors might be disappointed in their expectations, has determined me not to intermeddle in the business at all. Knowing how much people going to America overrate the resources of living there, I have made a point never to encourage any person to go there, that I may not partake of the censure which may follow this disappointment. You have more courage than I have to take upon yourself the risk of transplanting and contenting so many persons. I beg you, therefore, not to alter your plan in any part of it on my account, but to permit me to pursue mine of being absolutely neutral.[12]

Under this plan French professors were to teach in the Academy and its branches and to investigate American minerals, flora, fauna, and the like. In 1788 Quesney made provisional arrangement to establish schools of foreign languages, mathematics, design, architecture—civil and military, painting, sculpture, engraving, experimental physics, astronomy, geography, chemistry, mineralogy, botany, anatomy—human and veterinary, and natural history. One professor was elected to be Mineralogist-in-Chief and Professor of Natural History, Chemistry, and Botany. The French Revolution intervened at this moment and Quesney's project passed into oblivion.[13] Long afterward at the University of Virginia Jefferson carried out Quesney's idea of separate schools and gave the same bias toward the sciences in the program of studies, but as these were in vogue at European universities with which he was familiar, it is impossible to show that he obtained any essential ideas from Quesney. Dr. Bruce suggests that Jefferson's unusual apathy, as shown in the letter to Quesney, may have been due to the fact that he was already meditating a university near Monticello and feared that the institution at Richmond would be an obstacle. He further points out that Jefferson felt no such concern for the Geneva professors he wished to transplant to Virginia six years later, and suggests that Jefferson feared that an institution at Richmond with branches in northern cities would promote the principles of political consolidation which he opposed with profound conviction.[14]

The proposal of the faculty of the University of Geneva to remove in a body to America gave Jefferson another project which interested him for years. He had long held this faculty in high esteem. In 1785 he wrote that the best seminary in Europe was either Geneva or Rome. For fine arts, archaeology, and Latin pronunciation he preferred the latter, but believed Geneva the best place for the learning of French. However, it was lacking in one particular:

I do not count on any advantage to be derived in Geneva from a familiar acquaintance with the principles of that government. The late revolution has rendered it a tyrannical aristocracy, more likely to give ill than good ideas to an American.[15]

Six years later conditions had somewhat improved in Jefferson's estimation. After declaring Edinburgh the best school in the world, he added:

On the continent of Europe no place is comparable to Geneva. The sciences are there more modernized than anywhere else. There, too, the spirit of republicanism is strong with the body of the inhabitants; but that of aristocracy is strong also with a particular class; so that it is of some consequence to attend to the class of society in which a youth is made to move. It is a cheap place.[16]

This high opinion was formed after meeting some of the Swiss professors in Paris.[17] When a revolution in Geneva gave control of the government to an aristocracy, it nearly destroyed the University, which had been supported largely by the former government.[18] Members of the faculty seem to have considered various projects for finding employment in more congenial surroundings. Quesney mentions *M. Pictet, Citoyen de Geneva,* as one of his associates. Probably he was the professor who consulted Jefferson about removing to Virginia—or his brother.[19] In 1794 M. D'Ivernois, whom Jefferson describes as a man of science and author of a history of Geneva, wrote both to him and to John Adams his proposal that the Geneva faculty remove to America. While he had consulted only Prevost and the two Pictets, he was confident that ten or twelve professors, most of whom spoke English well, would gladly remove to America if assured of profitable employment. He proposed to establish a university "comprehending a college of languages, preparatory to the principal one of sciences, and also a third one for the gratuitous teaching of reading and writing to the poor." [20]

Although Jefferson does not seem to have expected that the Geneva professors could give instruction in English, he grasped eagerly at the opportunity to transplant such a body of scholars to America. On November 22, 1794, he wrote to Wilson C. Nicholas, asking him to find out how the members of the Virginia legislature would feel toward a proposal to establish the Geneva professors under state auspices. He recognized the obstacles of expense and of teaching in French and Latin, but enthusiastically characterized Edinburgh and Geneva as "the two eyes of Europe." [21] Ten weeks later he regretfully wrote to D'Ivernois that he had consulted a leading member of the legislature who had discussed the plan with others but that they had agreed that it was impracticable because: 1. Their youth were not prepared for instruction in any but the mother tongue; 2. Expense would make it impracticable; 3. Its extent was disproportioned to the narrow state of population.[22] The same day he wrote to John Adams, thanking him for sending a letter from D'Ivernois, explaining that he had received a similar one himself, and that he had referred it to Nicholas, whose reply was received "three days since." He added the following significant comment:

I have found so much tranquillity of mind in a total abstraction from everything political, that it was with some difficulty I could resolve to meddle even in the splendid project of transplanting the academy of Geneva, *en masse,* to Virginia; and I did it under the usual reserve of *sans tirer en conséquence.*[23]

Although he sent this discouraging reply to D'Ivernois because he felt that he must not keep him and his colleagues waiting, Jefferson did not abandon the project. In his message to Congress of January 8, 1790, President Washington had recommended the establishment of a national university. The proposal was repeated in his last annual message, but did not lead to action by the national congress.[24] As early as 1786 Jefferson was in correspondence with Washington about the shares in the Potomac and James river companies which the General was thinking of using to found charity schools.[25] Perhaps his guarded suggestions had their influence, for nine years later Washington was still considering how best to devote these shares to education. A few days after writing D'Ivernois Jefferson communicated his proposal to Washington. He suggested that the canal shares be used to establish a national university near the capital but within the state which should contribute most generously to maintain it. He thought the accession of such a body of professors would give the National University such advantage that it would attract youths from all states and probably from all parts of America.[26] Three weeks later Washington replied that John Adams had shown him D'Ivernois' communication some months before but that he did not think the plan to be practicable because, in the first place, plans were so uncertain that no real assurance could be given to the Geneva professors. Secondly, he doubted the wisdom of transplanting them *in a body,* because they "might not be all good characters nor all sufficiently acquainted with our language." And again, having been at variance with the levelling party in their own country, the measure might be considered as an aristocratical movement by more than those, who, "without any just cause that I can discover, are continually sounding the bell of aristocracy." And, third, because "it might preclude some of the first professors in other countries from a participation, among whom some of the most celebrated characters in Scotland, in this line, might be obtained."[27] The same letter stated that on January 28 he had announced to the commissioners of the federal city that he would give the shares in the Potomac company for a university in that city, and that he would like to apply the James River shares in the same way, but, considering their source, he was writing to the governor of Virginia asking the legislature at its discretion to apply them to some seminary within the state. "Hence," he added, "you will perceive, that I have in a degree anticipated your proposition." * The next day he referred his proposal, to give the Potomac shares to a national university and the James shares to a preparatory school, to the legislature of Virginia, as they had been presented to him by that body.[28] On December 1 the House of Delegates approved the disposition of the Potomac shares and suggested that the James shares be applied to a seminary in the upper country wherever Washington might deem it most convenient to the majority of the people.[29] By his will he gave the fifty shares in the Potomac Company for the university in the federal city. This laid the foundations of George Washington University. The hundred shares in the James River Company were given to Liberty Hall Academy, Rockbridge County, Virginia. For a time they yielded a substantial income, but later became valueless. Endowed by the Society of Cincinnati and by other benefactors, this academy grew into Washington College, the chief rival of Central College in the competition for the state university, and later became Washington and Lee University.

As late as 1803 in writing to M. Pictet, who wished to remove to America, Jefferson stated his intention to ask the Virginia legislature to establish a university, and added:

I hoped that some canal shares which were at the disposal of General Washington, might have been applied toward the establishment of a good seminary of learning; but he had already proceeded too far on another plan to change their direction.[30]

Later Jefferson cherished for some time the hope of bringing the faculty of the University of Edinburgh to America, but, as no opportunity offered, the project was reluctantly abandoned.[31]

A national university was long one of Jefferson's cherished ambitions. In 1800 when Dupont de Nemours visited Monticello, Jefferson asked him to draw up a plan for American education. This plan Dupont made to center in a national

---

* Washington began this letter by acknowledging the receipt of Jefferson's communication of January 23, "but not so soon as might be expected from the date of it." This equivocal expression leaves the reader in doubt whether Jefferson's letter was received before or after the President promised the Potomac shares to the federal commissioners on the 28th. Perhaps it was intended to leave Jefferson also in the dark.

university at Washington consisting of separate schools of Medicine, Mines, Social Sciences and Legislation, and Higher Mathematics. With these were to be associated a national library and museum.[32] * At the same time he was in correspondence with Joel Barlow who had an elaborate plan for a national university. On September 15, 1800, Barlow wrote to Senator Baldwin:

> I have been writing a long letter to Jefferson on quite another subject. . . . It is about learned societies, universities, public institutions, and the advantages you now have for doing something great and good if you will take it up on proper principles. If you will put me at the head of the Institution there proposed, and give it that support which you ought to do, you cannot imagine what a garden it would make of the United States. I have great projects, and only want the time and means for carrying them into effect.[33]

Although in the preceding January Jefferson had written to Dr. Priestley very definitely about his plan to establish a liberal university in central Virginia,† he heartily supported the project for a national university. He could scarcely have hoped to obtain this institution for his own state. It seemed to be taken for granted that the national institution would be situated in the capital city. His zeal for higher education seems to have been broad enough to support both proposals with the hope that the more practicable one would be realized. Barlow drew up an elaborate *Prospectus of a National Institution to be established in the United States,* which is dated January 24, 1806. This plan was an attempt virtually to duplicate French institutions. It provided for district colleges throughout the United States and a central university composed of a large number of distinct schools.[34] It was circulated widely and was favorably received. Barlow had drafted a bill for the incorporation of the institution. It was introduced into congress by Senator Logan of Pennsylvania and passed to a second reading, but was referred to a committee which never reported, and so was lost. The opposi-

---

* In an unpublished letter to James Madison written October 9, 1809, Jefferson stated that he was hopeful that Virginia would establish a university when he asked advice about the arrangement of professorships from Dupont and Dr. Priestley, and intended to give it his library. When, however, he saw this to be hopeless he conceived the idea that Congress might establish one at Washington. He thought Dupont would be willing to become president or a professor of this national university.—(*MS., L. C.*)

† See Appendix C.

tion of the colleges already in existence helped bring about its defeat.[35]

Jefferson's letter to Barlow of February 24, 1806, shows that he lent his advice to the preparation, if not of the prospectus, at least of the bill to establish the institution:

> I return you the draft of the bill for the establishment of a National Academy and University at the city of Washington, with such alterations as we talked over the last night. They are chiefly verbal.[36]

While having some resemblance to Jefferson's plan, Barlow's proposals differ so widely from anything Jefferson ever systematically advocated that the latter must have had little influence upon the plan except in the effort to have it realized.

Believing that an amendment to the constitution would be required to legalize federal support of a university, Jefferson, in his sixth annual message, December 2, 1806, recommended that such an amendment be initiated. After pointing out that the duty on imports would soon pay the public debt and thereafter would yield a surplus, he suggested that the rates might be reduced. While he believed that duties on necessities should be abolished, he feared giving the foreign manufacturer an advantage over the domestic and favored the retention of duties on luxuries purchased only by the rich:

> Their patriotism would certainly prefer its continuance and application to the great purposes of the public education, roads, rivers, canals, and such other objects of public improvement as it may be thought proper to add to the constitutional enumeration of Federal powers. By these operations new channels of communication will be opened between the States, the lines of separation will disappear, their interests will be identified, and their union cemented by new and indissoluble ties. Education is here placed among the articles of public care, not that it would be proposed to take its ordinary branches out of the hands of private enterprise, which manages so much better all the concerns to which it is equal, but a public institution can alone supply those sciences which though rarely called for are yet necessary to complete the circle, all the parts of which contribute to the improvement of the country and some of them to its preservation. The subject is now proposed for the consideration of Congress, because, if approved, by the time the state legislatures shall have deliberated on this extension of the Federal trusts, and the laws shall be passed and other arrangements made for their execution, the necessary funds will be on hand and without employment. I suppose an amendment to the Constitution by consent of the States, necessary, because the objects now recom-

mended are not among those enumerated in the Constitution, and to which it permits the public money to be applied.

The present consideration of a national establishment for education particularly is rendered proper by this circumstance, also, that if Congress, approving the proposition, shall yet think it more eligible to found it on a donation of lands, they have it now in their power to endow it with those which will be among the earliest to produce the necessary income. This foundation would have the advantage of being independent of war, which may suspend other improvements, by requiring for its own purposes the resources destined for them.[37]

The following winter Jefferson wrote in characteristic style to Barlow:

The desire of peace is very much strengthened in me by that which I feel in favor of the great subjects of your and Mr. Fulton's letters. I had fondly hoped to set those enterprises into motion with the last legislature [Congress] I shall meet. But the chance of war is an unfortunate check. I do not, however, despair that the proposition of amendment may be sent down this session to the [state] Legislatures. But it is not certain. There is a snail-paced gait for the advance of new ideas on the general mind, under which we must acquiesce. A forty years' experience of popular assemblies has taught me that you must give them time for every step you take. If too hard pressed, they balk, and the machine retrogrades.[38]

The "chance of war" led to the reality too swiftly for the "snail-paced gait" of the general mind and the National University never was established.

It is impossible to determine when Jefferson first concluded that the University of Virginia should be a new institution in a new locality. After his return from France in 1789, he showed no further interest in the reorganization of William and Mary. His proposal in 1794 to bring the Geneva professors to Virginia implied nothing about where they should be established. La Rochefoucauld traveled in America in 1795–97 and visited Monticello. He records that there was then a rumor that the legislature would soon establish a new college in a more central part of the state.[39] On January 18, 1800, he wrote to Dr. Priestley about his desire to establish in the upper country a university "on a plan so broad and liberal and modern as to be worth patronizing with the public support, and being a temptation to the youth of other states to come and drink of the cup of knowledge and fraternize with us."[40] This letter expresses ideas by which Jefferson was guided in the organization of the University and is properly regarded as the first plan for a new institution in the upper country.*   Three years later he had constantly in mind to propose to the Virginia legislature the establishment of a university on as large a scale as circumstances would permit.[41]   In 1807 his private secretary, Isaac A. Coles, after discussing the subject with the President, wrote to Cabell that William and Mary was declining and that a new institution "on an extended and liberal scale" was needed.   He urged Cabell to go into the legislature and labor to "found a new one which shall be worthy of the first state in the union." [42]   Significantly, this was the very time when Jefferson was planning for a national university.   The year before, Mr. Semple had presented a bill for the establishment of the University of Virginia by subscription, and Governor George Cabell, Joseph's brother, had spoken strongly on the need of literary institutions.[43]   In 1809 Governor Tyler, after an interview with Jefferson, urged upon the legislature the need of appropriations for public education, and for higher education in particular.[44]   This led to the establishment of the Literary Fund, which later paid for many of the university buildings.   In 1816 Jefferson outlined his plan for a university to Governor Nicholas at the time he and the other directors of the Literary Fund were preparing the report on a university, colleges, academies, and schools called for by the legislature.[45] The discussion following this report led on to the great legislative struggle of 1817–18 which ended in Jefferson's supporters accepting a plan for primary schools which they did not approve and compelling their opponents to accept a general provision for a university.   The *Bill for Establishing a System of Public Education* which Jefferson drafted in October, 1817, provided for primary schools, district colleges, and a university.   On February 11, 1818, it was offered in the House of Delegates but received only a few votes.   In its stead was adopted a provision merely for primary schools.[46]   Believing the plan had completely failed, Jefferson wrote:

We must turn to the affairs of the college, under our particular charge, and consider what we can do for it on its own scanty funds.[47]

* See Appendix C.

I hasten to apprise you [wrote Cabell four days later] that our proceedings now seem likely to eventuate differently from what I have heretofore expected. The school bill came up to the Senate in the form of Mr. Hill's amendment. We engrafted upon it a provision for an University. In that shape, it passed here by a majority of fourteen to three. This important vote took place yesterday.[48]

Two days later Cabell wrote a letter beginning, "The University bill has passed." [49]   Thus, engrafted upon a bill for the education of the poor, and wrung from a democratic House by a conservative Senate, began the University of Virginia.   Jefferson's labors for Albemarle Academy and Central College and their adoption as the University are a part of that remarkable story, worthy of a separate telling, in which we see how he came to be indeed "Father of the University of Virginia."

CHAPTER VI

THE BUILDING OF THE UNIVERSITY

IT IS true that Thomas Jefferson was one of the chief contributors to the funds of Central College. He was one of twelve who subscribed one thousand dollars each, although he was already heavily burdened with debt. The very day of the Rockfish meeting he notified his Richmond agent that his grandson would begin grinding his wheat and would send down a boat load of flour as soon as possible. He hoped this would arrive in time to pay twelve and one half per cent on a note for three thousand dollars soon to fall due, as the bank was curtailing its loans to that amount.[1] Such a gift under such circumstances shows a greater devotion than the millions with which the wealthy have founded or endowed favored institutions. However, no one thinks of Jefferson as the founder of the University of Virginia. He called himself its father. Scarcely an institution exists which can so aptly be described in the words of Emerson as "the lengthened shadow of one man." He bought the site for the university and surveyed it. He planned the buildings and superintended their construction. He wrung funds from a niggardly legislature while he sought even the smallest economy in the cost of bricks. The course of study, the plan of organization, the rules for admission, graduation, and government—all were his work. He set standards of democracy for the faculty and of manly self-reliance for the students. Nearly every detail of material construction, of organization, or of method was his. He was more than a founder. He was Father of the University of Virginia.

It is reasonable to ask how it was possible for one man thus to control a board of seven visitors composed of able and strong men. His election as rector of the board, March 29, 1819, and his tenure of this office until his death is, at best, but a partial explanation.[2]   In his mature knowledge and painstaking study of the matters to be determined, his forceful personality, and the sincere deference felt by his associates for him and for his views, we find the more significant explanation.   This was well expressed by Tucker:

> Though every essential part of the establishment required the sanction of the Board of Visitors, yet on almost all occasions they yielded to his views, partly from the unaffected deference which most of the Board had for his judgment and experience, and partly for the reason often urged by Mr. Madison, that as the scheme was originally Mr. Jefferson's and the chief responsibility for its success or failure would fall on him, it was but fair to let him execute it in his own way.[3]

General Cocke disapproved of some of Jefferson's expenditures for mere beauty and referred to the buildings as a "raree show."   However, he never obstructed Jefferson in carrying out his building plans,[4] though clothed with equal authority on the Committee of Superintendence.[5]   In February, 1818, Johnson, Cabell, and Cocke were opposed to the reappointment of Dr. Thomas Cooper.   The two former yielded to Jefferson's influence, but the Puritan conscience of the latter made him resist to the last, though he opposed the venerable Rector with great regret.[6]   In 1826, after repeated failures to secure a professor of law, the visitors overrode Jefferson's opposition and elected William Wirt President of the University and Professor of Law.   The Rector entered his objections in the minutes,[7] but voted with his colleagues and wrote the letter of notification to Wirt, urging him to accept.[8]

N. F. Cabell, editor of the Jefferson-Cabell correspondence, wrote:

> Mr. Cabell was wont to relate several pleasant anecdotes . . . relative to the dissent of the other visitors, not only from the plan of the buildings, but other novel and cherished ideas of the author; to the respectful manner in which their counter opinions were conveyed to the venerable Rector, and to the adroitness with which they were met.[9]

In their private correspondence Cocke and Cabell affectionately called Jefferson the "Sachem."[10]   The arrangement and limited size of the lecture rooms in each pavilion, as planned by Jefferson, were regarded as serious defects.   In April, 1819,

Cabell and Generals Breckenridge and Cocke agreed that they should be made larger. "We must move in concert," wrote Cabell, "or we shall perplex and disgust the Old Sachem." [11] The changes were not made, so apparently the Old Sachem prevailed.[12]

More significant was Jefferson's remarkable ability to command the services of faithful lieutenants and supporters, to fill them with the zeal of crusaders and the devotion of fanatics, and to hold them to their tasks through years of disappointment and defeat. Most notable among these was Joseph Carrington Cabell, more than thirty-five years his junior. Son of a Revolutionary officer and of a prominent Virginia family, educated at Hampden-Sidney, William and Mary, and prominent European universities, this remarkable man met Jefferson for the first time in 1806. He entered the Virginia legislature in 1809 and was a member of one or other house during all but two of the following twenty-six years. He was early attached to Jefferson's educational projects, and soon came to be recognized as his spokesman and the center of his influence at the Capital.[13] Referring to the petition and bill for Central College, Jefferson wrote: "We always counted on you as the main pillar of their support." [14]

Cabell long suffered from a serious pulmonary trouble which frequently made moderate exertion difficult or dangerous and was a heavy burden to his eager spirit. After thirteen sessions of the legislature, when the University was definitely established but when no prospect of improving its situation appeared, he announced his intention to retire to the domestic and literary leisure he long had desired, as he feared the rigors of a political canvass would carry him to the grave.[15] Jefferson's reply was unequivocal:

But the gloomiest of all prospects is in the desertion of the best friends of the institution; for desertion I must call it. I know not the necessities which may force this on you. General Cocke, you say, will explain them to me; but I cannot conceive them, nor persuade myself they are uncontrolable. I have ever hoped that yourself, Gen. Breckenridge, and Mr. Johnson, would stand at your posts in the Legislature until everything was effected and the institution opened. If it is so difficult to get along with all the energy and influence of our present colleagues in the Legislature, how can we expect to proceed at all, reducing our moving power? I know well your devotion to your country, and your foresight of the awful scenes coming on her sooner or later. With this foresight, what service can we ever render her equal to this? What object of our lives can we propose, so important? What interest of our own, which ought not to be postponed to this? Health, time, labor, on what in the single life which nature has given us, can these be better bestowed than on this immortal boon to our country? The exertions and the mortifications are temporary; the benefit eternal. If any member of our college of visitors could justifiably withdraw from this sacred duty, it would be myself, who *quadragenis stipendiis jamdudum peractis,* have neither vigor of body nor mind left to keep the field. But I will die in the last ditch. And so, I hope, you will, my friend, as well as our firm-breasted brothers and colleagues, Mr. Johnson and Gen. Breckenridge. Nature will not give you a second life wherein to atone for the omissions of this. Pray then, dear and very dear sir, do not think of deserting us; but view the sacrifices which seem to stand in your way as the lesser duties and such as ought to be postponed to this, the greatest of all. Continue with us in these holy labors, until having seen their accomplishment, we may say with old Simeon, *"nunc dimittis, Domine."* Under all circumstances, however, of praise or blame, I shall be affectionately yours,

Thomas Jefferson.[16]

A week later, Cabell replied:

It is not in my nature to resist such an appeal. I this day handed into the office of the *Enquirer* a notification that I shall again be a candidate. . . . I have shown your letter to Gen. Breckenridge and Mr. Johnson, who seemed (and particularly the former) to be as much affected by it as myself.[17]

Cabell was a Visitor of the University until his death in 1856, and Rector for thirteen years. When he retired from the legislature and resigned the presidency of the James River Canal Company, he retained this office as his one public interest.[18]

When the legislature passed the bill to establish the University, February, 1818, the battle for the institution which Jefferson and his friends wanted was far from won. He had long hoped to see the University within sight of his home, and had been developing Central College as an embodiment of his principles with the very definite hope that these ideals would gain a broader expression through the adoption of the college by the state. He had long felt that the University should be located in the upper country for reasons of health as well as to bring it nearer to the majority of the people. In 1788 he regarded Williamsburg as a very healthy situation, but a dozen years later he declared it to be eccentric in its position and exposed to the bilious diseases of the lowlands.[19]   This contradiction is better understood in the light of a letter written in 1816 in which he declares that Williamsburg is exposed to bilious fever during the months of August, September, and October, but is a very healthy situation after the first October frost.[20]

In 1814 he definitely mentioned Charlottesville as the location.   Writing to Dr. Cooper on January 16 about the university he long had contemplated, he added: "This would probably absorb the functions of William and Mary College and transfer them to a healthier and more central position; perhaps to the neighborhood of this place." [21] *

There is no doubt that Jefferson realized that no college would carry out his principles and ideals adequately unless it were under his immediate influence and supervision.   He believed in these principles so profoundly that their realization came to seem necessary to the highest well-being of his state and of the South.[22] A personal motive appears in his correspondence with D'Ivernois about the removal of the Geneva professors to Virginia:

> I should have seen with peculiar satisfaction the establishment of such a mass of science in my country, and should probably have been tempted to approach myself to it, by procuring a residence in its neighborhood at those seasons of the year at least, when the operations of agriculture are less active & interesting.[23]

In old age he sought to bring the scholarship to him.   His enthusiastic acquaintance or correspondence with men of science during many years and his pleasant relations with members of the faculty when the University at last was opened show how much these associations meant to him.

The act providing for the University required the governor to appoint one commissioner from each of the twenty-four senatorial districts to meet at Rockfish Gap on the Blue Ridge, August 1, 1818, to determine and report to the legislature at its next session:

First —   A proper site for the University.
Secondly — A plan for the building thereof.
Thirdly —   The branches of learning which should be taught therein.
Fourthly — The number and description of professorships; and

* This was less than ten weeks before his election as a trustee of Albemarle Academy set in motion the chain of events which led to the realization of his hope.

Fifthly —   Such general provision as might properly be enacted by the
Legislature, for the better organizing and governing the
University.[24]

To the friends of Central College the first problem was the
selection of commissioners. "The Executive, I think, will do
us justice," wrote Cabell, explaining how he had prevented the
selection of commissioners by the directors of the Literary
Fund. "All I want in this business is fair play—to put this
subject on a footing of just reciprocity between the two sides of
the mountain." [25]   Two days earlier he had written: "We have
fifteen districts on this side of the Ridge and I think we are safe
in the hands of the Executive." [26]

In the same letter he asked if Jefferson would serve as a commissioner, suggested Madison as another, and urged rapid work
at Central College to strengthen its claim. The reply was
prompt:

you seem to doubt whether Mr. Madison would serve if named a Commissioner . . . but there can be no doubt that he would, & it is most
important that he should.   as to myself, I should be ready to do anything
in my power for the institution, but that is not the exact question.   would
it promote the success of the institution most for me to be in or out of it?
out of it, I believe.   It is still to depend ultimately on the will of the
legislature, and that has its uncertainties.   there are fanatics both in religion and politics, who without knowing me personally have long been
taught to consider me as a raw head & bloody bones, and as we can afford
to lose no votes in that body I do think it would be better that you should
be named for our district.   do not consider this as mock-modesty.   it
is the cool & deliberate act of my judgment.   I believe the institution would
be more popular without me than with me, and this is the most important
consideration . . . I regard nothing but the good of the cause.[27]

Cabell felt that his own appointment would arouse as much
opposition as that of Jefferson, and finally left the matter in the
hands of a group of their friends, expecting neither of them to
be named.[28]   When the commission was named it included both
Madison and Jefferson and a number of others who had contributed to Central College or were its recognized friends.

The commission, appointed in March, was to meet on the first
of August and to make such adjournments as might be necessary
until its work should be done.   Adjournment to Staunton had
been urged,[29] but Jefferson favored prompt action:

My own opinion will be against any adjournment as long as we can get bread and water and a floor to lie on at the Gap . . . but my information is that we shall be tolerably well off at the Gap; that they have forty lodging rooms and are now making ample preparations. A waggonload of beds has passed through Charlottesville which at this season, however, we shall not need.[30]

During the early summer the friends of Central College were active. Written authority to transfer the property to the state was obtained from a majority of the subscribers and a deed was regularly executed by the proctor.[31] Through Alexander Garrett, Jefferson had written to every court clerk in Virginia for information about the distance of his courthouse from some well-known town and for facts about population, roads, and transportation. There is a tradition that he prepared a long list of persons over eighty years of age in Albemarle as evidence of its healthful climate.[32] His chief argument was to be the central situation of Central College. The very name had been selected years before to emphasize a fact of geography as well as to symbolize one of organization.[33] But other localities claimed to offer greater advantages. Staunton regarded itself as the center of the state and wanted the capital moved there from Richmond. The location of the University there would help these aspirations just as its location east of the Ridge would weaken them.[34] The year before Cabell had written: "When I was at Staunton the very spot where the University was to be placed was pointed out to me. And should there be a bank at Staunton, you may expect to hear it called the Central Bank." [35]

Washington Academy at Lexington, endowed by Washington and the Society of Cincinnati, was the other competitor and the one feared by Jefferson. Staunton had not been enterprising enough to make tangible offers of land or money, but Lexington offered, besides its plant and endowment, a substantial subscription and the promise of the entire estate of an old man. This consisted of 3353 acres of land, much of it valuable, fifty-seven slaves, and other property, estimated to be worth in all $100,-000.[36] Against this, Central College could offer only 200 acres of land, some unfinished buildings, and about $45,000 in cash and subscriptions.[37] To practical commissioners, buildings and actual money would be a powerful argument, and it would be easy to defeat the pretensions of Staunton; but to checkmate Lexington Jefferson must make the most of his argument from central location. He carefully prepared on cardboard a map of the state, showing its geographical center and the center of white population. From the mouth of the Chesapeake to the Ohio he drew a straight line, passing through or near Charlottesville and Staunton, thus dividing the state into two nearly equal parts. His statistics showed that there was a difference of only 15,000 in the white population north and south of this line. A line from the same point to the Ohio through Lexington would leave 91,009 more people to the north than to the south. A dividing line north and south would naturally follow the crest of the Blue Ridge. This would leave 150,121 more on the east than on the west. Drawn parallel to the Ridge but through Staunton, it would leave 221,733 more on the east. Through Lexington this would be 175,191, but through Central College it would be only 36,315. If the argument were to be based upon physical distances, it would be equally favorable to Central College when compared with Lexington. In a straight line Staunton was 110 miles from the Potomac and 112½ from the North Carolina line—a difference of 2½ miles. Similar measurements for Lexington showed a difference of 52½, and for Charlottesville of 11½ miles. Thus the Central College was nearly as central as Staunton and much more than Lexington.[38] Later, in the legislature, the friends of Staunton or of Lexington argued that these lines were not properly drawn and did not fairly represent the center of white population. Their arguments were that the southern part of the state should be laid off as a rectangle and the northern part as a triangle, that the line of equal population should start north of the mouth of the Chesapeake, and that it should run due west and the transverse line due north and south.[39] Jefferson's answer to these arguments throws light upon his whole computation:

I take up my pen now on the subject of my estimate of the center of white population. You say, it is objected, that the commencement at the mouth of the Chesapeake is nearer the southern than the northern limit on the coast. That is true; but the greatest part of what is north is water. There is more land on the south than north. I do not think a fairer point of commencement can be taken, and being a remarkable one, I therefore took it. The point of commencement being determined, the direction of the line of equal division is not a matter of choice, it must from thence take whatever direction an equal division of the population commands; and the census proves this to pass near Charlottesville, the Rockfish Gap, and Staunton. The Blue Ridge again, in the cross division, is so natural a dividing line, as to have been universally so considered, and a parallel course with that should therefore be taken for the line of equal division that way. They talk of a division by an east and west line, but our northern boundary tends north of northwest, while the southern is east and west, the fair direction is between the two, as that is which I took. Why should they divide by a parallel to our southern, more than to our northern boundary? What reason can be given for laying off the southern half in a parallelogram, and the northern in a triangle? Not a single one but to bring the course of that line nearer to Lexington. The state itself, being triangular, each half should be so. An east and west line would take the line of equal division entirely from Staunton, but I do not believe it would from Charlottesville; and while a north and south line would take it entirely from Lexington, I believe it would be still as near to Charlottesville; and, in my opinion, run your lines in what direction you please, they will pass close to Charlottesville, and for the very good reason that it is truly central to the white population.[40]

The commission met at Rockfish Gap on Saturday, August 1, as directed by law. Jefferson made the journey from Monticello on horseback, being so infirm that he thought it well to divide the ride of twenty-eight miles between two days.[41] He had invited Madison and Judge Roane to be his guests for a day or two before his departure that they might advise on what should be proposed, adding, in his letter to the latter, "I mention this to nobody but yourself and him, to avoid jealousy, and that even this little conciliabulum may be unknown and unsuspected." [42]

At least twenty-one commissioners attended the meeting. Jefferson was recognized as the moving spirit among them and was chosen to be their chairman.[43] During the first day of discussion he listened in silence until conflicting arguments had caused hopeless confusion in the minds of the commissioners. As delightfully expressed by Dr. Bruce, "It was at this critical moment that he modestly drew forth that innocent-looking blunderbuss, his map, and quietly spread it out for the inspection of the body." [44] * This argument was unanswerable. When the vote was taken on Monday, Breckenridge, Pendleton, and J. M.

* Quoted by permission of the Macmillan Co.

Taylor voted for Lexington, Stuart and Wilson for Staunton and the remaining commissioners for Charlottesville. The vote was made unanimous. A committee was chosen to prepare the report of the commissioners. It consisted of Thomas Jefferson, James Madison, General Breckenridge, and Judges Roane, Stuart, and Dade—one advocate of Staunton, one of Lexington, and four of Charlottesville.[45] On Tuesday twenty-one commissioners signed the report, and their work was done.

This remarkable report was written by Jefferson in June. He and Madison had been expected by the other commissioners to draft a report,[46] but the latter "perseveringly threw back the undertaking" upon Jefferson.[47] Late in June a copy was sent to Madison for criticism with a letter explaining that the body of the report was intended primarily to attract wavering votes in the House of Representatives. With these were enclosed on detached sheets population statistics and that part of the report which recommends that Central College be adopted as the University.[48] It is doubtful if Madison made any changes, and those made by the commissioners seem to have been slight.*

The struggle for the adoption of the Rockfish Report was the most dramatic of Jefferson's great battles for the University. At the opening of the legislature in December, 1818, Mr. Taylor of Chesterfield presented the report to the House. Cabell wrote to Jefferson:

> The report was read and received with great attention in both the houses. . . . The ability and value of the report, I am informed, are universally admitted. Present prospects are very favorable to a successful issue. Some votes about William and Mary may be lost; but nothing like a serious diversion in favor of a western site is, I believe, to be apprehended. . . . All that I can now positively affirm is, that the clouds seem to be scattering, and the prospect to smile.[49]

This forecast proved to be unduly hopeful. Taylor introduced a bill, largely copied from Jefferson's of the preceding year, and it was referred to a committee less favorable to Central College than Cabell had expected to obtain.[50] The friends of Lexington and Staunton tried to show that Jefferson's computation of the center of population was incorrect and that the westward movement would soon place the center farther west. Ca-

---

* See Appendix J.

bell showed these claims to be unfounded.[51] The friends of William and Mary demanded an appropriation of $5,000 per year as the price of their support. Cabell refused to compromise.[52] The Lexington supporters tried to induce the House committee to report the bill with the location blank, but it recommended Central College by a seven to six vote.[53] The Valley interests made common cause with the West, with the William and Mary group, and with a number of members along the eastern foot of the Blue Ridge. Cabell met combination with combination. He united Eastern interests in support of the bill. He districted the state and induced prominent citizens to influence delegates from their vicinity. He wrote careful discussions of the questions at issue, or had them written by others, and published them for the public information. He rose early to make computations of population. He was up until three in the morning discussing means of success with prominent men. He "passed the night in watchful reflection and the day in ceaseless activity." He wrote to Jefferson:

The course of things here will surprise and distress you. But be assured, sir, I do not exaggerate; and we have been compelled to meet the opposition on their own ground. The liberal and enlightened views of great statesmen pass over our heads unheeded like the spheres above. When we assemble here, an eastern and western feeling supersedes all other considerations.[54]

Under these conditions his frail health gave way again and hemorrhage followed hemorrhage, but his indomitable spirit yielded to nothing. Spitting blood in debate, at times unable to stand, but refusing to leave the capital until the question should be settled, he united and led the friends of Central College, brought to its support many members of the House of Delegates, and broke through the hostile alliances. The decisive vote was taken in the House, January 18, on the motion to strike Central College from the bill. It failed by 69 to 114. To escape the strain upon his feelings, Cabell had left the lobby before the vote, and he missed the eloquent and generous speech of Mr. Baldwin, an ardent advocate of Staunton, who, now that he was defeated, urged the West to come heartily to the support of the University. The next day the bill passed the House with only twenty-eight adverse votes. It was immediately taken up in the Senate.

The committee would admit no amendments. The motion to strike out Central College was beaten by sixteen to seven, and the bill passed the Senate by twenty-two to one on January 25, 1819.[55]

In Jefferson's answer to Cabell's joyous letter, announcing the victory for Central College, he gave one line to congratulation, then plunged into the problems of the future—buildings and equipment, faculty and funds.[56] His general plan for buildings had already been adopted for Central College—May 5, 1817.[57] He had explained this plan to the trustees of East Tennessee College in 1810. Declaring a large common building a mistake, he advised a small lodge for each professor, with a hall below for his class and two rooms above for him. These, joined by barracks for the students and a covered way connecting all, "around an open square of grass and trees would make it an academical village instead of a large and common den of noise, of filth and fetid air. It would afford that quiet retirement so friendly to study, and lessen the dangers of fire, infection, and tumult. Every professor would be the police officer of the students adjacent to his own lodge, which should include those of his own class of preference, and might be at the head of their table, if, as I suppose, it can be reconciled with the necessary economy to dine them in smaller and separate parties, rather than in a large and common mess." [58]

This plan was expressed in less sensational style in the letter to Governor Nicholas, April 2, 1816:

As the buildings to be erected will also enter into their report, I would strongly recommend to their consideration, instead of one immense building, to have a small one for every professorship, arranged at proper distances around a square, or rather three sides of a square to admit extension, connected by a piazza, so that they may go dry from one school to another. This village form is preferable to a single great building for many reasons, particularly on account of fire, health, economy, peace and quiet.[59]

In 1817 Jefferson said he formed the idea of the academic village about fifteen years before.[60] Bernard C. Steiner has argued that he adopted the idea of a hollow square from the *Essay on a System of National Education* by Reverend Samuel Knox, but Dr. Fiske Kimball thinks the differences are greater than the resemblances and that Jefferson arrived at the

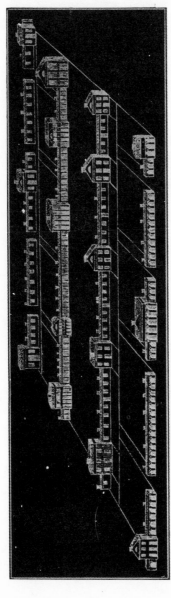

JEFFERSON'S PLAN FOR THE UNIVERSITY OF VIRGINIA

This drawing was made by Jefferson and shaded by his granddaughter, Cornelia J. Randolph. It shows his plan for the University after he had adopted Latrobe's suggestion to place the pavilions at the corners but before he had determined the style and location of the Rotunda.

plan by independent thinking from what he had observed in European universities, and experienced at William and Mary.[61] Until the building of the first pavilion, the plan was Jefferson's without modification. On May 9, four days after his plan was adopted, he wrote to William Thornton, the architect, asking for some rough sketches. Thornton sent two sketches with additional suggestions, of which some were followed.[62] This seems to have been all that Thornton contributed to the plan.[63] On June 17 Jefferson wrote also to the architect Latrobe, who sent him bulky drawings. The idea of an imposing building in the north line seems to have been his. He sent preliminary suggestions on July 24 and his drawings arrived on October 6. On August 3, Jefferson had written that they would leave the north side open so it could be filled with "something of the grand kind" if Central College should be adopted by the state as the University of Virginia. On October 12, after the visitors had decided to build two more pavilions the ensuing season, he wrote to Latrobe: "We shall certainly select their fronts from these" [drawings]. Latrobe's influence is plain in Pavilions III and V, and it seems to have been he who led Jefferson to modify his plan and place pavilions at the corners.[64] Jefferson traveled in England during his mission to France and is supposed to have derived his idea of the serpentine walls from those he saw in the gardens of rural England.[65] Between February and October, 1819, he drew the plans and wrote out specifications for five pavilions with their adjacent dormitories and for five hotels. In 1821 he drafted plans and specifications for the Rotunda and after his eightieth birthday he prepared plans for an observatory and for an anatomical hall.[66] The drawings preserved by his descendants show how thoughtfully he planned every detail, whether for utility or adornment.* An essential part of his plan was that each principal building should, for its educational value, show some model of classic architecture. His main drawings were copied or adapted from *The Architecture of A. Palladio,* edited by Inigo Jones, two volumes, London, 1742.[67] Dr. Lambeth said that he removed from the classic forms of the Caesars the architectural rubbish of the centuries.[68]

---

* About sixty of Jefferson's drawings for the university buildings are now in the possession of the University of Virginia besides several in other collections. Kimball, *Thomas Jefferson: Architect,* 200–205.

CHART II

PLAN USED IN THE SURVEY OF CENTRAL COLLEGE

July 18, 1817

a. The place at which the theodolite was fixed, being the center of the northern square[e] and the point destined for some principal building in the level of the square l.m.n.o.

The fall from a. to d. 18f from a. to d. the bearing
magnetically   S.21°W
add for variation   2½
                                            ————
                                           S 23½W

The true meridian was that day 2½° to left of magnetic.

b. Is the center of the middle square and at g. we propose to erect our first pavilion. *c.* is the center of the southern square. Locust stakes were driven at e.a.f./g.b.h./i.c.k. and at d. is a pile of stones.

Each square is to be level within itself, with a pavilion at each end, to wit at ef, gh, ik and ten dormitories on each side of each pavilion, filling up the sides of the squares.

From a. to b. was measured 255f or 85 yds, b.c. the same and c.d. the half, from the points a.b.c. was measured 100f each way to ef, gh, ik, making each square 255f by 200f = .8521 of an acre or nearly $\frac{17}{20}$.

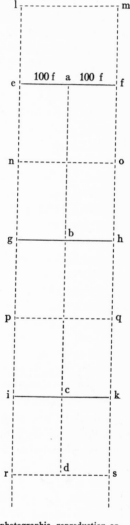

From the first page of Jefferson's pocket notebook. A photographic reproduction appears in Lambert, *Thomas Jefferson as an Architect,* Plate XIII.

This adornment was expensive. Tucker thinks the ornamental parts of the pavilions cost more than those which were indispensable.[69] For this large expense Jefferson was severely criticized, and this criticism seems the more just when we consider the scanty resources at his command and the long delay in opening the University for want of funds.[70]

On July 18, 1817, Jefferson made the first survey for Central College. A rectangle 200 feet wide was laid out and divided into three parts, each 255 feet long. Opposite the middle of these lesser rectangles were to be built the first six pavilions, or prolars, are known as East and West Range. This part of the pavilion would fill up the sides, and at the center of the northern square was to be built some principal building.[71] This plan admitted of indefinite extension to the south. During Jefferson's rectorship the pavilions were increased to ten, six hotels were built on outer lines parallel to those of the pavilions, and the Rotunda became the principal building at the center of the northern square. The two rows of pavilions and dormitories with their striking colonnades of round white pillars are known respectively as East and West Lawn. The hotels, built on lower levels, with covered ways supported by square brick pillars, are known as East and West Range. This part of the University today shows few important modifications of Jefferson's plan. Even the great trees that border the lawns were planned by him, though they were not planted until after his death.[72] On May 5, 1817, the visitors of Central College appointed Thomas Jefferson and John Hartwell Cocke a committee of superintendence "with authority, jointly or severally, to advise and sanction all plans and the application of moneys for executing them."[73] Two years later the same appointment was renewed by the reorganized visitors of the University.[74] If for no other reason, his residence near the College would have made most of these duties devolve upon Jefferson. "Our Central College gives me more employment than I am equal to," he wrote to Cabell on the day when Jefferson sent him the *Bill to Establish a System of Public Education*.[75] He bargained with bricklayers in Lynchburg, and, as their prices seemed high, he had Cabell make careful inquiry in Richmond, with the hope of making a better bargain.[76] Through his granddaughter's husband he obtained prices on a clock and a bell in Boston. He hired stonecutters from Italy to carve the ornamental capitals from Virginia stone, but when he discovered that the quality of the stone was poor and the cost greater than for the same articles in Italian marble, he ordered them carved in Italy.[77] He bought land to insure an adequate water supply,[78] he planned for an observatory, he studied the practicability of lighting with gas,[79] he taught the workmen how to cover the flat roofs with tin. These are a few of the many and varied ways in which every phase of the physical needs of the University was considered, planned, and provided for by Jefferson.

Naturally a large part of such a task was to find the resources to pay for the buildings. When Central College became the University of Virginia, its assets barely equalled $50,000.[80] The subscriptions to Central College amounted to $43,808 but some subscribers were very slow in making payment. In 1822 the Committee of Superintendence was authorized to employ a collector.[81] A year later the collector was directed to call again upon subscribers who had not paid and to institute court proceedings against those who would not pay nor give notes or bonds, payable in ninety days.[82] During that year he had collected $4,825.77½ and obtained bonds or promises for $10,107.-93¾.[83] During the next year he collected $2,069.88½ and considered $7,468.92½ outstanding to be sperate.[84] The next year he collected $2,734.89. Of the balance he regarded $4,306.53½ as sperate and $4,500 as desperate.[85] This loss of more than ten per cent and the discouraging slowness with which the rest was paid were a serious hindrance to the visitors who were depending upon these payments to meet the costs of building.

The act providing for the University appropriated $15,000 per year from the Literary Fund toward its expenses.[85] As estimated by Jefferson this would have made it possible for the University to open with a minimum of accommodations for faculty and students at the end of thirteen years. He clung to the belief that the buildings must be provided for before the institution should be opened, lest the public should be satisfied and no further funds could be obtained to finish the buildings.[86] He explained this view to several of his associate visitors:

We have proceeded from the beginning on the sound determination to finish the buildings before opening the institution; because, once opened, all its funds will be absorbed by professors' salaries, etc., and nothing remain ever to finish the buildings. . . . Of the wisdom of this proceeding and of its greater good to the public finally, I cannot a moment doubt. . . . I am not at all disheartened with what has passed nor disposed to give up the ship. We have only to lie still, to do and say nothing, and firmly avoid opening. The public opinion is advancing; it is coming to our aid and will force the institution on to consummation.[87]

To hasten the building the visitors borrowed from the banks, giving outstanding subscriptions and the credit of individual visitors for security. They borrowed from the Literary Fund, pledging the future annuities to the University. They borrowed money claimed by the state from the federal government, then they induced the government to allow the claim and pay the money. Then the state was induced to suspend interest on the loan and finally to cancel the principal.[88] To gain this necessary support for the University, Cabell toiled year after year in the legislature with his old time vigor and devotion. How great were the difficulties to be overcome we realize from his reports of sectional or sectarian combinations to prevent appropriations to the University or to obtain them for other institutions.[89] How sensitive both he and the legislature were toward these frequent appeals for funds can be seen in his admonition, repeated after nearly every triumph—"We must never come here again for money to erect buildings."[90] From Monticello Jefferson directed these annual struggles for means, suggesting overlooked possibilities for funds, recommending methods of campaigning, furnishing his lieutenant with reports, estimates, and plans to be used in answering critics and satisfying the doubtful.[91] Late in 1820 he wrote:

To rebut exaggerated estimates of what our institution is to cost, and reproaches of deceptive estimates, $162,364 will be about the cost of the whole establishment when completed. Not an office at Washington has cost less. The single building of the courthouse of Henrico has cost nearly that; and the massive walls of the millions of bricks of William and Mary could not be now built for a greater sum.[92]

With this letter, written on November 28, 1820, Jefferson enclosed a statement of more than usual interest:

A general view of what the lands, buildings, and all other expenditures for the University will have cost when completed, estimated from the moneys actually received, and what the Proctor states as further necessary.

Received of the subscriptions about	$ 19,000
Loan from the Literary Fund	60,000
Annuities of 1819, '20	30,000
To be received, the annuity of 1821, included in Proctor's estimate	15,000
Further necessary to complete the Pavilions, Hotels and Dormitories by do	38,364
Probable actual cost of whole establishment, (exclusive of Library)	$162,364

Estimates Heretofore Made

10 Pavilions for accommodation of Professors at $6,000 each	$ 60,000
6 Hotels for dieting the students, at $3,500 each . .	21,000
104 Dormitories, at $350 each	36,400
200 Acres of land, and buildings purchased, may be stated as worth	10,000
Covering with tin instead of shingles, levelling grounds and streets, bringing water in pipes, and numerous other contingencies, say	10,000
Excess of actual cost above the estimates (about 18 per cent)	24,964
	$162,364

To liberate the funds of the University, and to open it in 1821, with only six professors, will require —

1.	A remission of the loan of	$60,000
2.	A supplementary sum to liberate the annuities of 1821, 2, 3,	45,000
3.	To make good the deficit estimated by the Proctor . .	8,364
4.	An additional sum for the building of the Library . .	40,000
5.	And to establish and maintain ten Professorships, an equal partition of the Literary Fund between the University and elementary schools will be necessary, say $30,000 a year to each.	

A building for an Observatory not having been mentioned in the Rockfish report, is not brought into view here. It will cost about ten or twelve thousand dollars, and may be accomplished by the balance of subscription money not taken into account in the report of 1820, and by the rents for the hotels and dormitories.[93]

Under date of November 9, Jefferson had written to Governor Randolph, his son-in-law, for communication to the legislature, a financial report based upon the same figures. After an explanation of the deficit of $8,364, came the confident sentence— "We are now so near the end of our work as to leave little room for future errors of estimate." [94] How pathetically over-confident these estimates were can be appreciated by comparing them with the actual costs of the buildings as reported by Dr. Bruce:

Pavilions		Hotels	
I	$ 9,992.05	A	$4,499.21
II	10,863.57	B	6,278.29
III	16,528.47	C	4,525.38
IV	11,173.30	D	6,245.39
V	11,723.41	E	4,638.71
VI	9,793.40	F	6,013.68
VII	9,399.73		
VIII	10,786.86	Dormitories	
IX	8,785.04		$78,509.58 *
X	11,758.06		

A comparison of these figures will show that the pavilions cost $110,803.89 instead of the $60,000 estimated by Jefferson, or an average of more than $11,080.38 instead of $6,000. The hotels cost $32,200.66 instead of $21,000, an average of $5,366.77 instead of $3,500. Where he allowed 18 per cent for an excess of actual cost above the estimates it should have been for the pavilions 46 per cent, for the hotels 35, for the dormitories 54, or for all combined 47. The balance sheet of the Proctor for 1828 shows that up to that year the residential buildings had cost $236,678.29 and the Rotunda $57,749.33. [95]

Once the pavilions, hotels, and dormitories were provided for, Jefferson became convinced that the library must likewise be made secure before the opening of the institution should divert all revenues to other channels. [96] In June, 1822, he wrote that these buildings would be completed in three months, and added:

Our late legislature refused to enable us to proceed with the Rotunda; it is said by those who attended it to have been truly the *Parliamentum indoctissimum* that ever assembled in this state. The late elections have

* Quoted by permission of the Macmillan Co.

changed a majority of the members and given us some valuable friends. Should the next session merely relinquish the debt of $120,000, which it is believed they will, our annuity will in three years enable us to finish the Rotunda and then to open the institution; should they give us $50,000 additional to build it, we may open within a year succeeding the gift.[97]

Proposals to borrow further from the Literary Fund or from private interests with state endorsements, requests for appropriations from interest due the state from the federal government and for permission to delay interest payments on loans already made, and various other expedients were urged by friends of the University. An additional loan finally made possible the completion of the Rotunda, and later legislatures cancelled these debts. His struggle for buildings was about ended in 1824 when Jefferson could write: "We are at this time about building a Dome to our principal edifice on De Lorme's plan." [98]

He was no less energetic in providing for the books of the library than for the building to shelter them. In September, 1824, he wrote to Madison about the catalogue and tables he had prepared, classifying and showing the size and cost of the 6,860 volumes which he regarded as the necessary nucleus for the university library. These would cost $24,076. If the $50,-000 being sought at that time should be received, it would pay for these books, would provide $10,000 for scientific apparatus, and would leave $16,000, which he believed should be invested in stocks to yield $1000 per year for the upkeep of the library.[99] By his will he left his own library to the University,[100] but the embarrassment of his estate prevented this bequest from being carried out. Only four of his books were given to the University, and this was during his lifetime.[101]

In Jefferson's first list of books for the library there were 409 touching the classics, 367 on jurisprudence, 305 on modern history, 175 on religion and ecclesiastical history, 160 on pathology, 118 on philosophy and literature, and lesser numbers on other subjects. Many of these were in foreign languages.[102] He classified them in forty-two groups, but when the library finally was arranged, other hands placed them in twenty-nine classes. His classification conformed in general to the time-honored psychology which recognizes memory, reason, and imagination as the faculties of the mind to which belong respectively, history, philosophy and the fine arts. This plan of classification is said to be derived from Bacon's subdivision of knowledge.[103]

Rules for the use of the library were drafted in March, 1825, three days before the opening of the University. By these, the faculty was allowed free use of the library, but students could get books only on request of the professors and not more than three at any time. They were allowed to enter the library only by ticket and not more than twenty were admitted in any one day. Fines for the late return of books were in proportion to the size of the books. Students were required to deposit a library fee of one dollar, which must be renewed when fines exceeded that amount.[104] These stringent regulations, so similar in character to those which Jefferson proposed for the state library in 1779, emphasize the comparative expensiveness and preciousness of books in his time.

CHAPTER VII

THE FACULTY OF THE UNIVERSITY

NONE realized more fully than Jefferson that his oft-repeated purpose that the University should teach "all the branches of science useful to us, and at this day, in their highest degree" could be fulfilled only by the work of a very superior faculty. "We mean to accept for our institution no person of secondary grade in his science if there be one of the first on either side of the Atlantic who can be tempted to come to us." [1] "No secondary character will be received among them. Either the ablest which America or Europe can furnish, or none at all." [2] "We are next to observe that a man is not qualified for a professor, knowing nothing but merely his own profession. He should be otherwise well-educated as to the sciences generally; able to converse understandingly with the scientific men with whom he is associated, and to assist in the councils of the Faculty on any subject of science on which they may have occasion to deliberate. Without this, he will incur their contempt and bring disreputation on the institution. . . . We have all, from the beginning, considered the high qualifications of our professors as the only means by which we could give to our institution splendor and pre-eminence over all its sister seminaries." [3] * "Besides the first degree of eminence in science, a professor with us must be of sober and correct morals and habits, having the talent of communicating his knowledge with facility, and of an accommodating and peaceful temper." [4] *Detur digniori* was the motto which Jefferson proposed for himself and his associates in the selection of professors. [5]

To Jefferson's mind the necessary qualifications in a professor seem to have been eminence in his own field of scholarship, broad culture, teaching ability, integrity and amiability. However, some other qualifications were not entirely without

* For a longer passage from this letter see Appendix O.

weight. In 1791 he approved both Edinburgh and Geneva because the spirit of republicanism had become strong among both students and faculty.[6] The resistance of the Geneva professors to a political aristocracy strengthened his desire to have them remove to America in 1794–95.[7] "In the selection of our law professor we must be rigorously attentive to his political principles," he wrote to Madison in 1826, and went on to explain that before the Revolution *Coke on Littleton* was a universal elementary text and made good Whigs of young lawyers but when it was superseded by Blackstone they began to slide into Toryism.[8]

He seems to have made it clear to Mr. Gilmer in 1824 that no minister was to be engaged as a professor.[9] Nevertheless, the first professor appointed to the faculty of Central College was the Reverend Samuel Knox, president of Baltimore College. This was in July, 1817.[10] This inconsistency is not hard to explain. Dr. Knox was a native of Ireland, a graduate of Glasgow University, and a strict Presbyterian who had preached and published a sermon condemning the views of Dr. Priestley. However, he had advocated Jefferson for the presidency, vindicating his religious conduct and principles, and was the author of a treatise on education supposed to have influenced Jefferson's plans for the University. The notice of his appointment as Professor of Languages, Belles Lettres, Rhetoric, History and Geography in Central College never reached him.[11] In September the Board received apparently unreliable information that Dr. Knox had "retired from business," [12] and they sought elsewhere, but without success, for a professor of these subjects.[13] More than a year later Dr. Knox learned of his nomination and wrote to Jefferson asking for a position. The reply was evasive, probably because at that time Jefferson was distressed by the opposition of religious bodies to the appointment of Dr. Thomas Cooper to the faculty.[14]

The criticism of the engagement of Dr. Cooper for the faculty of Central College was comparatively mild, but became more widespread and acrimonious when he was reappointed after the College was adopted as a state institution. It was based chiefly upon the belief that because of the liberality of his religious views he was an improper person to be an instructor of youth.

Many Virginians believed that Jefferson intended the University to be a center of Unitarian propaganda; others were convinced that he was opposed to all religion.[15]   There is no doubt that Dr. Cooper's views were far from orthodox.   This was abundantly proved by Dr. John Rice, a Presbyterian minister and editor, from Dr. Cooper's own writings.[16]   The whole story of Jefferson's relations with Cooper seems to show that he never considered his religious beliefs to have any relation to his fitness as a teacher of science or of law.

In 1810, Jefferson sent to a friend a letter from "Judge Cooper, of Pennsylvania, a political refugee with Dr. Priestley from the fires and mobs of Birmingham"; he declared him one of the ablest men in America in several branches of science, including chemistry and mineralogy.   In Jefferson's opinion his writings on political economy were the best produced in America and his legal opinion in "Dempsy vs. The Insurers" the most luminous he had seen and one destined to effect a revolution of opinion on the question treated.[17]   For many years he was in correspondence with Dr. Cooper, asking advice about such matters as subjects to be taught, admission requirements, or faculty personnel.[18]   On October 7, 1817, the Visitors of Central College— Madison, Monroe, Watson, Cocke, Cabell, and Jefferson being present—offered Cooper the professorship of chemistry, zoölogy, botany, and anatomy, and also the professorship of law.[19]   In December Jefferson received Cooper's acceptance.[20]   Fourteen months later he wrote of their obligations to receive Dr. Cooper and advised that an usher be induced to open a grammar school in Charlottesville and that Dr. Cooper instruct the upper classes and open his Law School.[21]

Some of the visitors did not recognize any obligation to Dr. Cooper, and Cabell frankly wrote Jefferson of his previous satisfaction in supposing their arrangement with him to be at an end.[22]   On March 1, Jefferson wrote at length, defending Cooper's character and habits and explaining the grounds of their obligation to him.   His concluding sentences show his feeling toward Cooper:

> From all this it appears to me that we are bound, not only in consistency and reputation, but in law, if Dr. Cooper accepts our propositions, and why should we wish otherwise?   Cooper is acknowledged by every enlightened

man who knows him, to be the greatest man in America, in the powers of mind, and in acquired information; and that without a single exception. I understand, indeed, that a rumor unfavorable to his habits, has been afloat, in some places, but never heard of a single man who undertook to charge him with either present or late intemperance; and I think rumor is fairly outweighed by the counter-evidence of the great desire shown at William and Mary to get him, that shown by the enlightened men of Philadelphia to retain him . . . . , the anxiety of New York to get him, that of ·Correa to place him here, who is in constant intercourse with him, the evidence I received in his visit here, that the state of his health permitted him to eat nothing but vegetables, and drink nothing but water, his declarations to me at table, that he dared not drink ale or cider, or a single glass of wine, and this in the presence of Correa, who, if there had been any hypocracy in it, would not have failed to tell me so.[23]

Apparently he sought verification of this opinion from some of his Philadelphia friends, for a few weeks later he received a letter from one of them saying that he had feared only two things about Dr. Cooper—his temper, said to be unaccommodating, and his temperance, which had often been questioned. He added that he had been set at rest on the latter point by a reliable friend who assured him that Dr. Cooper was only a water drinker and that the story of his intemperance probably was started by the appearance of his face, though at an earlier time it may have had some foundation because of domestic infelicity.[24] What relationship may have existed between the unaccommodating temper and either the domestic infelicity or the religious independence it is now idle to inquire.

Cooper's nomination in 1817 had been unanimous,[25] but in 1819 Cabell and Johnson were opposed on grounds of expediency [26] and General Cocke for conscientious reasons.[27] However, the Old Sachem prevailed; Johnson and Cabell acquiesced; and Cooper was reëlected Professor of Chemistry, Mineralogy, and Natural Philosophy and Professor of Law, with a guaranteed income of not less than $3500 per year, on March 29.[28] The public opposition to Dr. Cooper continued and operated to damage the standing of the University in parts of the state. The lack of funds made necessary a long postponement in the opening of the University, and in 1820 the Visitors released Dr. Cooper, paying him $1500 to indemnify him for the inconvenience and loss this engagement had cost him.[29] Dr. Cooper had trouble at the College of South Carolina, to which he went after the termination of his contract with the Visitors. Jefferson seized the opportunity to renew his proposal to bring him to the University, expecting only one dissentient among the Visitors.   Madison advised against it, and the Rector reluctantly abandoned his fond hope.[30]   Opinions of Cooper's real ability in scholarship differ widely.   Dr. Adams believed him the ablest professor of economics and politics in the country and wished he had been allowed a fair chance among the first faculty of the University, though he recognized that "the eccentricities of Dr. Cooper's character and genius stood in the way of academic success." [31]   Dr. Bruce believes that he was overrated by Jefferson, whose judgment seems to have been colored by his sympathy with Cooper and Priestley as martyrs to intellectual freedom.[32]   And Dr. Malone's extensive study of Cooper bears out this opinion.[33]

In general, Jefferson seems to have ignored the religious affiliations of the professors.   His objection to ministers was because of their active association with sectarian groups, in his day a fruitful source of social friction.   The charge that he intended the University to be a center of Unitarian influence is totally groundless, though his friendly attitude toward the tenets of that sect is shown in his letter of January 8, 1825, to Benjamin Waterhouse:

Your favor of Dec. 24 is received.   the Professors of our University, 8 in number are all engaged.   those of ant. and Mod. lang. are already on the spot.   3 more are hourly expected to arrive, and on their arrival the whole will assemble & enter on their duties.   there remains therefore no place in which we can avail ourselves of the services of the rev'd mr. Bertrum as a teacher.   I wish we could do it as a Preacher.   I am anxious to see the doctrine of one god commenced in our state.   But the popul'n of my neighb'hood is too slender, and is too much divided into other sects to maintain any one preacher well.   I must therefore be contented to be an Unitarian by myself, although I know there are many around me who would become so, if once they could hear the questions fairly stated.[34]

On May 28, 1856, Professor George Tucker wrote to Henry S. Randall that he did not remember hearing Jefferson discuss or inquire into the religious views of either professors or visitors. On June 1, Professor Robley Dunglison wrote the same to Mr. Randall, and added that he had not been asked anything about religion by Mr. Gilmer.   Both stated that all the first professors were Episcopalians except Blaetterman, who was a German Lutheran.[35]

To Jefferson the qualities which make a great man would likewise make a great professor. Perhaps the distinctive work for which a professor is set apart would have led him to attach greater value to knowledge than in the case of men found in other kinds of work. In 1808 he wrote to Dr. Rush:

for thus I estimate the qualities of the mind 1. good humor. 2. integrity. 3. industry. 4. science. the preference of the 1st to the 2d quality may not at first be acquiesced in, but certainly we had all rather associate with a good humored light principled man than with an ill tempered rigorist in morality.[36]

This high standard for professors created the problem of finding men who could measure up to it. While preferring Americans, Jefferson early came to the conclusion that most of the professorships must be filled by men from Europe if the desired eminence in science were to be maintained. In 1783 he sought in vain at Princeton and Philadelphia for a master for the proposed Albemarle grammar school, and finally concluded that the best chance would be to seek one in Scotland when the school should be so far established as to warrant it.[37] His enthusiasm for the transfer of the Geneva professors to America was based largely upon his opinion that they were the most eminent scientists on the continent.[38] After the failure of this project he proposed that the faculty of Edinburgh University be invited to America. He believed Edinburgh to be the best school in the world, so abandoned his plan with reluctance.[39] In 1800 he wrote to Dr. Priestley about the projected university and explained that they proposed "to draw from Europe the first characters in science by considerable temptations, which would not need to be repeated after the first set should have prepared fit successors, and given reputation to the institution.[40] In 1815 he wrote to Cabell:

I have lately received a letter from Say. He has in contemplation to remove to this country, and to this neighborhood particularly; and asks of me answers to some enquiries he makes. Could the petition which the Albemarle Academy addressed to our Legislature have succeeded at the late session, a little aid additional to the objects of that would have enabled us to have here immediately the best seminary of the United States. . . .

If we could obtain a loan for four or five years only of seven or eight thousand dollars, I think I have it now in my power to obtain three of the ablest characters in the world to fill the higher professorships.[41]

The three "ablest characters" seem to have been Say, Cooper and Correa. A year before this, Cabell and Jefferson were discussing Say's economic writings in terms of the highest praise and comparing them with the writings of Adam Smith, very much to the advantage of the French economist.[42] Say himself was thinking of coming to Virginia to engage in farming and cotton manufacture.[43] In 1818 Jefferson wrote to Nathaniel Bowditch of Salem, Massachusetts, urging him to accept the professorship of mathematics. He explained that they had concluded to employ no professor not of the first order of science, and that they would prefer Americans, but when they could not find professors of proper ability in this country, they would get them wherever possible.[44] Two years later the Board of Visitors directed the Committee of Superintendence to negotiate with Mr. Bowditch of Salem and Mr. Ticknor of Boston with a view to engaging them for professors in the University at the same time that they terminated their contract with Dr. Cooper.[45] The year before Jefferson had written to John Adams about Messrs. Bowditch and Ticknor:

Our wish is to procure natives where they can be found, like these gentlemen, of the first order of requirement in their respective lines; but preferring foreigners of the first order to natives of the second, we shall certainly have to go for several of our professors to countries more advanced in science than we are.[46]

In 1820 a letter to William Roscoe, an Englishman, showed that Jefferson had tempered his enthusiasm for European teachers by recognizing the necessity of having instruction given in the English language.[47] Two years later he explained to Cabell his anxiety to have the buildings completed before the opening of the University:

The great object of our aim from the beginning, has been to make the establishment the most eminent in the United States, in order to draw to it the youth of every State, but especially of the south and west. We have proposed, therefore, to call to it characters of the first order of science from Europe, as well as our own country; and, not only by the salaries and the comforts of their situation, but by the distinguished scale of its structure and preparation, and the promise of future eminence which these would hold up, to induce them to commit their reputation to its future fortunes. Had we built a barn for a college, and log huts for accomodations, should we ever have had the assurance to propose to an European professor of that character to come to it.[48]

When the time finally came for the selection of professors, Jefferson determined to send a special agent to the universities of England and Scotland.   Cabell at first consented to go, but business difficulties compelled him to give up the mission.[49] Francis Walker Gilmer, an active friend of the University, was induced to undertake the task and sailed in the spring of 1824. On April 26 Jefferson wrote letters of introduction to the American ambassador and to numerous friends in England and Scotland.   Several of these letters asked assistance for Mr. Gilmer and explained that he hoped to engage professors of mathematics, natural history, and natural philosophy at Cambridge, of the classics at Oxford, and of anatomy and medicine at Edinburgh.[50] The letter to Samuel Parr, an eminent classical scholar and a strong Whig, reveals Jefferson's purpose most completely:

> We are anxious to place in it none but professors of the first grade of science in their respective lines, and for these we must go to countries where that highest grade exists, and of preference to Great Britain, the land of our own language, morals, manners, and habits.   For a professor of the classical languages particularly, of the highest attainments in them, Oxford necessarily offers itself as the institution most eminent in the world in that branch of learning. . . .   Characters of the degree of science we seek, of sober and correct morals and habits,—indispensable qualities in a professor in this country,—and of accommodating and peaceable dispositions, so necessary for the harmony of the institution.[51]

Mr. Gilmer discharged his mission well, though at the cost of much suffering on his homeward voyage and of impaired health during the short remainder of his life.   He engaged five professors in Great Britain, three of them English, one Scotch, and one German.   Immediately after his return to America, he employed another who was of Irish nativity.   They all reached the University early in 1825, and only one proved to be a notably unfortunate selection and that was because of defects in personality rather than of scholarship.[52]   This policy of going to Europe for men of sufficient scholarship to give instruction in the University was highly offensive to the aggressive nationalism of some Americans who asserted that it was an insult to American scholarship. Jefferson defended this policy in a notable letter to Edward Everett, Professor of Greek, and later President, of Harvard.

I know the range of your mind too well ever to have supposed for a moment you could view but with contempt the miserable sneers of our seeking abroad some of the professors for our University. Had I thought them worth notice I should have asked of those wits and censors these questions only. The seminaries of the United States being all of them first served for the choice of the talents of our own country, were we to take the refuse and place ourselves thus at the fag end of the whole line? Would it have been either patriotism or fidelity in us to have sunk the youth of our State to a half-lettered grade of education by committing them to inferior instruction and rejecting that of the first order merely because offered from without the limits of our own Union, and the mass of science among us still further reduced by the refusal of many eminent characters to accept academical instructions, and is this the way to advance the American character? We thought otherwise and as yet believe we have reason to be satisfied with the course we have pursued. I hope the only rivalship with our elder sisters will be in honorable efforts to do the most good possible. I am happy in the expectation which your letter authorizes that you will think our institution worthy of a visit and I shall even hope from your experience and kindness to receive suggestions for its further improvement than which none would be more respected by me. I beg you to be assured also that no visit will be received with more welcome than yours.[53]

There were exceptions to Jefferson's willingness to obtain the most eminent men for professors regardless of the country from which they might come. When establishing the eight professorships in the spring of 1824 the Board of Visitors considered it expedient that the professors of law and moral philosophy should be citizens of the United States.[54] This was because they were "connected with a science calculated to give tone and direction to the public mind, on the most important subject that can occupy the human understanding."[55] No great difficulty was experienced in finding an American professor of ethics, but the professorship of law was long a source of perplexity to the Visitors and their Rector. There were American lawyers of recognized ability, but they were judges or practising attorneys with established incomes which they could not give up for the modest salary and uncertain fees offered by the University.

Dr. Cooper was an English immigrant, but he had served so long in Pennsylvania as attorney, judge, and lecturer on law that Jefferson never doubted his Americanism. When the time came actively to seek a full faculty, Francis Walker Gilmer was asked to be the first professor of law. His mission to England so impaired his health that he was forced to resign. Not knowing where to find a professor whose Americanism was not infected with Federalism, Jefferson proposed that the Visitors safeguard the instruction in government by prescribing the books to be used. A letter to Cabell places this proposal in an interesting setting:

In most public seminaries, textbooks are prescribed to each of the several schools, as the *norma docendi* in that school; and this is generally done by authority of the trustees. I should not propose this generally in our University, because, I believe none of us are so much at the heights of science in the several branches as to undertake this; and therefore that it will be better left to the professors, until occasion of interference shall be given. But there is one branch in which we are the best judges, in which heresies may be taught, of so interesting a character to our own State, and to the United States, as to make it a duty in us to lay down the principles which shall be taught. It is that of government. Mr. Gilmer being withdrawn, we know not who his successor may be. He may be a Richmond lawyer, or one of that school of quondam federalism, now consolidation. It is our duty to guard against the dissemination of such principles among our youth, and the diffusion of that poison, by a previous prescription of the texts to be followed in their discourses. I therefore inclose you a resolution which I think of proposing at our next meeting; strictly confiding it to your own knowledge alone and to that of Mr. Loyall, to whom you may communicate it, as I am sure it harmonizes with his principles. I wish it kept to ourselves, because I have always found that the less such things are spoken of before hand, the less obstruction is contrived to be thrown in their way. I have communicated it to Mr. Madison.[56]

The letter to Madison had mentioned the belief of numerous friends that even Gilmer was infected with the doctrines of the Richmond Federalists—a belief which Jefferson did not share —and asked Madison's criticism of the protective resolution.[57] Madison proposed that Washington's *Farewell Address* be added to the works proposed by Jefferson,[58] and with this change the resolution was adopted at the March meeting, Jefferson, Madison, Loyall, Cocke, and Cabell being present.[59] At the same meeting they nominated Chancellor Henry St.

George Tucker, and, in case he declined, Judge Philip P. Barbour.[60] Both declined. Chancellor Carr, Jefferson's nephew, was proposed by Cocke and Cabell, but declined.[61] Jefferson proposed Judge Dade, one of the Rockfish commissioners, but he declined, and in August he wrote a circular letter to the Visitors stating that Mr. Gilmer's health was so much restored that he was willing to undertake the work.[62] Accordingly, in October, Francis Walker Gilmer was reappointed Professor of the School of Law.[63] With visible relief, Jefferson wrote to his granddaughter: "Our professors . . . continue to be what we wish them. Mr. Gilmer accepts the Law chair, and all is well."[64]

Gilmer's improvement was brief, and on February 25, 1826, he died.[65] Confronted again by the old perplexity, the Board for once overrode the opposition of their venerable rector and as an additional inducement created the office of President of the University with an independent salary. This and the professorship of law were offered to William Wirt, attorney general of the United States. The same meeting nominated John Taylor Lomax, in case Mr. Wirt should decline.[66] This he did, but Mr. Lomax accepted, planning to open his school on the first of July.[67] He long held this professorship with distinction, and it became the most famous of the schools at the University. Among its professors have been Henry St. George Tucker and John B. Minor. Woodrow Wilson was one of its graduates. Its traditions have exercised a profound influence upon the political thought and the statesmanship of the South, for the most part in harmony with those basic principles which Jefferson guarded so jealously.

As it was no part of Jefferson's plan that professors should be easily removed, it was all the more necessary that care should be taken to select men who could be trusted with the largest measure of academic freedom through a long term of years. When writing to Nathaniel Bowditch in 1818, urging him to accept the professorship of mathematics in Central College, Jefferson stated the circumstances of salary, living costs, and climate which might induce him to come to Virginia, and added:

Our society is neither scientific nor splendid, but independent, hospitable, correct and neighborly. But the professors of the University of themselves compose a scientific society. They will be removable only by a vote of two-thirds of the Visitors; and when you are told that the Visitors are Mr. Madison, President Monroe, and myself, all known to you by character, Senator Cabell, General Cocke, Mr. Watson, gentlemen of distinguished worth and information, you will be sensible that the tenure is in fact for life.[68]

Six years later the same security was promised to candidates for professorships in the state university. "Your tenure of office is such that you can be removed only by the concurrence of five out of seven, all the first men in our country, with Mr. Jefferson at the head," wrote Gilmer to the prospective professor of ancient languages in 1824.[69] "You know the emoluments and that the tenure is in fact for life," wrote Jefferson to Cabell in suggesting George Tucker for the professorship of ethics later in the same year.[70]

Freedom from dismissal for light or temporary reasons has always safeguarded the freedom of teaching which each professor has enjoyed. Jefferson admirably stated this principle in 1820 in a letter to one of his English correspondents: "This institution will be based on the illimitable freedom of the human mind. For here we are not afraid to follow truth wherever it may lead, nor to tolerate any error so long as reason is left free to combat it." [71]

Another safeguard of academic independence was to be the democracy of the faculty within itself. All professors were to be on an equal footing in rank and authority. Assignment to the various pavilions was by lot. There was to be no president of the University, but a member of the faculty should be elected annually by his colleagues to discharge the inevitable executive duties. He was to be known as chairman of the faculty and could hold the position for one year only.[72] Garnett believes that Jefferson derived this idea from the annual election of a Rector Magnificus in the German universities.[73] Jefferson intended that the office should be held in turn by each member of the faculty, and Professor Minor says that he attached much importance to the principle of rotation.[74] It was continued for about twenty years after the opening of the University, no professor being chairman for more than two years. It was finally abandoned, chiefly because some professors disliked the duties of the office too much to be attracted by the additional salary which it brought and left it to those who were willing to hold it for longer periods.[75]

Jefferson's objection to having a president in the University seems to have arisen largely from the belief that such an officer would rule arbitrarily and that this would lead to intrigue among members of the faculty who would seek his favor for personal ends.[76] He seems to have had in mind the college presidents of his youth, all clergymen, who governed paternally but arbitrarily. Although his association with Bishop Madison made possible the reorganization of William and Mary in 1779 by this method after his plan to reorganize by legislature authority had failed, as a general principle it was in conflict with his democratic convictions.[77]

In the spring of 1826 when the University had been open for more than a year without the Visitors being able to provide a professor of law, it was proposed that the office of president be established and offered as an additional inducement to William Wirt, then attorney general of the United States. In March, Judge William H. Cabell had written to his brother Joseph that he thought Wirt could be obtained for the professorship of law by a salary of $3000 besides student fees. He suggested that he be given a greater fixed salary than the other professors, that his students be required to pay larger fees, or that he be made president with an additional salary. Both Gilmer and Johnson had suggested the association of the presidency with the professorship of law.[78] They and Judge Cabell knew about the incomes of Virginia lawyers and knew that the really able ones would not be attracted by the regular university salaries.[79] At their meeting in April, 1826, the Visitors voted to establish the office of president with an independent salary of $1500. The president was to be the executive officer of the University, the proctor and all subordinate agents being subject to his control. He should convene the faculty and preside at meetings, having one vote as professor and a casting vote as president in case of a tie. He should also have power to suspend students for two weeks. This office, together with the professorship of law, was offered to Mr. Wirt; though the Board voted that if he declined, the resolution establishing the presidency should be null and void.[80]   This action conflicted so sharply with Jefferson's ideals of faculty equality that he claimed the right to enter in the record the following protest:

> From the enactments establishing the office of president, the rector dissented. His dissent is ordered to be entered in the journal, and is in the words following: "The subscriber, rector of the University, fully and expressly concurring in the appointment of William Wirt to the professor of the School of Law, dissents from, and protests against, so much of these enactments as to the establishment of the office of President of the University, for these reasons:
>
> 1. Because the law establishing the University, delineating the organization of the authorities by which it should be directed and governed, and placing at its head a Board of rector and Visitors, has enumerated with great precision the special powers it meant to give to that Board, in which enumeration is not to be found that of creating a president, making him a member of the faculty of professors, and with controlling powers over that faculty; and it is not conceivable that, while descending, in their enumeration, to give specially the power of appointing officers of the minutest grade they should have omitted to name him of the highest, who was to govern and preside over the whole. If this is not among the enumerated powers, it is believed it cannot be legitimately inferred, by construction, from the words giving a general authority to do all things expedient for promoting the purposes of the institution; for, so construed, it would render nugatory the whole enumeration and confer on the Board powers unrestrained within any limits.
>
> 2. Because he is of opinion that every function ascribed to the president by this enactment, can be performed, and is now as well performed by the faculty, as now established by law.
>
> 3. Because we owe debts at this time of at least 11,000 dollars beyond what can be paid by any means we have in possession, or may command within any definite period of time; and fixes on us permanently an additional expense of 15,000 [sic] dollars a year.
>
> 4. Because he thinks that so fundamental a change in the organization of the institution ought not to be made by a thin Board, two of the seven constituting it being now absent.
>
> "For these reasons the subscriber protests against both the expedience and the validity of the establishment of this office.
>
> Th. Jefferson [81]

General Breckenridge and Mr. Loyall were absent, but Jefferson, Cabell, Cocke, Johnson, and Madison were present. While the board was not extremely "thin," with the Rector opposed, it left but four, a bare majority of the full board, actively favoring the change.

While Jefferson seems to have accepted the decision of his colleagues and to have urged Wirt to accept the appointment,[82] there was doubtless an element of satisfaction in writing his circular letter of April 21 informing his colleagues that Mr. Wirt had declined, but that the law professorship at last was provided for by the acceptance of Mr. Lomax.[83] Dr. Bruce thinks that Wirt was privately informed of Jefferson's opposition to the establishment of the presidency.[84] Whether this or some other consideration was the reason for his refusal, the wishes of the Old Sachem were respected for seventy-eight years.

Although the professors were to be protected in a maximum of individual freedom, Jefferson believed that some direct stimulation to effort would not be amiss. Besides a fixed salary each professor was to be paid a uniform fee by each student enrolled in his school. This was expected to be an additional encouragement for the professor to progress in scholarship and to conduct his classes in the satisfactory way which would attract large numbers of students to his school. The poverty of the institution may have been another reason for avoiding too large fixed charges.[85] This was no new plan, for La Rochefoucauld tells us that when Jefferson was a student at William and Mary, each professor received $400 besides the fees of the men who entered his classes.[86]

In every instance the Visitors offered each professor the free use of a house. Besides this, they offered Dr. Knox, in 1817, $500 and a fee of $25 from each student. The same year Dr. Cooper was offered two professorships with a salary of $1000 and a fee of $20 from every student in either school. The largest fixed salaries were those of $2000 offered to Bowditch and Ticknor in 1820, but these were to be supplemented with fees of only $10 per student. The largest fees were offered in 1819 to Dr. Cooper, who was to have $30 from each student in two schools besides a salary of $1500 with a guaranteed total of $3500 per year. When the faculty finally were engaged, Mr. Gilmer was authorized to offer salaries from $1000 to $1500 and fees of $25 per student with a total guaranteed at not less than $2500 per year for five years. On September 30, 1825, when the enrollment for the first year was about complete, there were 116 students in the seven schools, varying from 68 in the School of Mathematics to 14 in the School of Moral Philosophy, an average of a trifle above 40. Most of these men were entered in three schools, so were paying $25 to each professor.

Table V shows the distribution of these students by schools and the amount of fees each professor would receive at $25 per student. Table VI shows the actual amounts offered at various times, and, taking 40 as an average first-year class, estimates the average amount of fees which the professors would have received under each offer:

TABLE V

DISTRIBUTION OF 116 STUDENTS BY SCHOOLS, SEPTEMBER 30, 1825 [87]

SCHOOL	NUMBER OF STUDENTS	PROFESSORS' FEES AT $25 EACH
Ancient Languages.....................	55	$1357
Modern Languages.....................	64	$1600
Mathematics...........................	68	$1700
Natural Philosophy....................	33	$ 825
Natural History.......................	30	$ 750
Anatomy and Medicine.................	20	$ 500
Moral Philosophy.....................	14	$ 350
AVERAGE..........................	40.57	$1014.28

It was contrary to Jefferson's plan that members of the faculty should have any regular occupations beyond the duties of their professorships. "We should propose that the professors follow no other calling, so that their whole time may be given to their academical function," he had written to Dr. Priestley in 1800.[89] This purpose was carried out at the organization of the University when the Visitors adopted the following resolution:

The collegiate duties of a professor, if discharged conscientiously, with industry and zeal, being sufficient to engross all his hours of business, he shall engage in no other pursuits of emolument unconnected with the service of the University without the consent of the Visitors.[90]

It is true that in 1814 he had urged Dr. Cooper to undertake a translation of Bracton's *De Legibus Angliae* with a glossary —"Could not such an undertaking be conveniently associated

TABLE VI

PROFESSORS' SALARIES AND FEES [88]

Date	To Whom Offered	Fixed Salary	Fees From Each Student	Aggregate Fees In Average Class (of 40)	Guaranteed Total Per Year	Total Income—Salary and Fees Only
July 28, 1817	Dr. Knox	$ 500 a	$25	$1000	None	$1500
October 7, 1817	Dr. Cooper	$1000	$20	$1600 b	None	$2600
October 26, 1818	Bowditch	$1000–$1500	$25	$1000	None	$2000–$2500
March 29, 1819	All professors	$1500	$30	$1200 c	None	$2700
March 29, 1819	Dr. Cooper	$1500	$30	$2400 b	$2500 d	$3900
October 3, 1820	Bowditch and Ticknor	$2000	$10	$ 400	$2500 e	$2400
October 5–7, 1824	Gilmer authorized to offer in Europe	$1000–$1500	$25 g	$1000	$2500 f	$2000–$2500

a *Cabell*, 396—$400 in *Library Ed.*, XIX, 365-366.

b Two professorships—Chemistry, etc., and Law.

c Professors holding two professorships to be allowed fees from students in both schools, but only one fixed salary.

d For two years.

e For three years.

f For five years.

g If attending three professors, $30 each if attending two, $50 if attending one.

Free use of a house always included.

with your new vocation of giving law lectures? I pray you to think of it." [91] In the same letter he told of his plans for a university "which should comprehend all the sciences useful to us, and none other," which probably would absorb William and Mary, and might be a worthy place for Dr. Cooper or Dr. Priestley. However, this suggestion was made to Dr. Cooper, whom Jefferson considered to be almost in a class by himself, and to his mind law lectures in the University of Pennsylvania were a much simpler matter than a professorship of law and government in the ideal university for which he planned. After Mr. Gilmer's resignation when the Visitors were unable to obtain a satisfactory man for the law professorship, Cabell had proposed Chancellor Tucker, with the suggestion that a small chancery district consisting of Albemarle, Orange, Louisa, Fluvanna, and Nelson counties be created and that the Professor of Law be made Chancellor of this district. He thought the combination would attract men of the first order.[92] The proposal does not seem to have impressed Jefferson, for a month later, the professorship was offered to Chancellor Tucker without any suggestion of other employment.[93] When Judge Barbour was offered the professorship of law he considered the offer for some time, proposing that he combine the new duties with those of his judgeship. Jefferson voiced his disapproval in the words, "Barber throws a greedy grapple at both places." [94] In October, 1825, the Visitors adopted a resolution stating that they believed the school would benefit by the professor of medicine keeping in mind the practical part of his profession and by his getting acquainted with the diseases peculiar to the climate and country. Therefore, he should be allowed, besides practice within the precincts of the University, to act as a consulting physician elsewhere, so timing these avocations as not to interrupt the work of the school.[95]

CHAPTER VIII

SUBJECTS AND METHODS OF INSTRUCTION

IF THE architecture of the University of Virginia showed Jefferson's love of beauty and the first faculty his respect for scholarship, still more did his plans for actual instruction reveal his own mental processes and interests. His plan for the University buildings probably reflected unpleasant physical surroundings at William and Mary, and his insistence upon free electives and more mature methods was equally the result of his own experiences as a student. The arrangement by which students were led to concentrate in chosen fields shows his fear of the superficial methods which were appearing in American education, as his enthusiasm for a broad and varied curriculum reveals his appreciation of the values in the study of subjects but little taught before his time.

An essential part of his plan was the division of the University into distinct "schools." Ten such schools were contemplated in the Rockfish report, but when the visitors organized the University, April 7, 1824, their limited resources permitted the establishment of only eight: Ancient Languages, Modern Languages, Mathematics, Natural Philosophy, Natural History, Anatomy and Medicine, Moral Philosophy, and Law.[1] At first these corresponded to the fields of individual professors, but the schools were intended to be distinct entities whether several professors or tutors should work in a single one or one professor give courses in more than one school.[2] The student entered one or more of these schools. The only degree at first intended was that of "Graduate," and the student who passed the examinations in any one school should be a "Graduate of the University of Virginia."[3]

Exactly where Jefferson obtained this idea of the distinct schools or when he adopted it for the University cannot be positively stated. In 1779 he found and abolished something resembling it at William and Mary. There was a school of Sacred Theology with two professors; one of Philosophy with two professors, and one of Ancient Languages. In their stead he established eight professorships without any groupings.[4]

However, the looseness with which these terms were used in this connection appears from the facts that Heatwole asserts that Jefferson abolished the grammar school and the two divinity schools and introduced in their stead "schools" of Modern Languages, Municipal Law, and Medicine [5] and that he himself states that he "got the two professorships of divinity and the grammar school put down and others of law and police, of medicine, anatomy, and chemistry, and of modern languages substituted." [6] Apparently the "schools" of William and Mary had slight relation to plans for university organization in Jefferson's mind in 1821.

Quesney's plan provided for fifteen schools in the proposed Academy, but Jefferson seems to have been no more impressed by this than by other features of the plan. It has been common to attribute to Dupont de Nemours a distinct influence upon Jefferson's educational plans and views. The two were acquainted while Jefferson was ambassador to France, and he sent a pamphlet by M. Dupont to Madison in 1788.[7] Dupont came to America in 1800 and visited frequently at Monticello. At Jefferson's request he drew up a plan of education for America which included a national university composed of four schools: Medicine, Mines, Social Sciences and Legislation, and Higher Mathematics.[8]

Certainly if Dupont had original ideas, Jefferson had ample opportunity to acquire them. Professor John B. Minor believed that Jefferson was considerably influenced by the gifted Frenchman.[9] Professor Adams felt that Dupont's plan of separate schools may have confirmed ideas already in Jefferson's mind, pointing out that the same plan of organization had long existed in the schools of Paris, which constituted the oldest university in Europe.[10] Dr. Bruce reached the same conclusion.[11]

The idea of distinct schools, like other important parts of Jefferson's plan, seems to have been long present in his mind without a visible influence upon his concrete proposals. Whether it was derived from observations of the University of Paris or from other sources, earlier or later, is immaterial. There is no suggestion of such a grouping in his correspondence with Washington or D'Ivernois in 1795 nor in his letter to Dr. Priestley in 1900. The letter to Peter Carr in 1814 proposes professional schools for highly specialized study but it suggests no such arrangements for the general sciences and arts. The letter to Governor Nicholas in 1816 and the bill for a system of education in 1817 are silent upon the subject. The Rockfish report makes vague references to schools of special subjects. The act establishing the University and the reports of the Visitors make no reference to distinct schools until the report of October 5, 1824,[12] giving an account of the enactment of the Visitors at the April meeting when they organized eight schools and established for the time being eight corresponding professorships.[13] Whatever its origin, this plan does not seem to have been definitely adopted by Jefferson until late in the development of his system of organization.

In determining subjects to be taught in the University, Jefferson's principle was simple. He desired an institution to teach "all the branches of science useful to us, and at this day . . . in their highest degree"—a university "which should comprehend all the sciences useful to us, and none others," "at this day and in this country." [14] About the subjects to be included he asked advice from many eminent men in Europe and America. Among others, he consulted Dr. Priestley in 1800,[15] M. Pictet in 1803,[16] John Adams [17] and Dr. Cooper in 1814.[18] To what extent he was influenced by these men or others, it is impossible to determine. Dr. Priestley seems to have commented upon the omission of the classics from the list of subjects suggested in Jefferson's letter of January 18, for the letter of January 27 contains an explanation, coupled with very high praise of Latin and Greek as cultural studies. In the letter to Peter Carr in 1814, Jefferson proposed a professorship of theology and ecclesiastical history among the strictly professional schools. He sent a copy of this letter to Dr. Cooper, who wrote three letters in reply on September 15, 21, and 22. In one of these Dr. Cooper advised against the teaching of theology because of its sectarian complications.[19] This coincided with views Jefferson had held since' 1779, and he omitted theology from all later lists of subjects to be taught at the University. At the reorganization of William and Mary in 1779 he must have worked in close harmony with Bishop Madison, but he later spoke of this as distinctly his own work.[20] He seems to have asked advice freely but to have been little influenced by it on points where he already held a definite opinion. Many influences, no doubt, contributed to the formation of such opinions, but for the most part they are very hard to trace.*

In Chart III an attempt is made to show what subjects Jefferson believed should be taught in the University, arranged in parallel columns as an aid in tracing the development of his plans for specific subjects and groups and the hampering of these plans by financial necessity when at last the University was organized. There are six enumerations of subjects to be taught, and this program may be taken as fairly representative of his views at various times. These were in the bill for amending the constitution of William and Mary College, proposed in 1779 but never enacted; the letters to Dr. Priestley in January, 1800, naming a declaredly incomplete list of subjects; the letter to Peter Carr, 1814, planning for general and professional schools; the bill for a system of public education, October, 1817; the Rockfish Gap report, 1818; and the enactment of the Board of Visitors, April, 1824.† In the Rockfish report, Jefferson arranges these subjects most systematically, so this may be taken as best representing his mature views of what a university ought to teach and of the grouping of these subjects into a small number of professorships. This arrangement is taken as the base of the chart and is shown in the fifth vertical column. The same or similar subjects appearing in the other lists are placed horizontally opposite the group in which they appear in the fifth column—unless they are arranged in distinct professorships, as in 1779, 1814, and 1824, when the group as a whole is placed opposite the 1818 group to which it most nearly corresponds. Roman numerals indicate the order in which professorship groups are named in the various documents. Subjects proposed for the professional schools in the letter to Peter Carr are shown

---

* This subject is further discussed in Chapter XI.
† The full text of these documents will be found in the Appendix.

CHART III

COLLEGE CURRICULA AS PROPOSED BY JEFFERSON

WILLIAM AND MARY— BILL OF 1779	LETTERS TO DR. PRIESTLEY—1800	LETTER TO PETER CARR—1814
VII Ancient Languages — Oriental and Northern	Latin Greek	I Language and History — Ancient and Modern, Belles Lettres, Rhetoric, Oratory
VIII Modern Languages (Missionary to the Indians to study their languages)		
IV Mathematics	Mathematics	II Mathematics — pure, Physico Mathematics Physics Anatomy Medicine — theory (Architecture) Military Naval (Projectiles) (Technical Philosophy)
	Astronomy Geography Arts	
VI Natural Philosophy and Natural History	Natural Philosophy Chemistry Agriculture Geology	III Chemistry Mineralogy Botany Zoölogy
	Botany, Zoölogy	(Rural Economy)
V Anatomy and Medicine	Anatomy Surgery Medicine	(Practice of medicine) (Materia medica) (Pharmacy) (Surgery)
III History — Civil and Ecclesiastical	Politics Commerce History	IV Philosophy — Ideology, Ethics, Law of Nature and Nations Government Political Economy
II Law and Police	Law	(Law — Municipal and Foreign)
I Moral Philosophy, Law of Nature and Nations, Fine Arts	Ethics Fine Arts	(Theology and Ecclesiastical History) (Fine Arts)
		NOTE. — In the General Schools were to be taught the subjects listed under the four professorships. Subjects in parenthesis were to be taught in separate professional schools.

CHART III

<small>COLLEGE CURRICULA AS PROPOSED BY JEFFERSON</small>

PROPOSED IN BILL OF 1817	THE ROCKFISH REPORT—1818	ESTABLISHED AT THE UNIVERSITY—1824
Languages	I Languages — Ancient: Latin Greek Hebrew	I Latin and Greek, higher grade, Hebrew, Rhetoric, Belles lettres, Ancient History, Ancient Geography
	II Languages — Modern: French, Spanish, Italian, German, Anglo-Saxon	II French, Italian, Spanish, German, English (Anglo-Saxon), Modern History, Modern Geography
Mathematics — Pure Mixed Military and Naval Science	III Mathematics — pure: Algebra, Fluxions Geometry, elemental and transcendental, Architecture, naval and military	III Higher Numerical Arithmetic, Algebra, Trigonometry, Plane and Spherical Geometry, Mensuration, Navigation, Conic Sections, Fluxions, or Differentials, Military and Civil Architecture
	IV Physico-Mathematics: Mechanics, Statics, Dynamics, Pneumatics, Acoustics, Optics, Astronomy, Geography	IV Mechanics, Statics, Hydrostatics, Hydraulics, Pneumatics, Acoustics, Optics, Astronomy
Natural Philosophy, Chemistry, Mineralogy, Geology, Agriculture	V Physics, or Natural Philosophy: Chemistry Mineralogy	Law and properties of bodies
		V Chemistry, Mineralogy, Geology, Rural Economy, Botany, Zoölogy
Botany, Zoölogy	VI Botany, Zoölogy	
Anatomy, Theories of Medicine	VII Anatomy Medicine	VI Anatomy, Surgery, History of Medicine, Physiology, Pathology, Materia medica, Pharmacy
Civil Government, Political Economy, Law of Nature and Nations, History and Geography, — Ancient and Modern	VIII Government, Law of Nature and Nations, Political Economy, History-interwoven with Politics and Law	VIII Common and Statute Law, Chancery, Laws Feudal, Civil, Mercatorial, Maritime, Law of Nature and Nations, Government, Political Economy
Law-Municipal and Foreign	IX Law Municipal	
Ideology, Ethics, Rhetoric, Belles lettres, Fine Arts	X Ideology, General Grammar, Ethics, Rhetoric, Belles lettres, Fine Arts	VII Mental Science Ideology, General Grammar, Logic, Ethics

in parentheses and do not belong to the four professorship groups proposed for the general schools.

The chart as a whole shows a high degree of uniformity from 1779 to 1824. The modern languages are not mentioned in the letters to Dr. Priestley, but the classics were not named in the first of these letters, which was frankly incomplete and hastily written. Different groupings of specific subjects, like the association of history with languages in 1814 and 1824, with geography in 1817, and with politics and law in 1818, call attention to varying theories about methods of teaching.

For one who thought as widely on educational subjects and was a master of as many as Jefferson was, he has left surprisingly few opinions about principles and methods of teaching. Where he did express his views, it was usually in specific advice to some of the first professors of the University or to some young friend seeking guidance. While he advocated progress in method as truly as in the subject matter of science, he had a hearty disdain for contemporary educational fads and short-cuts to knowledge. Those sciences which he believed to be of enough value to justify study were to be mastered thoroughly by the tried and proved method of intense study aided by intelligent explanation.[21] In 1816 he gave a friend this advice, about the education of her son:

As far as I am acquainted with the colleges & academies of the U.S., and I will say more especially of Princeton, which you name I have found their method of instruction very superficial & imperfect, carrying their pupils over the ground like race horses to please their parents and draw custom to their school. This was never the character of Wm. & Mary while I knew it, nor do I suppose it is now. whatever they learned, they learned thoroughly, and the principles in which it was founded. for the languages there, for Mathematics and Natural philosophy I prefer it to any college I know, except that of Philadelphia; and for boys to that also because that is a great city while Williamsburg is but an academical villege.[22]

The languages were fundamental to all his plans. When he did away with the teaching of Latin and Greek at William and Mary, it was with the expectation that the essentials of these languages would be taught in the grammar schools, and he proposed to substitute for them oriental and northern languages, the latter because of their relationship to English.[23] These were to include Moeso-Gothic, Anglo-Saxon, and Old Icelandic.[24] This part of his plan had to be dropped, but he established a professorship of modern languages, the first in America.[25] A part of his plan which never was realized was the appointment of a missionary to the Indians—a missionary who was to study their languages and construct grammars and vocabularies.[26] He early recognized that the learning of languages is primarily a memory task and thought it should constitute a large part of a boy's education between the ages of eight and fifteen or sixteen.[27] In the Rockfish report, he suggested the tenth to fifteenth years as the time for learning languages. In the same document he spoke of Latin, Greek and Hebrew as being "the foundation common to all the sciences." Midway between these expressions, in his second letter to Dr. Priestley in January, 1800, he stated his views in an interesting manner:

> I do not think them [languages] essential to the obtaining eminent degrees of science; but I think them very useful towards it. I suppose there is a portion of life during which our faculties are ripe enough for this, & for nothing more useful. I think the Greeks & Romans have left us the purest models which exist of fine composition, whether we examine them as works of reason, or of style & fancy; and to them we probably owe these characteristics of modern composition. I know of no composition of any other antient people which merits the least regard as a model for its matter or style. to all this I add that to read the Latin & Greek authors in their original is a sublime luxury; and I deem luxury in science to be at least as justifiable as in architecture, painting, gardening, or the other arts. . . . I thank on my knees Him who directed my early education for having put into my possession this rich source of delight; and I would not exchange it for anything which I could then have acquired, & have not since acquired.[28]

He seems to have admired the Greek classics but to have found greater pleasure in reading Latin authors.[29] In 1785 he regretted that the movement against the Turks was not likely to restore the language of Homer and Demosthenes because real freedom for the Greeks was not intended.[30] While living in Paris he recommended to his future son-in-law the study of Latin, Greek, French and Spanish, saying that he regarded Greek to be the least useful of these.[31] A few days later he advised his nephew to study French and Spanish, but not Italian because he would be apt to confuse the latter with the others. He thought Spanish should be studied with great care because future connections with Spain and Spanish America would make it valuable to Americans.[32] A notable passage in the Rockfish report emphasizes the value of French because of its use in the intercourse of nations and as a depository of science, of Spanish because the language in which much early American history was written, of Italian because of fine style and composition, of German because of its scientific value, and of Anglo-Saxon because of its aid in a study of the common law.

Beside its legal and political significance, Anglo-Saxon was of great interest to Jefferson as an aid in the study of English as a language, and he was the first in America to incorporate it in a college curriculum.[33] In 1818 he wrote an *Essay on the Anglo-Saxon Language*. It was intended for use in the University, but a copy was sent to Herbert Croft, an eminent Englishman who was preparing an etymological dictionary. It contained discussions of the Anglo-Saxon alphabet, spelling, and grammar, criticisms of current grammars which attempted to organize the language on classical patterns, and suggestions for teaching.[34] Seven years later he added extensive criticisms and suggestions.[35] Akin to this scholarly work is his *Thoughts on English Prosody*. It was sent to F. J. Chastellux undated, but probably was written while he was Secretary of State after 1789. It is a critical and instructive discussion of the basis of rhythm in English verse.[36] He had clear views of the invigorating influence which dialects exert upon a language. Forty years before Max Müller, he apprehended the process called "dialectic regeneration," [37] as the following letter shows:

It is much to be wished that the publication of the present county dialects of England should go on. It will restore to us our language in all its shades of variation. It will incorporate into the present one all the riches of our ancient dialects; and what a store this will be may be seen by running the eye over the county glossaries and observing the words we have lost by abandonment and disuse, which in sound and sense are inferior to nothing we have retained. When these local vocabularies are published and digested together in a single one, it is probable we shall find that there is not a word in Shakespeare which is not now in use in some of the counties of England, from whence we may obtain its true sense.[38]

Dr. Bruce suggests that Jefferson's comparative indifference to English literature, as compared with grammar or the literature of other languages, has left a lasting impression upon the University, which has failed to encourage the same eminence in literature as in other fields.[39] However, it should not be forgotten that the man frequently spoken of as the most illustrious graduate was Edgar Allan Poe.

In one particular Jefferson anticipated modern methods in the teaching of languages. When his future son-in-law wrote from Edinburgh asking advice about his studies, and requesting that the advice be sent to his father in Virginia also, Jefferson wrote to the latter, recommending that the son spend two years in legal study within an hour's walk of Paris, boarding in a French family in order to learn the language.[40] Thirty years later the visitors of Central College voted to build a pavilion "until otherwise wanted for a boarding house to be kept by some French family of good character, wherein it is proposed that the boarders shall be permitted to speak French only with a view to their becoming familiarized to conversation in that language." [41]

Various phases of mathematics were always included in Jefferson's plan—"common arithmetick" in the ward schools, "vulgar and decimal fractions and the extrication of the square and cube roots" in the grammar schools, and higher mathematics in the University.[42] "I have never thought a boy should undertake abstruse or difficult sciences, such as mathematics in general, till fifteen years of age at soonest," he wrote in 1788.[43] Probably it was a realization of the inadequate preparation of prospective students which led the visitors to include "higher numerical arithmetic" with the more advanced mathematics to be taught at the University, April, 1824,[44] for the following autumn they thought it necessary to exclude from the schools of mathematics and of natural philosophy those who lacked this preparation.[45]

Natural science was always held by Jefferson in very high esteem, though in his crusade for the advancement of science he commonly used the term in its broader and more literal sense. It is in a letter giving general suggestions for the teaching of the sciences to Dr. Emmett, first professor of natural philosophy, that he incidentally suggested the normal program for students taking work in that department. At entrance, he assumed, the student would be so well qualified in ancient and modern languages that one year in the University would suffice for a final polish. The student, therefore, would do well to study the languages and mathematics the first year, mathematics and physics the second, physics and chemistry, with other subjects, the third. If about twelve dozen lectures were to be given in Emmett's school, dealing with botany, zoölogy, mineralogy, chemistry, geology, and rural economy, he suggested that about two dozen be given to botany and zoölogy, two dozen to mineralogy and geology, and eight dozen to chemistry—or mineralogy, geology, and chemistry might be blended, giving them two thirds of the year, and one third to botany and zoölogy. He recognized that two thirds of a year would be inadequate time for the teaching of chemistry, but said that the University did not attempt to produce finished scientists, but rather to give enough of a start so the students could go farther by their own efforts. He advised giving the least possible time to geology, because speculations about the origin of the earth are useless, though it is helpful to learn the ordinary arrangement and associations of minerals.[46] On another occasion he expressed the same lack of interest in geology because it lacked practical value:

What difference does it make whether the earth is six hundred or six thousand years old? And is it of any real importance to know what is the composition of the various strata, if they contain no coal or iron or other useful metal? [47]

This strange disdain for geology is strikingly at variance with his almost universal interest in every other scientific phenomenon. The same letter to the president of Yale which discusses the restoration of classical Greek as a spoken language, explains that he had sent old almanacs because of their valuable catalogues of fixed stars and discusses the location of Herschel, describes a screw propeller recently invented by a Frenchman and its probable use by Bushnell in his submarine during the revolution, and thanks Dr. Stiles for information about bones found in Ohio and a Connecticut flower which grows in air.[48] This was during his residence in France at a time when that nation was much interested in experimental science. There were chairs of the sciences at the universities of Paris, Toulouse, and

Montpellier. This undoubtedly deepened his interest in these subjects and strengthened his purpose to have them more extensively taught in his native state.[49] By his will he left his own not inconsiderable museum of minerals and curiosities to the University.[50]

Chemistry occupied a position opposite to that of geology in Jefferson's estimation. "I think it amongst the most useful of sciences," he wrote, "and big with future discoveries for the utility and safety of the human race. It is yet indeed a mere embryo." [51] He recommended to Dr. Emmett that chemistry, including its applications to agriculture, should be given twice as much time in his school as should be allotted to botany, zoölogy, mineralogy, and geology combined.[52]

He had long considered the teaching of agriculture as very important, classing it as a branch of chemistry. In the same letter in which he suggested to Washington the bringing of the Geneva professors to the proposed national university, he urged a professorship of agriculture and recommended that the professor come from no country but England. "Indeed I should mark Young as the man to be obtained," he wrote.[53] In 1803 he recognized "too strong a current from the country to the towns," and advised agricultural education as a means of checking the over-crowding of the learned professions to the neglect of others:

the class principally defective is that of agriculture. it is the first in utility, & ought to be the first in respect. the same artificial means which have been used to produce a competition in learning may be equally successful in restoring agriculture to its primary dignity in the eyes of men. it is a science of the very first order. it counts, among it's handmaids, the most respectable sciences, such as chemistry, natural philosophy, mechanics, mathematics generally, natural history, botony. in every college & university a professorship of Agriculture, & the class of it's students, might be honored as the first. young men, closing their academical education with this as the crown of all other sciences, fascinated with it's solid charms, & at a time when they are to chuse an occupation, instead of crowding the other classes, would return to the farms of their fathers, their own, or those of others, & replenish and invigorate a calling, now languishing under contempt & oppression. the charitable schools, instead of storing their pupils with a lore which the present state of society does not call for, converted into schools of agriculture, might restore them to that branch, qualified to enrich & honor themselves & to increase the productions of the nation instead of consuming them. a gradual abolition of the useless offices, so much accumulated in all governments, might close this drain also from the labors of the field, and lessen the burthens imposed on them. by these, & the better means which will occur to others, the surcharge of the learned, might in time be drawn off to recruit the laboring class of citizens, the sum of industry be increased, & that of misery diminished.[54]

In the *Notes on Virginia,* written before his sojourn in France, Jefferson shows an excellent acquaintance with the natural history of his native state. Physics, botany, and zoölogy were prominent in all his programs of higher studies. In 1815 when he thought it within his "power to obtain three of the ablest characters in the world to fill the highest professorships, . . . three such characters as are not in a single University of Europe," [55] beside Say and Cooper, who are mentioned in the letter, he seems to have had in mind the Abbé Correa, ambassador from Portugal, a noted savant and botanist. In the spring of 1826 he advised Dr. Emmett to suspend all other work in his school and give his whole attention for a few weeks to preparations for the instruction in botany which he would begin the following year. Following suggestions previously given him by Correa, who preferred a combination of the methods of Linnaeus and Jussieu, he recommended for the present year—(1) the selection of about six acres of ground with proper soil and moisture; (2) the inclosure of this land within serpentine brick walls seven feet high (this would cost about $800, and rails could be used if the necessary funds could not be obtained); (3) the grading of the hillside into level terraces and of level ground into beds and alleys; (4) a listing of the trees and plants needed. Among the trees to be cultivated he recommended "exotics of distinguished usefulness and accommodated to our climate—larch, cedar of Lebanon, cork oak, the marronnier, mahogany, the catachu or Indian rubber tree of Napul (30°), Teak tree or Indian oak of Burman (23°), various woods of Brazil." [56]

Astronomy was one of the sciences which Jefferson always intended should be taught. In his bill to reorganize William and Mary in 1779 he included a provision having so little to do with the rest of the bill as to have much the appearance of a legislative rider, and probably growing out of his friendship for Dr. Ryttenhouse:

And that this commonwealth may not be without so great an ornament, nor, its youth such a help towards attaining astronomical science, as the mechanical representation, or model of the solar system, conceived and executed by that greatest of astronomers, David Ryttenhouse; Be it further enacted, that the visitors first appointed under this act, and their successors, shall be authorized to engage the said David Ryttenhouse, on the part of this commonwealth, to make and erect in the said college of William and Mary, and for its use, one of the said models, to be called by the name of the Ryttenhouse, the cost and expense of making, transporting and erecting whereof shall, according to the agreement or allowance of the said visitors, be paid by the Treasurer of this commonwealth, on warrant from the Auditors.[57]

When the site for Central College was chosen, Jefferson selected a neighboring hilltop as an appropriate location for an observatory. This advantage he emphasized in the Rockfish report.[58] Because the Southwest Mountains slightly obstructed the view of the eastern sky from this site, he at one time considered the advisability of locating the observatory on the summit of one of those mountains. Shortly before his death he drew careful plans for the building, but it was not erected until long afterward.[59] Realizing that the necessary funds for an observatory would not soon be available, he conceived a plan to give the students some of the advantages of visual instruction at little cost. This proposal may have been an outgrowth of his interest in the Ryttenhouse model of the solar system many years before:

The concave ceiling of the Rotunda is proposed to be painted sky-blue, and spangled with gilt stars in their position and magnitude copied exactly from any selected hemisphere of our latitude. A seat for the operator, movable and flexible at any point in the concave, will be necessary, and means of giving to every star its exact position. A white oak sapling is to be used as a boom, its heel working in the center of sphere, with a rope suspending the small end of the boom and passing over a pulley in the zenith, and hanging down to the floor, by which the boom may be raised or lowered at will. A common saddle with stirrups is to be fixed as the seat of the operator; and seated in it, he may, by the rope, be propelled to any point in the concave.[60] *

Today the ceiling of the Rotunda is blue, but the stars are significantly absent.

Jefferson consistently planned for the teaching of anatomy

* Quoted by permission of the Macmillan Co.

and medicine as a major subject, partly as the basis of a professional training, but also for its practical value to any person. In 1825 he thought the professor of medicine might well take part in consultations in order to get acquainted with the diseases peculiar to the climate and country.[61] The following spring a dispensary was provided for, a part of the plan being that assisting at minor examinations and in mixing medicines would be valuable training for the students.[62] In 1824 when the proposal to remove William and Mary to Richmond and associate it with a medical school threatened the prosperity of the University, Jefferson wrote an entertaining discussion of medical education as he understood it, pointing out the advantages of Charlottesville over Richmond for the abstract studies and that Norfolk was the only place in the state where clinical experience could be obtained.

This letter contains the following passage, written with delightful seriousness:

And I will ask how many families in Richmond would send their husbands, wives, or children to a hospital, in sickness to be attended by nurses hardened by habit against the feelings of pity, to lie in public rooms, harassed by the cries and sufferings of disease under every form, alarmed by the groans of the dying, exposed as a corpse, to be lectured over by a clinical professor, to be crowded and handled by his students to hear their case learnedly explained to them, its threatening symptoms developed, and its probable termination foreboded? [63] *

His own professional experience, first in law and later in politics, would have given Jefferson an interest in these subjects if other circumstances had not. Law and government, sometimes separate, sometimes treated as a single subject, appear in all his programs of study. In 1814 government was classed with economics as a philosophy, but in 1818 these were grouped with history. In 1824 the necessity of condensing ten departments into eight placed them in the School of Law. In 1779 the law of nature and of the nations was classed as moral philosophy, and at that time it partook more of the nature of philosophy than of law. In 1814 it was again classed as philosophy. In 1818 it was grouped with government and history, and continued with these in the School of Law in 1824.

* A longer passage from this letter appears in Appendix L.

When Jefferson arranged in 1779 that George Wythe should give lectures on law at William and Mary, he was establishing the first professorship of law in the United States.[64] He long regarded his old preceptor as the ablest as well as the safest authority on law in America [65]—and in this field he felt that instruction must be safe. His disdain for the "whimsies, puerilities, and unintelligible jargon" of Plato's *Republic* and his amazement that the Roman and Christian world had given "reputation to such nonsense as this" [66] seem prompted rather by unpalatable political principles than by crudity of style. Perhaps his chief reason for wishing Anglo-Saxon taught was because it would introduce the student to the sources of free institutions. This is well expressed in a letter of 1824, describing some of the innovations in the University:

There are some novelties in it. Of that of a professorship of the principles of government you express your approbation. They will be founded in the rights of man. That of Agriculture I am sure you will approve; and that also of Anglo-Saxon. As the histories and laws left us in that type of dialect must be the textbooks of the reading of the learners, they will imbibe with the language their free principles of government.[67]

When Dr. Smith, President of William and Mary, asked Jefferson to recommend a textbook on the principles of government because Dr. Smith was dissatisfied both with Locke and Rousseau, Jefferson promptly named De Tracy's *Review of Montesquieu*.[68] It was adopted and the edition was soon exhausted.[69] He also praised highly *The Federalist* and Chipman's and Priestley's *Principles of Government*.[70] The year before he had declared Montesquieu to be "the ablest work of the age . . . giving the most correct analysis of the principles of political association which has yet been offered." [71] When the resignation of Mr. Gilmer left Jefferson fearful that they might have to take "a Richmond lawyer" (presumably trained under the influence of his Federalist cousin, John Marshall) for the law professor, he advised that the Visitors prescribe the textbooks to be read,[72] and offered the following resolution, which they adopted:

Whereas it is the duty of this Board to the Government under which it lives and especially to that of which this University is the immediate creation, to pay especial attention to the principles of government which shall be inculcated therein, and to provide that none shall be inculcated which are incompatible with those on which the constitutions of this State and of the United States were genuinely based, in the common opinion; and for this purpose it may be necessary to point out specially where these principles are to be found legitimately developed:

Resolved, that it is the opinion of this Board that as to the general principles of liberty and the rights of man, in nature and in society, the doctrines of Locke in his *Essay concerning the true original extent and end of Civil Government,* and of Sidney in his *Discourses on Government* may be considered as those generally approved by our fellow citizens of this, and the United States, and that on the distinctive principles of the government of our State and of that of the United States, the best guides are to be found in (1) the *Declaration of Independence,* as the fundamental act of union of these states, (2) the book known by the title of *The Federalist,* being an authority to which appeal is habitually made by all, and rarely declined or denied by any as evidence of the general opinion of those who framed, and of those who accepted the Constitution of the United States, on questions as to its genuine meaning, (3) The *Resolutions of the General Assembly of Virginia* in 1799 on the subject of the alien and sedition laws, which appear to accord with the predominent sense of the people of the United States, (4) The valedictory address of President Washington, as conveying political lessons of peculiar value; and that in the branch of the School of Law, which is to treat on the subject of civil polity, these shall be used as the text and documents of the school.* [73]

For the more strictly legal studies Jefferson recommended *Coke on Littleton,* as methodized by Thomas, declaring it to be much superior to Blackstone.[74] Madison recognized difficulties in prescribing texts and advised the selection of a politically orthodox professor who could be trusted to make his own choice.[75] Jefferson agreed with his younger colleague on the importance of political orthodoxy but in the following characteristic style emphasized the influence of reading:

In the selection of our Law Professor, we must be rigorously attentive to his political principles. You will recollect that before the Revolution, Coke on Littleton was the universal elementary book of law students, and a sounder Whig never wrote, nor of profounder learning in the orthodox doctrines of the British constitution, or in what were called English liberties. You remember also that our lawyers were then all Whigs. But when his black-letter text, and uncouth but cunning learning got out of fashion, and the honeyed Mansfieldism of Blackstone became the students' hornbook, from that moment, that profession (the nursery of our Congress) began to slide into toryism, and nearly all the young brood of lawyers now are of that

---

* Washington's *Farewell Address* was included at Madison's suggestion.—To James Madison, February 12, 1825, *Ms., L. C.,* Vol. 228.

hue. They suppose themselves, indeed, to be Whigs, because they no longer know what Whigism or republicanism means. It is in our seminary that that vestal flame is to be kept alive; it is thence it is to spread anew over our own and the sister States. If we are true and vigilant in our trust, within a dozen or twenty years a majority of our own legislature will be from one school, and many disciples will have carried its doctrines home with them to their several States, and will have leavened thus the whole mass. New York has taken strong ground in vindication of the Constitution; South Carolina had already done the same. Although I was against our leading, I am equally against omitting to follow in the same line, and backing them firmly; and I hope that yourself or some other will mark out the track to be pursued by us.[76]

History was always included in Jefferson's plan for higher education, and in 1779 he proposed even for the elementary schools that "the books which shall be used therein for instructing the children to read shall be such as will at the same time make them acquainted with Graecian, Roman, English, and American history."[77] This reading of history, by the larger number who would have no higher education, he believed would make "the people the safe, as they are the ultimate, guardians of their own liberty."[78]

In 1779 he proposed for William and Mary a professorship of history—civil and ecclesiastical. In 1814 he would associate ancient and modern history with the corresponding languages. "History," he wrote, "is here associated with languages, not as a kindred subject, but on a principle of economy, because both may be attained by the same course of reading, if books are selected with that view."[79] In 1818 he grouped history with government with the proviso that it be interwoven with politics and law. The next year the legislature adopted this classification, but in 1824 the Visitors reverted to the older plan and placed ancient history in the school of ancient languages and modern history in the school of modern languages. Professor Long was fully in harmony with the plan to teach the history and geography of a people simultaneously with its language.[80] As he himself was the author of a history of Rome and of a classical atlas,[81] Jefferson's plan received a fair trial. A letter of October, 1825,* shows that Jefferson thought that history should be taught so far as possible from original authors and that

* Appendix P.

he regarded it as one of the most fruitful sources of political opinions, whether good or bad.[82]

By this plan geography was to be taught along with the history and language of a people. In 1800 Jefferson named it as a separate subject. In 1817 he associated geography and history—ancient and modern. In 1818 geography, like astronomy, was grouped with the physico-mathematical subjects. In 1779 it was named as a subject to be taught in the intermediate schools, but in the letter to Peter Carr, it was proposed for the elementary schools and was not otherwise mentioned. The bills of 1817 place geography in all three grades of schools. The Rockfish report places it among the applied mathematics in the University and proposes elementary geography for the district colleges. This seems to show that Jefferson considered it a subject which could be taught in its rudiments to children, more broadly in the colleges, and in its technical or professional applications in the University.

Philosophy was included in every proposal for university courses, and was limited to the highest grade of schools—except in the letter to Peter Carr where it was included among the subjects to be taught in the greatly enlarged secondary or general schools. In seeming contradiction to this consistent recognition of the value of philosophy, Jefferson held some curious views regarding some of its branches. In a letter of advice to a nephew in 1787 he declared that the study of moral philosophy was a waste of time because this is a natural endowment which may be developed by exercise but is distorted by artificial rules. However, he suggested that the writings of Sterne formed the best course of morality that ever was written, and added positive advice about moral development:

> Above all things, lose no occasion of exercising your dispositions to be grateful, to be generous, to be charitable, to be humane, to be true, just, firm, orderly, courageous; consider every act of this kind, as an exercise which will strengthen your moral faculties and increase your worth.[83]

Thirty-three years later, he gave the same advice regarding the education of his grandson:

> It would be time lost for him to attend professors of ethics, metaphysics, logic. The first of these may be as well acquired in the closet as from living lecturers; and supposing the two last to mean the science of the mind, the

simple reading of Locke, Tracy, and Stewart will give him as much in that branch as is real science.[84]

In the former letter he advised the study of religion free from "bias in favor of novelty and singularity of opinions" and from all fears and servile prejudices. He urged his nephew to judge everything in the light of reason, to read the Bible like Livy and Tacitus, and to study the life of Jesus like that of any historical character—"Do not be frightened from this inquiry by any fear of its consequences." He declared that our own reason is the only oracle given by Heaven, and that we are answerable not for the rightness but for the uprightness of our decisions.[85]

In 1779 Jefferson abolished the professorships of divinity at William and Mary to make room for those of law, medicine, chemistry, and modern languages,[86] though he had included civil and ecclesiastical history in the reorganization bill of that year. In 1814 he proposed among the professional schools a professorship of theology and ecclesiastical history. By the advice of Dr. Cooper, he omitted theology from all future proposals of subjects to be taught.[87] On October 7, 1822, the Visitors embodied in their annual report a plan by which they hoped to harmonize the demand for theological education with the principles of religious freedom and sectarian equality. This report, written by Jefferson, proposed that the various religious bodies be invited to establish their own theological schools near the University so that the divinity students might have the opportunities for general education which the University offered.[88] A month later Jefferson wrote to Dr. Cooper that the absence of a professorship of divinity had been used to spread the idea that the University was not only an institution of no religion but was against all religion. He explained the proposal that the denominations establish their own theological schools at the University and expressed the opinion that some sects would do so from candid motives and others from jealousy and rivalry. He expected that bringing the sects together and their mingling with other students would soften asperities, neutralize prejudices, and make the general relation one of peace, reason, and morality.[89] Three months later, Cabell wrote: "I think . . . that your suggestion respecting the religious sects has had great influence. It is the Franklin that has drawn the lightning from the cloud of opposition." [90]

Jefferson's enthusiasm for architecture and music insured the inclusion of the fine arts in every program of studies planned by him. In 1819 when the legislature passed the bill carrying out the recommendations of the Rockfish report, they conspicuously omitted the fine arts from the enumeration of subjects to be taught. As this was the only subject positively omitted, this action has the appearance of an implied injunction that the fine arts should not be taught. Under the title *Pure Mathematics*, the Rockfish report had enumerated as subdivisions algebra, fluxions, geometry and architecture (military and naval). The legislature adopted the general title without naming any subdivisions. Jefferson got around the tacit limitation on the teaching of the fine arts by inducing the Visitors to include "military and civil," instead of "military and naval," architecture among the subjects offered in the School of Mathematics.[91] His practical purpose in designing the Rotunda and pavilions along classical lines at so great pains and expense he explained as follows:

We therefore determined that each of the pavilions . . . should present a distinct and separate sample of the art. And these buildings being arranged around three sides of a square, the lecturer, in a circuit, attended by his school, could explain to them successively these samples of the several orders.[92]

I have been quite anxious [he wrote] to get a good drawing master in the military or landscape line for the University. It is a branch of male education most highly and justly valued on the Continent of Europe.[93]

He had reserved a room in the Rotunda "for instruction in those arts which are employed to embellish life." In April, 1825, the Faculty tried, in turn, to get a music teacher in New York, Philadelphia, and Richmond.[94] The stern regulations of the Visitors, forbidding students to make disturbing noises, contained the one exception—"the proper use of musical instruments shall be freely allowed in their rooms, and in that appropriated for instruction in music." [95]

Jefferson was a firm believer in military training. "We must make military instruction a regular part of collegiate education.

We can never be safe till this is done," he wrote to Monroe in 1813.[96] The next year he included military and naval architecture and projectiles among the subjects to be taught in professional schools and recommended general military training for the younger students as a form of recreation.[97]

In 1817 he wrote to Judge Brooke that, having heard that the Society of Cincinnati was considering the establishment of a professorship of gunnery and fortification, possibly at Central College, the visitors authorized him to offer to provide the buildings and professor within a year, to supplement the funds of the society (about $20,000) to the $25,000 considered sufficient to endow a chair, and to call the foundation the Cincinnati Professorship.[98] This move failed, and the funds of the society finally were bestowed upon Washington College at Lexington. The Rockfish report recommended that military drill be taught by special teachers, on the same basis as manual arts, dancing, music, and drawing—paid for by the students but provided with rooms by the University.

In October, 1824, the Visitors gave the faculty authority to employ a military instructor who should drill the entire student body from 1:30 to 3:30 on Saturdays, the School of Modern Language being pretermitted on those occasions. This instruction was compulsory, and those absent or insubordinate were to be "animadverted on by the faculty." [99] In April, 1826, the military training was made voluntary. General Cocke, himself an artillery officer of the War of 1812, supported Jefferson in this policy, but Madison was opposed to military instruction on a large scale.[100]

Jefferson's plan of vocational education is most fully stated in the letter to Peter Carr:

To [the school] of technical philosophy will come the mariner, carpenter, shipwright, pump maker, clock maker, machinist, optician, metallurgist, founder, cutler, druggist, brewer, vintner, distiller, dyer, painter, bleacher, soap maker, tanner, powder maker, salt maker, glass maker, to learn as much as shall be necessary to pursue their art understandingly, of the sciences of geometry, mechanics, statics, hydrostatics, hydraulics, hydrodynamics, navigation, astronomy, geography, optics, pneumatics, acoustics, physics, chemistry, natural history, botany, mineralogy and pharmacy.

The school of technical philosophy will differ essentially in its functions from the other professional schools. The others are instituted to ramify and dilate the particular sciences taught in the schools of the second grade on a general scale only. The technical school is to abridge those which were taught there too much in extenso for the limited wants of the artificer or practical man. These artificers must be grouped together, according to the particular branch of science in which they need elementary and practical instruction; and a specific lecture or lectures should be prepared for each group—and these lectures should be given in the evening, so as not to interrupt the labors of the day. The school, particularly, should be maintained wholly, at the public expense, on the same principles with that of the ward schools.[101]

In 1824 the Visitors resolved to erect workshops where students might learn the use of tools free. These shops were to be let rent-free to reliable artisans who would allow students to use their tools. These mechanics were to be allowed free instruction in the University in subjects related to their respective crafts.[102] This provision does not seem to have been carried out.[103]

Jefferson's proposals regarding admission, election of courses, and graduation were simple. For admission, he believed the University should "require elementary qualifications only, and sufficient age" [104] in order that any student capable of doing the work with profit might enter. The age requirement was to free the University from the "stricter government necessary for young boys, but unsuitable for youths arrived at years of discretion" and from "the intrusions and the noisy turbulence of a multitude of small boys." [105] In 1818 Jefferson believed that students ordinarily would come to the University at about the age of fifteen,[106] but in 1824 the Visitors enacted the rules that no student be received under sixteen.[107]

The "elementary qualifications" rested upon considerations equally practical. Notwithstanding his statement about the languages to Dr. Priestley in 1800—"I do not think them very essential to the obtaining eminent degrees of science; but I think them very useful towards it" [108]—he seems to have come to regard them as a necessary basis for a liberal education. In the Rockfish report he described the ancient languages as "being the foundation common to all the sciences," and urged the establishment of district colleges in which the elements of these languages would be taught as a preparation for entrance into the University. He was opposed to any part of a professor's time

A CORNER OF AN ACADEMIC VILLAGE

The northern part of the lawn of the University of Virginia, showing the Rotunda and some of the pavilions with their connecting colonnades. Jefferson regarded this arrangement of buildings as safer from fire or disease than a single large building, which he described as a "den of noise, of filth and fetid air." He planned for the trees as well as the building, and gave Virginia a university campus of unusual beauty.

being given to drilling a primary class, and intended the instruction to be so advanced in character that only the student well grounded in languages could follow it with profit.[109]   The many books in foreign languages, ancient or modern, selected for the University library, show that he expected the majority of students to be able to make free use of them, at least before the end of their attendance.   Chapman Johnson, one of the visitors, thought Jefferson demanded too high a standard for admission, declaring it to be "better . . . than most of our teachers." [110] Exactly what the standard was, as measured by conventional units, it is impossible to say, but it appears to have been substantially that recommended by Dr. Cooper to Governor Nicholas in 1816.   This letter may reasonably be taken as showing what he probably recommended to Jefferson in his letters of September, 1814.   He advised that no student be admitted unless he could read easily Virgil, Horace, Xenophon, and Homer, could render English into Latin at sight, and had mastered six books of Euclid and cubic and quadratic equations.[111]   As Jefferson held Cooper's learning and ability in very high esteem, and as about this time he expected Cooper to hold two of the four or five professorships in Central College, he would be apt to be influenced by his opinion of the preliminary training necessary for university students.   There could be no question of the practical necessity of a thorough grounding in Latin and Greek for students in the classical school.   And here it was that Jefferson suffered grievous disappointment, as shown in a letter written late in 1825:

We were obliged the last year to receive shameful Latinists into the classical school of the University, such as we will certainly refuse as soon as we can get from better schools a sufficiency of those properly instructed to form a class.   We must get rid of this Connecticut Latin, of this barbarous confusion of long and short syllables, which renders doubtful whether we are listening to a reader of Cherokee, Shawnee, Iroquois, or what.[112]

Dr. Bruce, himself a Harvard graduate, thinks Jefferson's condemnation of Connecticut Latin sprang more from hatred of Yale Federalism than from the supposed inferiority of the Yale accent, and he regrets that Yale could not have furnished more instructors to Virginia academies.[113]

Once admitted, the student enjoyed one of the most notable

of those forms of freedom of which Jefferson was a lifelong advocate; he was free to enter any school of the University. It was not until after Jefferson's death that the titled degrees were established and that candidates for these degrees were required to graduate in certain specified schools.[114] The elective system was a new idea in American education, though Jefferson had observed its operation in Europe. His views are explained in an interesting letter to George Ticknor:

> I am not fully informed of the practices at Harvard, but there is one from which we shall certainly vary, although it has been copied, I believe, by nearly every college and academy in the United States. That is, the holding of students all to one prescribed course of reading, and disallowing exclusive application to those branches only which are to qualify them for the particular vocations to which they are destined. We shall, on the contrary, allow them uncontrolled choice in the lectures they shall choose to attend, and require elementary qualifications only, and sufficient age.[115]

This letter not only sets forth the elective principle but implies that the concentration necessary for effective specialization is its chief justification. None of Jefferson's ideas gained a wider acceptance in American education. Ticknor, a Dartmouth graduate, visited Monticello in 1815 at the age of twenty-three and a lasting friendship grew up between Jefferson and the young man. In 1817 Jefferson wrote him an account of his plans for the University and the next year suggested that he take the professorship of ethics, belles lettres, and the fine arts.* In 1820 the Visitors elected him to a professorship,[116] which he declined. In the letter of 1823 partly quoted above, Jefferson scouted any rivalry between Harvard and the University of Virginia, alluding to the latter as Harvard's "yoke-mate," and urging Ticknor to visit the University. This he did in December, 1824, being much interested in the buildings and plans of instruction. "It is more practical than I feared but not so practical that I feel satisfied of its success," he wrote to his friend William H. Prescott.[117] Apparently he considered parts of the plan to be practical enough to be tried at Harvard. In 1821 he had set on foot a movement for the reform of Harvard, and in 1825 his proposals were adopted, chiefly

---

* He declined this informal proffer of a professorship because of the age and ill health of his father and of his anticipation of a position at Harvard.—Ticknor to Jefferson, Feb. 13, 1819, *Ms., M. H. S.*

A SAMPLE OF JEFFERSONIAN ARCHITECTURE

Pavilion No. 111, University of Virginia, Palladian Corinthian, designed by Jefferson with possible suggestions from Latrobe. From a manuscript letter to his nephew, Chancellor Carr, urging him to accept the professorship of law, we know that Jefferson regarded this as the most beautiful and convenient of the pavilions.

through the influence of William Prescott (father of the historian) and Judge Story. These changes as summarized by President Eliot in his report for 1883–1884 were; (1) the admission of persons not candidates for a degree; (2) the division of instruction into departments with a professor at the head of each; (3) division of classes according to proficiency; (4) consideration to a limited extent of the desires of students in arranging their studies. This plan was opposed by the faculty and was successful only under Ticknor in the department of modern languages. At the time of his resignation in 1835 he wrote that within his department he had entirely broken up classes, establishing the principle and practice of progress according to proficiency, and that he had introduced a system of voluntary study which for years had embraced from 140 to 160 students, making it possible to rely very little upon college discipline "but almost entirely on the good disposition of the young men and their desire to learn." [118] These were distinctly Jeffersonian methods. Longfellow succeeded Ticknor, and in the main followed his system. "The reform gradually gained new ground" until it came to be definitely established at Harvard.[119] Late in 1821 Ticknor had written to Jefferson of the way in which he hoped to see Harvard influenced by her southern rival:

I am very anxious to hear more about your University and to learn something of its success. Every day persuades me anew of the truth of an opinion I have long held, that at Cambridge we never shall become what we might be very easily unless we are led or driven to it by a rival. I see no immediate prospect of such a rival except in your University, and therefore I long to have it in successful operation.[120]

Francis Wayland, president of Brown University, was much interested in Jefferson's plans. In his report to the trustees, March 28, 1849, he recommended the elective system and within the next six weeks he and Zechariah Allen, a trustee, visited the University of Virginia to study the plan in actual operation.[121] Professor William B. Rogers had been a professor in the University of Virginia, and when he founded the Massachusetts Institute of Technology he adopted the system of free electives.[122] By 1885, at least thirty-five southern colleges had adopted the elective system, besides many in the North and West. With

greater freedom in the selection of studies had gone other mani-
festations of Jefferson's liberalizing spirit—mildness in discipline
in the lower schools as well as in the colleges and a growing confidence and coöperation between students and instructors.[123]
Dr. Bruce believes that Ticknor was influenced to adopt the
elective system chiefly by Jefferson, as he had previously shown
no interest in it after travel in Europe where he could have observed it. However, he thinks that the growth of science, and
not the influence of the University, was the chief cause of the
general spread of the system through the country [124] after its beginning in Virginia.

According to Jefferson's plan, graduates were not to receive
the usual academic degrees, but those satisfying the requirements of any school should be known as graduates of the University of Virginia. The doctorate was intended for advanced
graduates, either academic or professional, but at first was given
only in the School of Medicine. He was strongly opposed to
honorary degrees, although he had accepted five such awards
himself. He seems to have feared that the freedom with which
contemporary colleges bestowed honorary degrees would
cheapen those conferred upon graduates, for at many com-
mencements the former were the more numerous. Moreover,
he feared that they would be given to politicians, clergymen, and
soldiers for partisan, sectarian or military service and that this
would compromise the freedom and reputation of the University.[125] One passage from the records of the Visitors for October
4, 1824, states well his views on graduation requirements, showing that his principles of free election were not without qualification, and that from the beginning there was one required subject
at the University:

But no diploma shall be given to anyone who has not passed such an
examination in the Latin language as shall have proved him able to read the
highest classics in that language with ease, thorough understanding and just
quantity; and if he be also a proficient in the Greek, let that, too, be stated in
his diploma. The intention being that the reputation of the University
shall not be committed but to those who, to an eminence in some one or
more of the sciences taught in it, add a proficiency in these languages which
constitute the basis of good education, and are indispensable to fill up the
character of a "well-educated man." [126]

Strict examinations, both oral and written, were prescribed. In some schools a rating of 75 per cent in others 80 per cent was required. These details were not dictated by Jefferson but they were in full accord with his views. In the autumn of 1825 the Visitors adopted the following resolution:

The rector and Visitors, impressed themselves with the beneficial effect and the necessity of strict examinations of the students, on the topics of the lectures and lessons delivered them, recommend this practice to the consideration and attention of the professors.[127]

The lecture method was not prescribed but was assumed by Jefferson to be the best way to conduct most of the advanced instruction he was contemplating. He believed lectures would stimulate independent thought, create a desire for original investigation, and discourage mere memorizing, though he expected them to be checked by oral examination at the next meeting of the class. He had established some lecture courses at William and Mary in 1779, and had derived the idea from Dr. William Small while a student in his classes about 1761.[128]

CHAPTER IX

UNIVERSITY GOVERNMENT

FUNDAMENTAL to Jefferson's theories was the belief that student government could be carried on more successfully among adolescent and mature students by the appeal to honor and self-respect rather than to fear. His views are admirably stated in the Rockfish report:

The best mode of government for youth, in large collections, is certainly a desideratum not yet attained with us. It may be well questioned whether *fear* after a certain age, is a motive to which we should have ordinary recourse. The human character is susceptible of other incitements to correct conduct, more worthy of employ, and of better effect. Pride of character, laudable ambition, and moral dispositions are innate correctives of the indiscretions of that lively age; and when strengthened by habitual appeal and exercise, have a happier effect on future character than the degrading motive of fear. Hardening them to disgrace, to corporal punishments, and servile humiliations cannot be the best process for producing erect character. The affectionate deportment between father and son, offers in truth the best example for that of tutor and pupil; and the experience and practice of other countries, in this respect, may be worthy of enquiry and consideration with us. It will then be for the wisdom and discretion of the Visitors to devise and perfect a proper system of government, which, if it be founded in reason and comity, will be more likely to nourish in the minds of our youth the combined spirit of order and self-respect, so congenial with our political institutions, and so important to be woven into the American character.[1]

Profoundly as he believed in the principle, Jefferson looked forward with trepidation to the time when it should be put to the test of experience. His attitude appears from letters written to Dr. Cooper in 1822 and to George Ticknor the following year:

The article of discipline is the most difficult in American education. Premature ideas of independence, too little repressed by parents, beget a spirit of insubordination which is the great obstacle to science with us and a principal cause of its decay since the revolution.[2]

134

The rock which I most dread is the discipline of the institution. . . . The insubordination of our youth is now the greatest obstacle to their education. We may lessen the difficulty, perhaps, by avoiding too much government, by requiring no useless observances, none which shall merely multiply occasions for dissatisfaction, disobedience, and revolt by referring to the more discreet of themselves the minor discipline, the graver to the civil magistrates, as in Edinburgh.[3]

An attempt was made to carry out his plan of vesting minor cases of discipline in the students when the Board adopted the following resolution in October, 1824. It shows that Jefferson recognized the intolerance of youth when dealing with human shortcomings:

The major punishments . . . shall be decreed by the professors themselves. Minor cases may be referred to a board of six censors, to be named by the faculty, from the most discreet of the students, whose duty it shall be, sitting as a board, to inquire into the facts, propose the minor punishment which they think proportioned to the offence, and to make report thereof to the professors for their approbation, or their commutation of the penalty, if it be beyond the grade of the offence. The censors shall hold their offices until the end of the session of their appointment, if not sooner revoked by the faculty.[4]

About a month after the opening of the University, the Rector voiced the following hopeful view of the situation in a letter to Cabell:

We await Mr. Tucker's arrival to form a board of faculty, that the professors may enter upon their functions of order and discipline, which some incipient irregularities of the students begin to call for. From a view which I took of their ages when the whole number was 61, I found 6 of 21 and upwards, 9 of 20, 23 of 19, 10 of 18, 10 of 17, and 3 of 16. Two-thirds, therefore, being of 19 and upwards, we may hope are of sufficient discretion to govern themselves, and that the younger third by their example, as well as by moderate coercion, will not be very difficult to keep in order.[5]

The "incipient irregularities" continued, but he was keeping up his courage late in August when he wrote to his granddaughter that the students numbered more than one hundred and that order was good, and significantly added: "We studiously avoid too much government, we treat them as men and gentlemen, under the guidance mainly of their own discretion. They so consider themselves, and make it their pride to acquire that character for their institution." [6]

Evidently Jefferson, as well as several of his colleagues, recognized the need for more stringent government some time before the meeting of the Visitors in October, 1825. In September, General Cocke wrote to Cabell:

> If you regard the future happiness and well-being of our State prepare yourself to make an effort at the next meeting of the Visitors to correct these evils. The old sachem is well prepared, from what I learned as I passed through Charlottesville, to adopt measures calculated to reform the symptoms of irregularity, that, if not corrected, will soon grow into enormities.[7]

Jefferson's circular letter of September 10, 1825, calling the regular meeting of the Visitors for October 3, has a distinctive interest not only because of the circumstances which kept them in session for nearly a week, but because of the light it throws upon their methods of procedure:

> The state of my health renders it perfectly certain that I shall not be able to attend the next meeting of the Visitors (October 3) *at the University*. Yet I think there is no one but myself to whom the matters to be acted on are sufficiently known for communication to them. This adds a reason the more for inducing the members to meet at Monticello the day before, which has been heretofore found to facilitate and shorten our business. If you could be here then on the Sunday to dinner that afternoon and evening and the morning of Monday, will suffice for all our business, and the Board will only have to ride to the University *pro forma* for attesting the proceedings. Permit me, therefore, to expect you to dinner on that day, (October 2) which as it is ever grateful to me, seems on this occasion to be peculiarly urgent.[8]

On the night of October 1, General Cocke's prediction was fulfilled. Fourteen students, "animated first with wine," masked themselves and made an uproar on the University lawn. Two professors, attempting to restore quiet, were insulted by the rioters and had brickbats thrown at them. The faculty demanded that the students make known who the offenders were, but fifty others joined the rioters and signed a declaration supporting them in their resistance to the faculty.[9] The Visitors, being in session at Monticello, adopted a resolution deprecating the false sense of honor which forbids the giving of information and calling upon the innocent to divulge the names of the guilty.* [10] The Board adjourned to the University and called

* See Appendix M.

the students before them in the Rotunda.   It was a dramatic occasion.   The students looked into the serious faces of Madison and Jefferson, former presidents of the United States, Brecken-ridge and Cocke, veteran officers of the army, Cabell, Johnson, and Loyall, proportionately eminent in politics or at the bar. Jefferson, now in his eighty-third year and weak from long ill-ness, attempted to address them, but was overcome by emotion and called upon Chapman Johnson to speak in his stead.   So powerful was his appeal that the fourteen rioters voluntarily came forward and declared themselves to be the offenders.[11] The faculty promptly expelled three, presenting one to the grand jury for civil punishment.   The other eleven were suspended, and the fifty signers were allowed to retract.[12]   The Visitors unanimously approved the expulsion of Carey, Eyre, and Thompson.[13]   One of these was Jefferson's nephew.   Although he was deeply humiliated that a member of his family should be a leader of disorder, the Rector was as inflexible as Brutus in insisting that justice be done without favor.[14]   The Board adopted several resolutions simplifying the rules, forbidding intoxication, profanity, the wearing of masks, and the like, in-creasing the police power of the faculty, enjoining upon the proctor and the professors the faithful enforcement of the laws of the University, and making students responsible for what occurred in their rooms.[15]

On the sixth day of this extraordinary meeting the Visitors adopted their report to the President and Directors of the Literary Fund.   Although the full board was present and the report was amended in some particular, it is essentially Jeffer-son's work.   It is couched in his style and phraseology and is filled with his philosophy.   The passage on discipline splendidly illustrates the readjustment of his theory to the conditions of experience:

A printed copy of the statutes and regulations enacted by the Board of Visitors for the government of the University is now communicated.   We have thought it peculiarly requisite to give to the civil magistrates the restraint and punishment of all offences which come within the ordinary cognisance of the laws.   At the age of 16, the earliest period of admission into the University, habits of obedience to the laws become a proper part of education and practice.   The minor provisions and irregularities alone (unnoticed by the laws of the land) are the peculiar subjects of academical authority. No system of these provisions has ever yet prevented all disorder. Those first provided by this Board were founded on the principles of avoiding too much government, of not multiplying occasions of coercion, by erecting indifferent actions into things of offense, and by having left enough room to the student for habitually exercising his own discretion. But experience has already proved that stricter provisions are necessary for the preservation of order. That coercion must be resorted to where confidence has been disappointed. We have accordingly, at the present session, considerably amended and enlarged the scope of our former system of regulations, and we shall proceed in the duties of tightening or relaxing the reins of government as experience shall instruct us in the progress of the institution, and we are not certain that the further aid of the legislature itself shall not be necessary to enable the authorities of the institution to interpose, in some cases with more promptitude, energy and effect than is permitted by the laws as they stand at present.[16]

A month later he wrote to his granddaughter that the recent riot had gone off with the best effect in the world. He explained how the authorities had let it be understood that they wished to trust the discretion of the students for their own government and that four fifths of them had done well, but fifteen or twenty bad subjects had tried whether their indulgence was without limit. To this he added some characteristic philosophy:

But when the whole mass saw the serious way in which that experiment was met, the Faculty of Professors assembled, the Board of Visitors coming forward in support of that authority, a grand jury taking up the subject. Four [sic] of the most guilty expelled, the rest reprimanded, severer laws enacted and a rigorous execution of them declared in the future—it gave them a shock and struck a terror, the most severe as it was less expected. It determined the well-disposed among them to frown upon everything of the kind hereafter, and the ill-disposed returned to order from fear, if not from better motives. A perfect subordination has succeeded, entire respect toward the professors, and industry, order, and quiet the most exemplary has prevailed ever since. Everyone is sensible of the strength which the institution has derived from what appeared at first to threaten its foundation. We have no further fear of anything of the kind from the present set, but as at the next term their numbers will be more than doubled by the accession of an additional band, as unbroken as these were, we mean to be prepared and to ask of the legislature a power to call in the civil authorities in the first instant of disorder and to quell it on the spot by imprisonment and the same legal coercions provided against disorder generally committed by other citizens, from whom, at their age, they have no right to distinction.[17]

A letter written to Mr. Coolidge just a month before Jefferson's death shows that he remained convinced that coercive methods and an element of fear were necessary to preserve order in a large student body.

Our University is going on well. The students have sensibly improved since the last year in habits of order and industry. Occasional instances of insubordination have obliged us from time to time to strengthen our regulations to meet new cases. But the most effectual instrument we have found to be the civil authority. The terrors of indictment, fine, imprisonment, binding to the good behavior, etc. have the most powerful effect. None have yet incurred them, but they have been sternly held up to their view. These civil coercions want a little accommodation to our organization, which we shall probably obtain, and I suppose the more easily as at the age of 16 it is high time for youth to begin to learn and to practice the duties of obedience to the laws of their country. It will make an important item in the Syllabus of the Moral Professor and be considered as forming a standing branch in the system of education established here. The competition among our hotel keepers has made them too obsequious to the will of the students. We must force them to become auxiliaries toward the preservation of order, rather than subservients to their irregularities. We shall continue under this evil until the renewal of their leases shall place them in our power, which takes place but annually. Our present number are over 170 and growing weekly.[18]

It is fair to ask why the regulations of October 4, 1824,* which were approved and probably drafted by Jefferson embody so many rules or prescriptions of penalties inconsistent with the lofty ideals which he expressed in the Rockfish report, why his system failed when put to the test, and why the changes of October, 1825, were made. The latter question has been in a measure anticipated.

In 1823, after writing, "The rock which I most dread is the discipline of the institution," Jefferson asked Ticknor for a copy of the Harvard rules.[19] Mr. Patton believes that he was influenced by a study of these rules and came to feel that the prescription of specific penalties for the infraction of definite rules would be the only safe course.[20] Such punishments as "restraint within the precincts, within their own chamber, or in diet," "a seat of degradation in his schoolroom of longer or shorter duration, removal to a lower class," "imposition of a task," and others authorized in October, 1824, have been re-

* See Appendix M.

peatedly thrown into contrast with the sentiments of the Rockfish report—"Pride of character, laudable ambition, and moral dispositions are innate correctives of the indiscretions of that lively age; and when strengthened by habitual appeal and exercise, have a happier effect on future character than the degrading motive of fear. Hardening them to disgrace, to corporal punishments, and servile humiliations cannot be the best process for producing erect character." Probably the Rector felt that in this untried field, with minor discipline intrusted to inexperienced students and little power in the hands of the faculty, his fond theory in its first trial must be hedged about with prescriptions to prevent the abuse of power. He saw the need of the faculty's being a check upon the student censors—as the Visitors should be upon the faculty.

He thought much about protecting students from the rigors of the civil law, and probably he was more conscious of omitting ordinances like those regulating church attendance at Harvard than he was of the puerile character of some of those which he included.

A comparison of parallel regulations of the two universities * shows marked similarities and equally marked differences. It is probable that Jefferson was guided to some extent by the Harvard laws, when he drafted those for Virginia, but the influence seems to have been slight. Patton assumes that the Harvard rules were much more stringent than those of Virginia. This does not seem to be true of the regulations as a whole. It is true, for example, that the Harvard regulations about the giving of information and the use of musical instruments were more strict than those of Virginia,[21] but the opposite is true of the rule against dueling and those on the use of library books.[22]

Jefferson's plan to have very little government—and that largely in the hands of students—failed to preserve order, partly because the students, instead of being sedate young men earnestly following serious plans of advanced study, were largely the undisciplined heirs to slave plantations, more accustomed to servility than to authority. The student censors seem to have entirely failed to function, owing largely to the natural shrinking from the necessary method of spying and giving in-

* Appendix N.

formation about fellow students and the inevitable unpopularity and the common feeling that it is dishonorable to give information.

Dr. Bruce points out that Jefferson's theory of a minimum of restraint is impractical in any closely packed community, and that the University had the same causes of friction and unrest as a town or city.[23]   In the absence of a most exceptional spirit of coöperation in the student body the imposition of discipline by student censors would be certain to arouse hostility.   During these early months the faculty seems to have done little more than the censors in preserving order.   It may be said that Jefferson's theories were not so much proved to be mistaken as that they were never given a fair trial.   He assumed that any large number of students would contain a controlling majority of the serious-minded and dependable.   In 1825 they seem to have been distinctly in the minority, for about two thirds of the students took an active part in the October revolt. Perhaps it should be said that this assumption of itself was a sufficient defect to rob Jefferson's theories of anything like universal application.

In September, the faculty had asked the Visitors to repeal the most degrading of the minor punishments.[24]   This they did on October 3.[25]   At the same time they gave the faculty greater power and made contumacy a major offense.[26]   Jefferson's correspondence, already cited, shows that he realized, probably with much mortification, that his plan of leniency was a failure so far as applied to the students then in the University or soon to be expected, and that the authorities must be prepared for strong action backed, if necessary, by the civil power.[27]

One of Jefferson's plans for University discipline deserves special notice.   It was the proposal to establish a university court with ordinary judicial power vested in some official with authority to employ the usual court methods.   This was proposed in the first draft of the bill to reorganize Albemarle Academy as Central College.   Early in the session of the first legislature to consider that bill, Cabell wrote that he found some objection among the principal members of the Senate to that part of the bill giving the professors the power of imprisoning the students and asking Jefferson for a statement of the reasons for this provision which could be shown to doubting senators.[28] Before receiving the reply he wrote again that there was objection to the Central College bill "because it confers on the Proctor of the College the powers and authorities of a justice of the peace, within the precincts of the institution.[29] Jefferson's reply, intended for circulation among the senators, was written before this second inquiry was received:

> The establishment of a Proctor is taken from the practice of Europe, where an equivalent officer is made a part, and is a very essential one, of every such institution; and as the nature of his functions requires that he should always be a man of discretion, understanding and integrity, above the common level, it was thought that he would never be less worthy of being trusted with the powers of a justice, within the limits of the institution here, than the neighboring justices generally are; and the vesting him with the conservation of the peace within that limit was intended, while it should equally secure its object, to shield the young and unguarded student from the disgrace of the common prison, except where the case was an aggravated one. A confinement to his own room was meant as an act of tenderness to him, his parents and friends. In fine, it was to give them a complete police of their own, tempered by the paternal attentions of their tutors. And certainly, in no country is such a provision more called for than in this, as has been proved from times of old, from the regular annual riots and battles between the students of William and Mary, with the town boys, before the Revolution, *quorum pars fui*, and the many and more serious affrays of later times.—Observe, too, that our bill proposes no exclusion of the ordinary magistrate, if the one attached to the institution is thought to execute his power either partially or remissly.[30]

The significant parts of this plan are that it would aid the faculty, through the proctor, in obtaining evidence of student delinquency, and that it would substitute for the ordinary civil authority one expected to be more considerate of the youth and distinctive characteristics of the students in dealing with that intermediate class of misdemeanors which are violations of the civil law, but of minor seriousness.

This was not entirely a new idea as proposed by Jefferson. On December 21, 1807, a communication was laid before the trustees of Hampden-Sidney from Bishop Madison, President of William and Mary College, and another from Reverend George A. Baxter, Principal of Washington Academy, asking the trustees of Hampden-Sidney to concur with those of the other two institutions in petitioning the legislature to grant them power to summon and compel the attendance of witnesses and to administer oaths to any person other than a student to answer all questions respecting students as to violations of rules and statutes of the seminaries. The Hampden-Sidney board resolved that it would be beneficial to the seminary to have the right to call upon the civil authorities to administer oaths to persons other than students, and joined with William and Mary and Washington Academy in the petition.[31]

This same careful distinction between requiring evidence from students and from others was long observed at the University. The regulation of October 4, 1824, provides:

When testimony is required from a student, it shall be voluntary, and not on oath. And if unwilling to give it, let the moral obligation be explained and urged, under which every one is bound to bear witness, where wrong has been done, but finally let it be left to his own sense of right.[32]

As amended the following March, this regulation more simply and definitely forbade any compulsion:

When testimony is required of a student, it shall be voluntary and not on oath. And the obligation to give it shall be left to his own sense of right.[33]

Jefferson's great expostulation in October, 1825, urging the worthy among the students to purge themselves of the common censure spread over all by the unworthy few, contained this significant passage:

The Visitors are aware that a prejudice prevails too extensively among the young that it is dishonorable to bear witness one against another. While this prevails, and under the form of a matter of conscience, they have been unwilling to authorize constraint, and have therefore, in their regulations on this subject, indulged the error, however unfounded in reason or morality. But this loose principle in the ethics of school-boy combinations, is unworthy of mature and regulated minds, and is accordingly condemned by the laws of their country, which, in offences within their cognisance, compel those who have knowledge of a fact, to declare it for the purposes of justice, and of the general good and safety of society. And certainly, where wrong has been done, he who knows and conceals the doer of it, makes himself an accomplice, and is justly censurable as such.* [34]

Four days later the Visitors especially charged the proctor with the duty of bringing before the proper authority the tres-

* Appendix M.

passes and misdemeanors of students.[35] This would imply placing them in the hands of authorities with power to compel testimony from all. By this time, Jefferson had become convinced that for the present, it would be best to leave to the civil authorities all cases coming within the ordinary cognizance of the laws,[36] and that the University needed an enlarged power from the legislature to call upon the civil authorities with promptness in case of need.[37]

That part of the bill for Central College which provided for the university court had to be dropped before the bill could be passed in 1816.[38] The enactment of 1824—"The minor punishment shall be restraint . . . within their own chamber—" * seems to embody the very power to which the senators had objected eight years before. This is the more surprising when we observe that the minor punishments were to be imposed by the student censors, subject to review by the faculty. Perhaps this is one reason why this punishment was discontinued in October, 1825, when the censorship was abolished and discipline placed more completely upon the faculty, backed by the civil authorities.

Once more Jefferson's plan of a University court was brought forward as a more permanent provision for serious cases of discipline. On October 6, 1825, the Visitors adopted the following resolution:

Resolved, that Mr. Johnson, Mr. Cabell, and Mr. Loyall be appointed a committee whose duty it shall be to consider and enquire what system may be digested for the better government of the University; and that they be especially charged with the duty of considering how far it may be practicable and prudent to connect with the University a court having cognizance over misdemeanors committed within the precincts of the University, and over those committed by members of the University, within the County of Albemarle; and that they report thereupon to the next meeting of the Visitors.[39]

The next meeting was to have been held in December but did not take place until April, and the report seems to have been delayed until October, three months after the death of the aged Rector.[40] At that time the Visitors adopted a report proposing a court with elaborate judicial machinery, but it was rejected by the legislature.[41] Jefferson's share in maturing this

* Appendix M.

plan must be conjectured. Evidently its essentials were understood in December, when the Visitors substituted correspondence for the meeting previously decided upon. At that time Cabell wrote to Jefferson from Richmond:

> I saw Dr. Cooper here on my way down the country. He seems to entertain great doubts of the practicability of establishing with success such as a tribunal as Mr. Johnson contemplates. He suggests the expediency of enquiring into the legal power of the civil magistrate to bind over or commit a man for refusing to give evidence against another charged upon mere suspicion. He expressed, however, the greatest interest in the experiment.[42]

A part of the plan was that the professor of law should be sole judge of this court and should receive an additional salary, not to exceed five hundred dollars. At the time this plan was being considered, several attempts to obtain a law professor had failed, and at the next meeting the Visitors in desperation established the presidency as an additional inducement to William Wirt. No doubt they thought of the judgeship of the University Court with its additional salary as a similar inducement, but, whether the plans for the court were not sufficiently matured for action, or the presidency with its much greater supplementary salary seemed the least adequate inducement, the Visitors determined to try the latter first.

One significant expression of Jefferson's faith in student self-government was not established at the University until sixteen years after his death. It had been the custom for formal examinations to take place under the supervision of three professors. In June, 1842, on motion of Henry St. George Tucker, Professor of Law, it was resolved that in future each student should attach to his examination paper a certification that he had received no aid. This was later extended to include the giving of aid and other matters. Since that time examinations have been free from faculty surveillance, and the rare cases of dishonesty have been handled by the students themselves.[43] This policy has been widely adopted in American colleges and seems to have been more successful where students have punished dishonesty themselves than where they have been required to report it to the faculty. However, it has not been an unqualified success, and has been abandoned by several institutions.

CHAPTER X

PRINCIPLES AND IDEALS

JEFFERSON was a consistent utilitarian. Time after time he stated his purpose to found a university to teach "all branches of science useful to us, and at this day." [1] He thought geology of little use unless the rock studied contained some useful metal. [2] In a broader sense the same view is stated in letters to Kosciusko and Ticknor: "The main objects of all science are the freedom and happiness of man." [3] "Knolege is power, knolege is safety . . . knoledge is happiness." [4]

Holding these views, he inevitably looked to education as a means of social, moral, and political uplift to society as well as an aid to personal and professional progress for individuals. This often necessitated the protection cf fundamental rights from encroachment—sometimes of the rich upon the poor, of Tidewater upon the Back Country, of the North upon the South, of religious organizations upon persons of liberal views, of Federalists upon Republicans, of the national government upon the states. He found a lifelong joy in the belief that two of these menaces had been greatly reduced by his own handiwork—the statute for religious freedom, taking from intolerance its power of legal compulsion, and the law abolishing entail and primogeniture, which deprived wealth of its artificial perpetuity. The sectarianism of the aggressive religious denominations and the reincarnated Federalism of the Centralists were the red flags which most promptly brought the old champion of democracy to the defense of what he conceived to be his principles. Naturally he misunderstood his opponents at times—as militant crusaders usually do. At times he confused ultimate principles with immediate ends and abandoned the former that he might gain the latter. Universal education and organized self-expression through political units small enough to voice a vital public opinion were the chief means upon which he relied. To understand the values which he expected to flow from these is to understand why he so persistently labored for the public schools, the University, and the organization of wards.

"Freedom, the first-born daughter of science," [5] was fundamental to Jefferson's plan—freedom of religious faith, freedom of political expression, freedom from social cast and from inherent prejudice. He sought to destroy the dual system of schools for the well-to-do and for the poor, and free all education from the stigma of pauperism.[6] In 1786 he wrote to George Wythe from Paris a notable criticism of the intellectual life of the common people of Europe:

> if all the sovereigns of Europe were to set themselves to work to emancipate the minds of their subjects from their present ignorance & prejudices, & that as zealously as they now endeavor the contrary, a thousand years would not place them on that high ground on which our common people are now setting out. ours could not have been so fairly put into the hands of their own common sense had they not been separated from their parent stock & been kept from contamination, either from them or the other people of the old world, by the intervention of so wide an ocean. to know the worth of this, one must see the want of it here.[7]

The moral value of education was discussed in a letter to Thomas Law, written in the summer of 1814:

> When it is wanting [moral sense] we endeavor to supply the defect by education, by appeals to reason and calculation, by presenting to the being so unhappily conformed, other motives to do good and to eschew evil; such as the love or the hatred or rejection of those among whom he lives and whose society is necessary to his happiness and even existance; demonstrations by sound calculation that honesty promotes interest in the long run; the rewards and penalties established by the laws; and ultimately the prospects of a future state of retribution for the evil as well as the good done while here. These are the correctives which are supplied by education, and which exercise the functions of the moralist, the preacher, the legislator; and they lead into a course of correct action all those whose depravity is not too profound to be eradicated.[8]

The broad social benefits which Jefferson expected to flow from universal education were many times stated, but never better than in two well-known expressions, written respectively in 1818 and 1822:

If the condition of man is to be progressively ameliorated, as we fondly hope and believe, education is to be the chief instrument in effecting it.[9]

I look to the diffusion of light and education as the resource most to be relied on for ameliorating the condition, promoting the virtue, and advancing the happiness of man.[10]

Not only was education for the immediate benefit of those receiving it, but was to train those of superior ability for larger leadership and service:

The greatest good [of the people] requires that while they are instructed in general, competently to the common business of life, others should employ their genius with necessary information to the useful arts, to invention for saving labor and increasing our comforts, to nourishing our health, to civil government, military science, etc.[11]

This was particularly true of the poor boys to be educated at public expense:

The object is to bring into action that mass of talents which lies buried in poverty in every country, for want of the means of development, and thus give activity to a mass of mind, which, in proportion to our population shall be the double or treble of what it is in most countries.[12]

Jefferson's long career in politics made it inevitable that he should take a special interest in the relations of education and government. He believed education necessary to the establishment and preservation of good government, and that the state should actively aid that which was almost a means of government itself. The latter thought appears in a letter written to Madison as early as 1787: [To give] "information to the people . . . is the most certain and the most legitimate engine of government." [13]

The duty of the state to provide educational opportunities was so axiomatic that he seldom felt the need of stating it. In his first inaugural address he said: "The diffusion of information, I deem [one] of the essential principles of our government and consequently [one] which ought to shape its administration." [14]

His great ambition was the division of the counties into wards or hundreds to give the fruits of education a fair expression in government. "My partiality for that division," he wrote in

1816, "is not founded in views of education solely, but infinitely more as the means of a better administration of our government, and the eternal preservation of republican principles." [15]

Six years earlier he had written to Governor Tyler:

these little republics will be the main strength of the great one, we owe to them the vigor given to our revolution in its commencement in the Eastern states, & by them the Eastern states were enabled to repeal the embargo in opposition to the Middle, Southern, & Western states & their large & lubberly division into counties which can never be assembled. general orders are given out from a center to the Foreman of each hundred, the whole nation is thrown into energetic action, in the same direction in one instant & as one man, and it becomes absolutely irresistible. could I once see this, I should consider it as the dawn of the salvation of the republic, & say with old Simeon *"nunc dimittis, Domine."* but our children will be as wise as we are, and will establish in the fulness of time those things not yet ripe for establishment.[16]

Through the years he grew more enthusiastic in urging the organization of wards within the counties, believing that it would lead to a more coördinated system of self-government and the jealous guarding and enthusiastic exercise of the rights of citizenship by the people.[17]   When this plan finally was tried in Virginia it only too quickly demonstrated the impracticability of Jefferson's fond ambition.   The constitution of 1850 divided the counties into districts for electoral and other purposes, but this soon weakened popular interest in the meetings of citizens at the county courts without the growth of a compensating interest in district affairs.[18]   After the Civil War the reconstruction party introduced the town system of government.   The sparseness of population and the growing complexity of public questions would have prevented success if it had not been foredoomed to failure by the circumstances of the times.[19]

To Jefferson's mind education was the only sure protection of political rights and institutions against unjust encroachments. In 1781 he wrote that the study of history by the people would help them to judge of the actions of men and would enable them to know ambition under disguise and to defeat it.[20]   In 1810 he wrote to Colonel Duane:

I have received information of Pestalozzi's mode of education from some European publications and from Mr. Keefe's book which shows that the latter possesses both the talents and the zeal for carrying it into effect. I sincerely wish it success, convinced that the information of the people at large can alone make them the safe, as they are the sole depositories of our political and religious freedom.[21]

One tendency which Jefferson fought as a supreme evil was the growing power of the federal government. This he regarded as an iniquitous encroachment upon the freedom of the states. The spirit of Federalism appeared in many forms—in the enlarging power of the Supreme Court, of Congress, of the President—and Jefferson was against them all. Here, as elsewhere, his reliance was upon his universal weapon—education. A few months after the Supreme Court in the case of McCulloch versus Maryland had held an act of the Maryland Legislature to be unconstitutional, and therefore void,[22] he wrote to William Jarvis, denying that the judges are the "ultimate arbiters of all constitutional questions" and asserting the old principle of separation of powers. He concluded with this significant comment:

When the legislative or executive functionaries act unconstitutionally they are responsible to the people in their elective capacity. The exemption of the judges from that is quite dangerous enough. I know no safe depository of the ultimate powers of the society but the people themselves; and if we think them not enlightened enough to exercise their control with a wholesome discretion, the remedy is not to take it from them but to inform their discretion by education. This is the true corrective of abuses of constitutional power.[23]

The bitter controversy over the extension or restriction of slavery which involved the Missouri Compromise filled the last years of Jefferson's life with the warnings of a growing sectional hostility. He hated slavery as an institution, but, like a true states-rights advocate, was irrevocably opposed to any limitation of slavery which might be effected through any increase of national control over the members of the union. The danger which he especially recognized was that the southern youths then attending northern colleges would acquire the pernicious political doctrines of the North. Early in 1821 he wrote to John Taylor about the policy of the University:

We shall receive only those subjects who desire the highest degree of instruction for which they now go to Harvard, Princeton, New York, and Philadelphia. These seminaries are no longer proper for Southern or

Western students. The signs of the times admonish us to call them home. If knowledge is power we should look to its advancement at home where our resource of power will be unwanting. This may not be in my day, but probably will in yours. God send to our country a happy deliverance.[24]

The following day he wrote to General Breckenridge that he feared the line of division lately marked out between the sections would never be obliterated, and added:

We are now trusting to those who are against us in position and principle to fashion to their own form the minds and affections of our youth, . . . imbibing opinions and principles in discord with those of their own country. This canker is eating on the vitals of our existence.[25]

A few days before he had written to Cabell about the hampered finances of the University:

Even with the whole funds, we shall be reduced to six professors, while Harvard will still prime it over us, with her twenty professors. How many of our youths she now has, learning the lessons of Anti-Missourianism, I know not; but a gentleman lately from Princeton, told me he saw there the list of the students at that place, and that more than half were Virginians. These will return home, no doubt, deeply impressed with the sacred principles of our holy alliance of Restrictionists.[26]

Just a year before he had written:

If, however . . . we are to go a-begging anywhere for our education, I would rather it should be to Kentucky than any other State, because she has more of the flavor of the old cask than any other. All the States but our own are sensible that knowledge is power. The Missouri question is for power. The efforts now generally making through the States to advance their science, is for power; while we are sinking into the barbarism of our Indian Aborigines, and expect, like them, to oppose by ignorance the overwhelming mass of light and science by which we shall be surrounded. It is a comfort that I am not to live to see this.[27]

Other letters of this period show the same sense of rivalry, but without the bitterness of sectional hostility:

Surely Governor Clinton's display of the gigantic efforts of New York toward the education of her citizens will stimulate the pride as well as the patriotism of our Legislature, to look to the reputation and safety of their own country, to rescue it from the degradation of becoming the Barbary of the Union. . . . The mass of education in Virginia, before the revolution, placed her with the foremost of her sister colonies. What is her education now? Where is it? The little we have, we import, like beggars, from other States; or import their beggars to bestow on us their miserable crumbs.[28]

I lately saw in a newspaper an estimate in square miles of the area of each of the states, of which the following is an extract: "Virginia 70,000 square miles, Massachusetts 7,250, Connecticut 4,764, Delaware 2,120, Rhode Island 1,580." By this it appears that there are but three states smaller than Massachusetts; that she is the twenty-first only in the scale of size, and but one-tenth of that of Virginia; yet it is unquestionable that she has more influence in our confederacy than any other State in it. Whence this ascendancy? From her attention to education, unquestionably. There can be no stronger proof that knowledge is power, and that ignorance is weakness. *Iuousque tandem* will the Legislature be dead to this truth? [29]

Two years later, urging the need of funds to finish the library, he wrote in another of these letters so admirably calculated to stimulate Virginia pride: "To stop where we are, is to abandon our high hopes, and become suitors to Yale and Harvard for their secondary characters to become our first." [30]

However, the sources of dangerous doctrines were not entirely in the North. In the letter recommending that the Visitors prescribe textbooks to be used in the study of government he stated his position very definitely:

Mr. Gilmer being withdrawn, we know not who his successor may be. He may be a Richmond lawyer, or one of that school of quondam federalism, now consolidation. It is our duty to guard against the dissemination of such principles among our youth, and the diffusion of that poison.[31]

Through these years of effort and anticipation Jefferson confidently expected the University to become the source from which the principles of sound democracy were to spread throughout the South. In 1822 he wrote of the widespread anxiety throughout the South for the opening of the University which would relieve the southerners from dependence upon northern universities.[32] After the University had been open for some months he expressed the opinion that as high a degree of education could be obtained there as in England and prophesied that within twelve or fifteen years the majority of the rulers of the state would be men who had there been educated in the correct principles of the times.[33] This thought was much in his mind during the last winter of his life:

Our sister states will also be repairing to the same fountains of instruction, will bring hither their genius to be kindled at our fire, and will carry back the fraternal affections which, nourished by the same alma mater, will knit us to them by indissoluble bonds of early personal friendships. The good Old Dominion . . . will become a center of ralliance to the states whose youth she has instructed, and, as it were, adopted.[34]

In 1820 Jefferson had written, "I contemplate the University of Virginia as the future bulwark of the human mind in this hemisphere," [35] but within a short time the sectional question had become so acute that he regarded it as primarily a bulwark of the South. This hope was in a large measure realized. When the University opened, its students were poorly prepared because of the inferior secondary schools of the South. Many teachers have been trained at the University and sent out to establish schools at which the University standards and ideals have been built up.[36] This has been true, not only of Virginia, but of the entire South. Fitz-Hugh ascribes to the University a great influence in the organization of the Texan republic and state and of the University of Texas. "That noble old school has done more for Texas than all other institutions of learning," said Allison Mayfield, Secretary of State—not a University man himself.[37] In 1860 there were estimated to be 13,204 pupils in academies taught by 720 teachers, so many of whom had been educated at the University that practically all had been influenced by its methods of teaching. Undoubtedly political principles and academic methods went together.[38]

Jefferson had one other major aversion; the spirit of sectarianism. He believed that the non-conformists opposed his reorganization of William and Mary lest it should benefit the Episcopal Church.[39] He believed that the churches, especially the Presbyterians, were opposed to his educational plans because of his liberal religious opinions, and to the University lest its influence should weaken their dominance over the minds of their members. In this opinion he misunderstood his critics as fully as they did him. In 1820 he disdained the opposition of the pulpit to the appointment of Dr. Cooper: "For myself I was not disposed to regard the denunciations of these satellites of religious inquisition." However, some of his colleagues felt that some attention must be shown to it, and favored the acceptance of Dr. Cooper's proffered resignation.[40]   In accepting this resignation Jefferson explained that one or two of the Visitors were alarmed by the cry of "Fire!" from the Presbyterian pulpits, but that the real ground for their decision was that the funds of the University were "hypotheticated" for five or six years.[41]   Earlier in the year he had written to William Short a letter of virulent vituperation:

> An opposition in the meantime has been got up.   That of our alma mater, William and Mary, is not of much weight.   She must descend into the secondary rank of academies of preparation for the University.   The serious enemies are the priests of the different religious sects, to whose spells on the human mind its improvement is ominous.   Their pulpits are now resounding with denunciations against the appointment of Dr. Cooper whom they charge as a monotheist in opposition to their tritheism.   Hostile as these sects are, in every other point, to one another, they unite in maintaining their mystical theogony against those who believe there is one God only. The Presbyterian clergy are loudest; the most intolerant of all sects, the most tyrannical and ambitious . . . .   They pant to re-establish by law that holy inquisition which they can now only infuse into public opinion.[42]

During these years the religious bodies were taking up the principle of the secular Sunday school.   The Episcopal and Presbyterian churches divided their catechetical schools into two parts, one teaching reading, writing, and arithmetic.   The Literary Fund aided the Sunday schools in some cases.   In Richmond in 1825 thirty cents were given for every pupil enrolled and thirty dollars for books and supplies.   These Sunday schools helped to accomplish one thing which Jefferson had vainly hoped to realize through the ward schools.   Bringing the children together on an equality in the name of religion, they did much to equalize the differences between rich and poor and to take the sting of pauperism from free education.[43]

He believed that those of superior ability should assume the burdens of leadership.   For a career in politics he urged broad and conscientious preparation.   In 1787 he wrote to the youth who later married his daughter, advising him to lay a foundation with mathematics, natural philosophy, natural history, anatomy, chemistry, botany, during his hours of relaxation, then to proceed to the main object—politics, law, rhetoric, and history.   He recommended that he continue this study for two years, living in a French family to learn the language, then travel four or five months in France and Italy, return to America, and pass a year in Williamsburg under Mr. Wythe. He advised the practice of law for a time to gain facility of speech, but urged exercise to preserve health "without which there is no happiness." [44] To one preparing for legislative service he is quoted as saying: "Go among the people, lounge upon their beds that you may see how hard they are; eat their food that you may be able, if possible, to put some meat in their kettle of vegetables." [45]

However, he recognized that some are not qualified to profit by the pursuit of science and that the indiscriminate giving of higher education leads to so serious an over-crowding of the professions with incompetent men that a measure of vocational guidance by the state may be necessary. As early as 1803 he wrote:

the greatest evils of populous society have ever appeared to me to spring from the vicious distribution of it's members among the occupations called for. I have no doubt that those nations are essentially right, which leave this to individual choice, as a better guide to an advantageous distribution than any other which could be devised. but when by a blind concourse, particular occupations are ruinously over-charged, & others left in want of hands, the national authorities can do much toward restoring the equilibrium. on the revival of letters, learning became the universal favorite, and with reason; because there was not enough of it existing to manage the affairs of a nation to the best advantage, nor to advance its individuals to the happiness of which they were susceptible, by improvements in their minds, their morals, their health, & in those conveniences which contribute to the comfort & embellishment of life. all the efforts of the society therefore were directed to the increase of learning, & the inducements of respect, ease & profit were held up for its encouragement. even the charities of the nation forgot that misery was their object, and spent themselves in founding schools to transfer to science the hardy sons of the plow. to these incitements were added the powerful fascinations of great cities. these circumstances have long since produced an overcharge in the class of competitors for learned occupations, & great distress among the supernumerary candidates; & the more, as their habits of life have dis-qualified them for reentering into the laborious class. the evil cannot be suddenly, nor perhaps ever entirely cured: nor should I presume to say by what means it may be cured. doubtless there are many engines which the nation might bring to bear on this object. Public opinion & public encouragement are among these.[46]

"I am not a friend to placing young men in populous cities, because they acquire there habits and partialities which do not contribute to the happiness of their after life." [47]   Thus briefly did Jefferson state his preference for country surroundings at the very time when he and Barlow were aiming at the establishment of a national university.   Although it was commonly assumed that such an institution would be located in the capital city, Jefferson had proposed to Washington a situation near the capital but within the state which should most liberally support the university. [48]   Apparently he had in mind a location on the southern side of the Potomac.   The committee of the trustees of Albemarle Academy who inspected various proposed sites in and near Charlottesville in 1814 recommended that it be located not more than one-half mile from the town, [49] and there was strong support of the proposal to purchase the tavern of Triplett T. Estes in the center of the town for the academy. [50] When Cabell and Cocke were the only other Visitors to attend the meeting called for April 8, 1817, Jefferson utilized the opportunity to visit the various sites with his colleagues and provisionally to authorize the purchase from John Perry of land a mile above the town.   When Madison and Monroe were shown this site by Cocke and Jefferson on May 5 they readily confirmed the action of their colleagues, [51] and the University was located at a substantial distance from the only town in the vicinity.

In planning the districts for the various grades of schools included in Jefferson's system his ruling consideration was one of distance.   The wards were to be five or six miles square so that all residents would be within walking distance of the school. [52]   The college districts of 1817 were to be about eighty miles square so that the most remote residents would be within a day's ride of the college.   The districts planned in 1779 were much smaller though less regular in shape.   The greater distances between the limits of the 1817 districts seem to reflect chiefly the improved means of travel.   If there was any justification for his insistence that the University be located centrally among the white population it was that this would make it most easily accessible to the greatest number.

Jefferson was a consistent believer in small boards of Visitors or trustees. In 1779 he proposed to reduce the Visitors of William and Mary from eighteen to five. In 1815 he had the eighteen trustees of Albemarle Academy changed to the six Visitors of Central College—with himself the only member of the old board to be continued in the new. The first bill to establish the University provided for a board of thirteen, but when it passed, this number had been reduced to seven. Practical considerations would be a sufficient reason. Of the eighteen trustees of Albemarle Academy, all resident within a single county, only eleven were present at the meeting on April 15, 1814, and it was considered unwise to transact important business until a larger attendance could be obtained.[53] When the college became a state institution it naturally would be expected that Visitors should be more representative of the state as a whole, and it would be much more difficult to bring together a quorum at any one place. If a large number were to be selected from the immediate vicinity they could seldom all be men of large ability and understanding of educational questions, vitally interested in the success of the institution. The small board of the University almost never failed of a substantial majority, and frequently all members were present, though they came from points as distant as Richmond and Fincastle. Moreover, Jefferson's forceful personality and matured views on education virtually made it necessary that he should dominate any board in which he hoped to work with harmony. Whether consciously or otherwise, this may have led him to prefer a small board including men personally attached to him like Cabell, Cocke, and Madison. A letter from Cabell at the time of the first appointment of Visitors for the University shows that Jefferson had wished them all to be selected from neighboring counties but that the governor had only complied with this wish in part. The same letter shows that the writer had actively tried to influence the appointments, but apparently not with any direct instance from Jefferson.[54]

These statements of ideals and principles show that Jefferson regarded education as the only sure means of promoting human happiness and the freedom and democracy of which he was a life-long advocate. Political organization, administrative systems were but means of advancing the well-being of the people.

Even democracy itself was but a means to the same end, and universal education was expected to pave the way for the successful advancement of an intelligent self-interest by all the people. How fondly the old man dwelt upon this thought appears in many of the letters written during his last years. Early in the great struggle for the complete system he wrote to his faithful lieutenant:

pray drop me a line when any vote is passed which furnishes an indication of the success or failure of the general plan. I have only this single anxiety in this world. it is a bantling of 40 years birth & nursing, & if I can once see it on it's legs, I will sing with sincerity & pleasure my *nunc demittas*.[55]

A few years later when all his thought was centered on the University he wrote to his old friend Judge Roane:

The University will give employment to my remaining years, and quite enough for my senile faculties. It is the last act of usefulness I can render, and could I see it open I would not ask an hour more of life.[56]

To form a just estimate of anything as far-reaching and vital but as intangible as the educational work of Thomas Jefferson and its influence upon America is not easy. Of the splendor of some of his ideals there can be no doubt. To keep alive for half a century the concept of schools for all the people with broad opportunity for the poor but promising youths, free alike from the blight of pauperism and paternalism, was in itself a worthy service to his state. His insistence upon the straightforward policy of direct tax support in opposition to the specious allurements of plans of indirect school finance contributed to the self-respecting independence of the people and prepared the public mind for the financial burdens which had to be assumed before an adequate system of public schools could be successfully established. The University, the pride and idol of his old age, undoubtedly became an immeasurable influence, promoting sound scholarship throughout the South and training many who carried their culture with them and became innumerable centers of local stimulation and uplift. This is what he most desired, and is the service most difficult to measure.

On the other hand it must not be forgotten that certain of his most fond hopes embodied elements both inexpedient and unwise. Experience has shown that the division of the counties into wards was no more practical for educational than for political purposes. Similarly it has shown that the enlightened self-interest which he expected to prompt the people of the wards and college districts to establish and improve their schools all too often is lacking and that a measure of compulsion from state authorities usually is necessary to open the doors of educational opportunity to all the people. Nor was he always consistent in carrying his plans into operation. He declared that the University would be founded upon the illimitable freedom of the human mind, but he would not trust the Professor of Law to select the textbooks on government. He adopted the system of free electives, but required proficiency in Latin from all graduates. The honor system is an application of his principles, but it has failed more often than it has succeeded. In his zeal to establish an educational bulwark against the centralizing tendencies of Federalism he mistook a natural and inevitable growth of national consciousness for the hostile propaganda of faction. Though he foresaw and deplored the horrors of civil strife forty years before they broke upon the country, he trained the leaders of the South in that very spirit and philosophy of sectionalism which made the struggle so long and costly.

These are some of the merits and some of the defects of Jefferson's philosophy of education and of the ways in which it gained a partial expression in the life of his state and nation. It is fruitless to try to balance the one against the other. They can no more be measured than can the influence of his political principles upon the civic life of the nation. One thing is certain: He dreamed a magnificent prospect of political, moral, and social progress for his countrymen and toiled incessantly that the dream might be realized. He may have been arbitrary and dogmatic and may have used the tools of the politician and of the boss, but never that he himself might profit save in that deeper selfishness which finds its chief joy in the doing of a service which will outlive the doer. In this sense he will always hold a high place in that worthy company of American educational pioneers.

CHAPTER XI

SOURCES OF JEFFERSON'S IDEAS ON EDUCATION

WHEN principles and plans are as significant as those of Jefferson, a distinct interest attaches to the sources from which they may have been derived. Several of his plans or ideas can be attributed to their true source without question,—such as the derivation of the plan to disfranchise the illiterate from the Spanish constitution.* However, the great majority of his proposals came from sources which cannot be definitely determined, and many of them were so thoroughly revised and adapted to Virginia conditions that they must be considered as his own ideas, regardless of the possible germs from which they grew. Doubtless he himself was not aware of the specific sources of some of the ideas which he developed in various combinations and modifications through the years. In a few cases he has left a record of the use of some educational manual or of a particular interest in it. In others we know that he had the opportunity to acquaint himself with certain significant educational plans, such as those found in books known to have been in his library. In either of these cases, when he can be shown to have held an idea set forth in such a work after contact with it which he does not appear to have held before, there is a reasonable probability that the source has been found. It is not so easy to determine the total influence of any person or work upon his general plan and philosophy. However, a survey of the significant similarities between Jefferson's views and those of another, duly counterpoised by the outstanding differences, should give a fairly balanced estimate of such an influence.

* See Chapter III.

The proposal to divide the counties into wards is one of Jefferson's plans which can be attributed to its source without question. Repeatedly he compares the wards to the towns of New England.[1] To what extent he may have observed the New England system in operation it is impossible to determine. In 1784 he went to France by way of Boston. On the way he studied the commercial conditions of all the states through which he passed. He seems to have waited some time for a ship, for it was eight weeks after he left Annapolis before he sailed from Boston. This time was divided between correspondence and an observation trip into New Hampshire,[2] and he probably observed more than purely commercial conditions. He was at Providence for two days in August, 1790, when Brown University conferred upon President Washington the degree of Doctor of Laws.[3] In the summer of 1792 he and Madison entered New England near Bennington, Vermont, crossed to the Connecticut Valley at "umbrageous Brattleborough," and followed the river to Long Island Sound.[4] It is probable that he learned much more about local government in New England from his long friendship and correspondence with such New Englanders as the Adamses and Dr. Stiles and from the many contacts with New England representatives and others during his years at the national capital.

Although deriving his idea of ward organization directly from New England, Jefferson was fully conscious of its Anglo-Saxon origin. On June 5, 1824, writing to Major John Cartwright, he described his plan and added that the wards should be "about six miles square, and would answer to the hundreds of your Saxon Alfred."[5] Probably his high opinion of Anglo-Saxon political principles increased his faith in the system of organization through which they gained expression.

In 1819 Jefferson received a tract on the literary institute of Liverpool. "Your Liverpool institution will also aid us in the organization of our new University," he wrote in acknowledgment.[6] When his third library was offered for sale in 1829 it contained, beside several tracts on education, Griscom's *Monitorial Instruction*, Garnett's *Lecture on Female Education* and Russel's *View of the System of Education in the Schools and Universities of Scotland*. The work of Russel is the only one of these which with any confidence can be said to have contributed to Jefferson's educational plans. In 1825 he wrote to his granddaughter's husband: "I owe you many thanks for the two last books you have been so kind as to send me. I have derived a great deal of information from Russel for the use of our University. I had only a borrowed copy, and had been disappointed in getting one from England." [7]

Nearly a year before this Cabell apologized for his delay in returning this borrowed copy to Jefferson, saying that he had loaned it in turn to General Breckenridge and Mr. Johnson, but that Mr. Loyall had never seen it. [8] This shows that Jefferson and his colleagues were interested in Russel's work and had the opportunity to study and adopt his ideas. That they did so in a limited way seems probable, though it is possible that they found ideas in Russel which they already held. It seems possible only to show that Jefferson held some of the specific views advanced by Russel after he had read the book. The most conspicuous examples can be briefly noted. Russel urged the necessity of regular examinations on recent lectures. [9] The Rector and Visitors recommended to the faculty "strict examinations of the students on the topics of the lectures and lessons delivered them." [10] Russel approved the public final examinations as carried out at Oxford and Cambridge. [11] Jefferson planned to have a room in the Rotunda for public examinations. [12] Russel commended the giving of prizes for excellence at the end of the session. [13] The Visitors authorized the giving of medals and books to the highly meritorious. [14] Russel urged the necessity of an attendance record, pointing out how little time need be occupied by a roll call. [15] The Visitors prescribed that the roll should be called at the beginning of every class and the absentees reported. [16] Russel advised two-hour classes daily as at Glasgow, rather than the single hour which was customary at Edinburgh. [17] The Visitors provided for two-hour classes to meet on alternate days. [18] Russel urged the necessity of mathematics, natural philosophy; then logic and ethics. [19] Jefferson suggested to Dr. Emmett, but not as a recommendation, that students follow the order—languages, mathematics, physics, and chemistry. [20] On the other hand it should be noted, lest this really significant influence should be exaggerated, that Russel sharply criticized the lecture method, especially as practised at Edinburgh.[21] This seems to have made no impression upon Jefferson, unless to lower his general estimate of Edinburgh, for he always assumed that the lecture method would commonly be employed. In 1791 he was sure that Edinburgh was the best school in the world,[22] but thirty-three years later he thought it had degenerated seriously,[23] and Gilmer was advised to find professors of the languages, mathematics, and the sciences at Oxford and Cambridge and to seek only the professor of medicine in Edinburgh. Possibly this may reflect Russel's account of the laxity of instruction and administration which had grown up at Edinburgh. Moreover, Jefferson planned for public examinations in 1818 and it is doubtful if he saw Russel's work earlier than 1823. At best it can only be said that Russel was one of the many sources of ideas on educational methods which Jefferson searched with eager enthusiasm to find any plan which might be useful, but that any ideas so gained were so completely analyzed and adapted to his plan as to be truly his own.

Another writer on education whose influence Jefferson acknowledged was Destutt de Tracy. Their relations were so intimate that Jefferson arranged for the translation and publication in America of several of Destutt's works.[24] In 1816 he declared Destutt de Tracy to be the ablest living writer on intellectual subjects and the operation of the understanding.[25] A few weeks later he alluded to the third volume of his *Ideology* as containing his commentary on Montesquieu "and a little tract on education." [26] This "little tract" seems to have exercised a very interesting influence upon Jefferson, at least for a time. On May 15, 1817, ten days after he bought land for Central College, he wrote to Destutt:

I have to aknolege the reciept of your two letters of Feb. 4 and Dec. 24, 16 and, with the last your *Principes logiques* and a 2d copy of your 4th vol. of which I had before received a printed one as well as the Ms. The analysis of Dupuy and the luminous tract on public instruction I had possessed some time before, and had availed myself of some of the leading ideas of the latter in the scheme of an institution here on a much smaller scale, and obliged to adapt its details to the localities, the ideas, character and circum. of our country.[27]

Destutt's tract on education is mentioned in the catalogue of the library which Jefferson sold to Congress in 1815 and in that of the library sold by his executors in 1829.[28] The quotation shows that he consciously made use of this source in the plans for Central College. This influence would be apt to appear in the letter to Peter Carr, as it contains the only "scheme of an institution" written by Jefferson for many years before the autumn of 1817. This gains color from his statement in the opening sentences of that letter—"I have lost no occasion of making myself acquainted with the organization of the best seminaries in other countries, and with the opinions of the most enlightened individuals on the subject of the science worthy of a place in such an institution." [29]

Destutt classified those to be taught in two groups, *ouvrière* and *savante*, and urged the need of two kinds of schools and of two complete systems of public instruction.[30] Jefferson divided the mass of citizens into the *laboring* and *learned* groups, and proposed that they should go through the elementary schools together, after which the latter should go through the general and professional schools and the former should go into agriculture or be apprenticed, with further training in trade schools.[31] Destutt intended the savants to go through domestic, general, and special schools, which correspond very closely to Jefferson's elementary, general, and professional schools except that the Frenchman expected this course to run through twenty years and Jefferson through twelve.[32] Destutt proposed that the general schools teach belles lettres and the physical and moral sciences.[33] Jefferson proposed the same with the addition of mathematics.[34] Some of the special schools advocated by Destutt were the same as those proposed by Jefferson, but several were different, so the similarity is not striking.[35]

Destutt included as an appendix to his tract the *Loi Sur L'organisation de L'instruction Publique. Du 3 Brumaire an 4.* The plan of studies for the central schools provided for by this law is strikingly parallel to that proposed by Jefferson for the general schools. These French schools were to be divided into three sections. In the first should be taught ancient and modern languages, belles lettres, and rhetoric; in the second, mathematics, natural history, geography, and chemistry;

and in the third, ideology, geography, grammar, ethics, law, and history.[36] In Jefferson's first classification of subjects to be taught in the general schools he names exactly these subjects in the same three groups except that geography is included only in the second (under physico-mathematics), history is transferred from the third to the first, and the theory of medicine and political economy are added respectively to the second and third groups.[37] He even includes a school for the deaf, dumb, and blind, which was a part of the French plan.[38]

The letter to Peter Carr is strangely inconsistent with Jefferson's other educational programs. The general schools offer a much broader curriculum and more advanced instruction than the academies which he proposed in 1779 or the district colleges advocated in 1817 and later. The professional schools are much more specialized and technical than the higher education planned by him at any other time. This comparison with the proposals of Destutt de Tracy makes it seem very probable that when the trustees of the Albemarle Academy asked Jefferson for a plan he used the French system as the basis of what he proposed, but when a renewed interest in the subject led him to further reflection he reverted to the main ideas of his plan of 1779.

In 1810 Jefferson received the *Essai general d' Education physique, morale, et intellectuelle* by Jullien, and seven years later his *Esquisse d'un ouvrage sur l' education comparée.*[39] The letter acknowledging the receipt of the former work shows that he had every opportunity to utilize Jullien's ideas and that he valued them highly:

I have safely received the very valuable present of your work on education, and I pray you to accept my thanks for this mark of your attention. I am now engaged in reading it, and have made sufficient progress to see it's great merit . . . . the plan of your work is so happily adapted to practice, that we may safely say it will have a greater effect in execution than has ever been produced by the works of mere theory; and at the same time the great branches of pursuit are so well combined, that little more will be necessary in any country than to adapt them by the small modifications which local circumstances may require to the use of any particular country, and the special circumstances of it's inhabitants, the benefits of your labours therefore are not confined to a single age or nation. multitudes unborn will owe to you their physical strength, moral correctness, & instruction.[40]

A perusal of this work shows at least one plan which Jefferson advocated soon after reading it, but he does not seem to have formed this plan earlier. In 1814 he proposed that the history of a people be taught along with their language.[41] Though he departed from this view in 1818, he returned to it in 1824, and provided that the language, history, and geography of nations should be taught together.[42] This method is mentioned by Jullien in his account of the educational and agricultural institution established at Hofwil, near Berne, Switzerland, by M. de Fellenberg:

L' enseignement des *langues anciennes, grecque et latine,* et celui des *langues modernes, allemande, française, italienne, anglaise,* sont combines avec l' étude de la *geographie* et de l' *historie* de chaque pays.[43]

Even this probable source is made less certain by the fact that at his death Jefferson's library contained a pamphlet on education by Fellingberg [*sic*].[44] This suggests the possibility that he learned of Fellenberg's method or had it brought again to his mind independently of Jullien's essay.

The writings and opinions of Dupont de Nemours are a presumptive source of Jefferson's ideas on education, but one which proves very disappointing when specific influences are sought. Dupont was one of Jefferson's earliest intimates in France, and their friendship continued for more than thirty years.[45] He came to America in 1800, and was a frequent visitor at Monticello in the years that followed. On April 12 of that year Jefferson requested Dupont to prepare a plan of subjects to be taught, mentioning his similar request to Dr. Priestley.[46] On December 12 he thanked Dupont for his "piece on education," saying that he had read it with great pleasure.[47] Fifteen years later Dupont asked Jefferson to criticize his translation of this essay into English. Jefferson frankly told him that the French version was too good to be spoiled, reminded him of Cicero's unfortunate attempts to write in Greek, and advised him to employ a competent translator.[48] A century later one of Dupont's descendants, native to the English language, performed this task.[49]

Dupont's essay, *Sur l' Education nationale dans les Etats Unis,* proposed a national university composed of four schools—

Medicine, Mines, Social Sciences and Legislation, and Higher Mathematics. It has been shown that this, its most marked resemblance to Jefferson's later plans,.was based upon the organization of the University of Paris with which Jefferson already was familiar. There are similarities between Dupont's and Jefferson's proposals, and it is not improbable that the latter was influenced by his French friend in ways which did not lead to specific and tangible changes in his plans.[50] Some of Dupont's proposals seem to be based upon Jefferson's plan of 1779, so the influence appears to have been mutual.[51]

Jefferson's friendship with Quesney de Beaurepaire, D'Ivernois, and Pictet undoubtedly brought him valuable ideas about educational plans and methods, but it seems impossible to trace specific lines of influence. It is equally difficult to show in what ways he may have utilized Pestalozzi's ideas, though his interest in these methods is shown by a letter written in 1810.[52] Jefferson's second library contained Lancaster's *Improvements in Education* and tracts on education by Lancaster and Ogilvie.[53] The widespread interest in Lancaster's methods might have been expected to attract Jefferson's attention, but in 1816 he wrote that he considered the Lancastrian system to be one which would go into operation with another generation, so he never had read a sentence about it.[54] Ogilvie was an Alexandria schoolmaster. His pamphlet, entitled *Cursory Reflexions on Government, Philosophy and Education,* was published in 1802. It advocates some of the methods proposed by Jefferson in 1779 and makes frequent use of his terms— especially the unusual expression, "the diffusion of knowledge." [55] Ogilvie seems to have been familiar with the *Bill for the More General Diffusion of Knowledge,* but apparently it is impossible to show that Jefferson was in any way influenced by him.

In 1795 the American Philosophical Society offered a prize of one hundred dollars for the best plan of public education to be proposed to the society.[56] Jefferson was not present at the meeting on February 6 when the plan was presented and a committee appointed, nor on March 6 when the committee reported,[57] but he was elected president of the society on January 6, 1797,[58] and presided at some of the meetings when the prize-winning essays were read.[59]   He was not present on December 15, 1797, when the society voted to divide the prize between the Reverend Samuel Knox of Bladensburg, Maryland, and Samuel H. Smith of Philadelphia,[60] but he presided on April 6, 1798, when Dr. Smith asked the society to apply the fifty dollars awarded to him toward a similar new prize.[61]   These circumstances would bring these two essays vividly to Jefferson's attention a short time after he was trying to bring the Geneva faculty to America and only a short time before he planned a national university with Joel Barlow and asked advice about a university in Virginia from Dr. Priestley.   Moreover, Jefferson owned a copy of Dr. Knox's essay,[62] and retained so high an opinion of the author that he proposed him for the first professor for Central College twenty years later.[63]   Dr. Smith was long Jefferson's friend, for it was through him that he offered his library to Congress in 1814.[64]   These circumstances give an unusual interest to these two essays as possible sources of Jefferson's ideas.

The society voted to publish Dr. Knox's essay,[65] but their printer declined the task,[66] so it was published by the author under the title *An Essay on the Best System of Liberal Education Adapted to the Genius of the Government of the United States.* This plan shows a general resemblance to that of Jefferson and a few points of interesting similarity.   It proposed elementary schools, academies, state colleges, and a national university to teach about the same subjects which Jefferson proposed for his three-fold system of schools in Virginia but with no more similarity of grouping than would naturally result from the character of the subjects.[67]   One proposal is strikingly similar to a later plan of Jefferson's.   Knox did not include theology among the subjects to be taught, proposing that each denomination establish its own theological school in each state, but at a distance from other institutions.[68]   Jefferson proposed this plan for Virginia in 1817, except that these schools were invited to locate near the University so that the students might have the benefit of both institutions.*

Other proposals by Knox are similar to Jefferson's plans. He pointed out the value of emulation as a stimulus to effort.[69]

* See Chapter VIII.

He favored the location of colleges in the country, fearing the corrupting atmosphere of large towns.[70]   He recommended public examinations and the awarding of prizes.[71]   He thought the manual of arms should be taught in every academy, both for exercise and for its military value.[72]   He advised that no clergymen be on the faculty of the national university.[73]   He declared that "a thorough knowledge of Euclid's Elements is preferable to the best system of logic that ever was taught," and advised only enough attention to moral philosophy to inculcate a scientific view of it.[74]   These opinions coincide with Jefferson's views, but some of them were subjects of common discussion at the time and some had been advanced by such well-known philosophers as Locke and Bacon, so it is unsafe to assume that Jefferson derived them from Dr. Knox.

There has been quite a discussion of the plan for university buildings proposed by Knox and of its supposed influence upon Jefferson.[75]   Knox recommended that the buildings be arranged in a rectangle with the administration buildings in front, the classrooms and professors' houses along the sides, and the library at the back.   Within this square should be another containing the dormitories and dining halls, and another square should be built in the center for the teachers of fine arts and for the printing office and bookshop.   An arched gateway was to be built in the center of each side.[76]   Jefferson advocated a range of buildings around an open space, instead of a single massive structure, and proposed that the professors' houses, containing their classrooms, should occupy the sides of the rectangle, but the fourth side was to be left open to admit of indefinite extension. This is so different from the three concentric squares proposed by Knox that it seems probable that Jefferson found the germ of his plan in the rambling buildings of some of the old universities of Europe.

The prize essay by Samuel Harrison Smith was promptly published under the title, *Remarks on Education Illustrating the close connection between Virtue and Wisdom*.   It contains many ideas which appear in the writings of Jefferson.   It uses the expression, "diffusion of knowledge," [77] urges the value of chemistry to farmers and of history to those who would recognize political ambition and preserve their liberties,[78] and declares popular enlightenment to be the only secure defence of civil rights.[79]   It proposed that one boy should be selected annually from the elementary schools to go to the college at public expense, and recommended that the modern languages be taught to those who could study them without neglecting their regular studies.[80]   As these views had long been held by Jefferson it seems probable that Dr. Smith made use of the plans and opinions of his older friend in the preparation of his essay.

When Jefferson was formulating his first plans for Central College he wrote to John Adams asking suggestions about the subjects to be taught and the way they should be grouped.[81] Adams replied promptly, recommending a number of the fundamental subjects and suggesting that they be grouped under five professors.[82]   These suggestions may have influenced Jefferson's grouping of subjects in the letter to Peter Carr, but the influence appears to have been very slight.   A few weeks later he wrote to Dr. Wistar, his successor as president of the American Philosophical Society, telling him of the plan to establish an academy on a moderate scale, but capable of enlargement to include every useful science.   As an aid in planning this institution he wished to know the organization of others which had attained celebrity, and, considering the university at Philadelphia first among these, he asked how the professorships were arranged and what subjects were included under each.[83]   What reply was received is not known.   The same day Jefferson wrote to Dr. Thomas Cooper, asking for similar suggestions, and two weeks later wrote again, enclosing a copy of his letter to Peter Carr, with a request for comments.[84]   Cooper replied to the first letter by sending the manuscript of an article on education with a request for criticism,[85] and a few days later sent his comments on Jefferson's plan.[86]   Beyond advising against the teaching of theology because of sectarian rivalries, these do not seem to have contributed to Jefferson's plans unless to strengthen his conviction that students should be well grounded in the classics and mathematics before entering a higher institution.* The next year Horatio Gates Spofford, an Albany Quaker, sent Jefferson a long essay on the establishment of a new school of science at Washington, asking his criticism and advice.[87]   Jef-

* See Chapter VIII.

ferson read a part of this plan,[88] but his opinion of its merits is unknown.[89]

In the spring of 1823 Jefferson received from Dr. Cooper a copy of the laws of South Carolina College from which Jefferson expected much help when the time should come to prepare similar rules for his own institution.[90]   Three months later he wrote to George Ticknor asking for a copy of the Harvard rules.[91]   A comparison of these three codes * shows many wide differences as well as some striking similarities.   It is probable that Jefferson had both the other codes before him when he drafted the rules for the University of Virginia and that he made use of the ideas and phraseology of either whenever it suited his purpose.

In view of the well-known influence of John Locke upon Jefferson's political principles it is natural to expect that his educational views were similarly influenced.   Jefferson's second library contained Locke's philosophical writings, including his essays on education.[92]   Jefferson held several of the views stated in these essays, so it is probable that his thinking was influenced by Locke or even that he adopted some ideas directly from that source at a time when his own views were in a formative state.

Locke declared the only fence against the world to be a thorough knowledge of it.[93]   He considered that talking a language into children is the best way to teach it and that Latin could be taught this way as well as French.[94]   He proposed that history, geography, and mathematics be taught in French and Latin as soon as the students should be able to learn in this way in order that they might be learning the language at the same time that they were mastering these other subjects.[95]   He considered Latin to be necessary for a gentleman, but declared it ridiculous to compel boys to master it if they had no taste for it nor use for it after leaving school.[96]   He held formal logic in small esteem, calling it "hog-shearing," [97] and considered ethics a subject to be learned more by practice than by rules.[98]   He recommended that when the student had digested Tully's *Offices* he should read the works of Puffendorf and Grotius, thus making ethics introductory to civic and international relations

* See Appendix N.

by an unusual association.[99]   With slight modification all these ideas appear among the plans or policies of Jefferson.*

Dr. Joseph Priestley was greatly admired by Jefferson, who corresponded with him until his death in 1804.   It was to Dr. Priestley that he wrote in 1800 of his purpose to found a university on a broad, liberal, and modern plan and asked recommendations about subjects to be taught.[100]   His second library contained Priestley's *Memoirs*, his *Lectures on History*, and a description of his *Biographical Chart*.[101]   With so high an opinion of the writer it would have been strange if he had not carefully studied Priestley's writings on education when he was developing his own plans.

It seems probable that Jefferson read Priestley's *Miscellaneous Observations relating to Education*.   It states one opinion which Jefferson held for many years, namely, that the classic languages were important to the scholar, though less necessary than formerly as the vehicles of learning, and that the fullest measure of benefit was to be derived from reading authorities in the original.[102]

Jefferson seems to have made a considerable use of Priestley's *Lectures on History and General Policy*, especially when planning for the teaching of history at the University of Virginia. In October, 1825, he wrote to an unnamed member of the faculty a long letter † suggesting authors and methods for the teaching of history.   A striking parallel exists between his recommendations and those of Dr. Priestley.   This is most striking in the long list of classical historical writers recommended for the course in ancient history.   Jefferson listed nearly twenty. They were almost identical with those named by Priestley, and in much the same order, except that Jefferson added "etc." where Priestley named a few others.[103]   Priestley called the *Universal History* "the most complete body of history."[104]   Jefferson called it "the most learned and most faithful perhaps *that ever was written.*"[105]   Priestley wrote, "Of all the general histories of our nation till the revolution none are so full, and so impartial, as that written by Rapin."[106]   Jefferson wrote, "Of England there is as yet no general history so faithful as Rapin's."[107]   Both praise Hume's style but criticize his

* See Chapter VIII.   † See Appendix P.

toryism.[108]   In his introduction, discussing the preparation necessary for his course in history, Priestley wrote, "A knowledge of the learned languages is not absolutely necessary, but is very desirable." [109]   In a letter to Dr. Priestley, written in 1800, regarding the classical languages Jefferson wrote, "I do not think them essential to the obtaining eminent degrees of science, but I think them very useful towards it." [110]   In a course of reading for a law student * revised by Jefferson in 1814 he recommended a number of works in English history and biography. Most of these had been favorably mentioned by Priestley.[111] In the absence of more explicit evidence these facts seem to show that Jefferson made free use of Priestley's recommendations for the study of history.

From all these evidences we see in Jefferson a splendid blending of the man of strong conviction, holding tenaciously to his opinion when once he has made a decision, with the man of open mind, seeking eagerly for suggestions from any source, respectful of the opinions of others, and promptly adopting any new ideas of value.   It was this which gave to his educational plans the originality of the new with its adaptability to new and changing conditions at the same time that they were balanced by the proved wisdom of experience.   In formulating his plans he drew directly from the wisdom and culture of western Europe.   Portugal, Spain, Italy, France, Switzerland, Holland, Germany, England, and Scotland all made contributions.   Back of this, he made classical Greece, prophetic Israel, and imperial Rome pay tribute to his native state.   In America he sought the guidance of the best minds in Massachusetts, Connecticut, New York, Pennsylvania, Maryland, South Carolina, and other states in order that his plans for Virginia might harmonize more fully with American conditions, and might be a worthy part of the great movement which was to build the new America of which he dreamed.

* See Appendix D.

CHAPTER XII

AUTHORITIES AND SOURCES

THE following references are given in a simpler and more brief form than that sometimes employed. Long titles are frequently shortened and publication data are omitted, as they can be found in full in the bibliography. Abbreviations for volume and page are omitted, as Roman numerals are almost universally used to indicate volumes while Arabic numerals are used for pages. Rare exceptions exist in which small Roman indicates the pages of an introduction so numbered. As Jefferson's writings are cited often and the nature of the source always appears from the context, brief forms are used. References to his collected writings are to the edition, volume, and page (e.g., *Ford Ed.*, V, 40). All material in Cabell's *Early History of the University of Virginia* is cited as *Cabell*, with the page. The autobiography of Jefferson is cited as *Autobiography*, with the page. Letters written by Jefferson are referred to, so far as possible, by the name of the person to whom addressed, the date, and the source (e.g., To J. C. Cabell, January 12, 1823— *Library Ed.*, X, 45). Manuscript materials, both in the Coolidge Collection of the Massachusetts Historical Society and the Thomas Jefferson Papers of the Library of Congress, are now arranged chronologically. The former are cited as *Ms., M.H.S.*, with the date; the latter as *Ms., L.C.*, with the date and volume number.

CHAPTER I

1. Bruce, Philip A.—*History of the University of Virginia*, I, 107.
2. *Autobiography*, 4–5.
3. Hirst, Francis W.—*Life and Times of Thomas Jefferson*, 15–17.
4. To John Adams, June 11, 1812—*Library Ed.*, XIII, 160.
5. *Autobiography*, 4.
6. Bruce—*op. cit.*, I, 109.

7. Hirst—*op. cit.*, 15.
8. *Autobiography*, 5.
9. Ibid.
10. Ibid.; Bruce—*op. cit.*, I, 115.
11. *Autobiography*, 5, Note 3; Hirst—*op. cit.*, 20.
12. *Library Ed.*, XX, 335.
13. *Autobiography*, 5, Note 3.
14. Ibid., 6.
15. Ibid.
16. Ibid.
17. Hirst—*op. cit.*, 15.
18. Ibid., 24.
19. Heatwole, Cornelius J.—*History of Education in Virginia*, 89.
20. Hirst—*op. cit.*, 24.
21. *Autobiography*, 6.
22. Parton, James—*Life of Thomas Jefferson*, 26.
23. To John Page, February 21, 1770—*Ford Ed.*, I, 370.
24. To Samuel Harrison Smith, September 21, 1814—*Ford Ed.*, IX, 485–488.
25. Manuscript *Catalog, M. H. S.*
26. Johnston, William D.—*History of the Library of Congress*, I, 84, 89.
27. Manuscript *Catalog, M. H. S.*
28. *Catalogue of President Jefferson's Library.*
29. Manuscript letters to and from Elisha Ticknor, 1816–17, *M. H. S.*
30. Chinard, Gilbert—*Thomas Jefferson, the Apostle of Americanism*, 21–31.
31. Ibid., 14–15.
32. *Early Proceedings of the American Philosophical Society*, 246; John Vaughan to Jefferson, January 4, 1815—*Ms., M. H. S.*
33. Certificate of Membership, June 1, 1814—*Ms., M. H. S.*
34. To Joel Barlow, February 24, 1806—*Ford Ed.*, VIII, 424.
35. Manuscript *Records of the Harvard Corporation*, April 10, 1787; Cf. *Harvard Quinquennial Catalogue.*
36. To Ezra Stiles, December 24, 1786—*Library Ed.*, VI, 25.

CHAPTER II

1. Eckenrode, H. J.—*The Revolution in Virginia*, 169–172.
2. Ibid.
3. Randall, Henry S.—*The Life of Thomas Jefferson*, I, 199.
4. Ibid., 201–202.
5. Ibid., 202–216.
6. Ibid., 217–228.
7. To John Adams, October 28, 1813—*Library Ed.*, XIII, 399–400.
8. To Colonel Charles Yancey, January 6, 1816—*Library Ed.*, XIV, 383–384.

9. Heatwole, Cornelius J.—*History of Education in Virginia*, 51.
10. Ibid.
11. Barnard, Henry—*Journal of Education*, XXVII, 535.
12. Heatwole—*op. cit.*, 51.
13. Hirst, Francis W.—*Life and Times of Thomas Jefferson*, 20.
14. Heatwole—*op. cit.*, 92.
15. Channing, Edward—*History of the United States*, III, 7.
16. Maddox, William A.—*The Free School Idea in Virginia before the Civil War*, 44.
17. *Ford Ed.*, II, 195–196, 220.
18. "Notes on the State of Virginia"—*Library Ed.*, II, 203.
19. Ibid., 206.
20. *Ford Ed.*, II, 229–235.
21. Ibid., 236–237.
22. To J. C. Cabell, January 13 and 28, 1823—*Cabell*, 267, 270.
23. To George Wythe, August 13, 1786—*Library Ed.*, V, 396–397.
24. To George Washington, January 4, 1786—*Library Ed.*, XIX, 23–25.
25. To Mann Page, August 30, 1795—*Ford Ed.*, VII, 24.
26. To John Tyler, May 26, 1810—*Library Ed.*, XII, 393.
27. To Dupont de Nemours, April 24, 1816—*Library Ed.*, XIV, 491.
28. To E. J. Dupont, August 11, 1817—*Library Ed.*, XV, 171.
29. To James Breckenridge, February 15, 1821—*Library Ed.*, XV, 314–318.
30. To J. C. Cabell, January 13, 1823—*Cabell*, 267–268.
31. To J. C. Cabell, January 28, 1823—*Cabell*, 270.
32. Madison to Jefferson, December 4, 1786—*Writings of James Madison*, II, 292.
33. To George Washington, January 4, 1786—*Library Ed.*, XIX, 23–25.
34. To M. Pictet, February 5, 1803—*Library Ed.*, X, 355.
35. Madison to Jefferson, February 15, 1787—*Writings of James Madison*, II, 308.
36. *Autobiography*, 76.
37. Maddox—*op. cit.*, 42–46.
38. Bruce, Philip A.—*History of the University of Virginia*, I, 85.
39. To Governor Tyler, May 26, 1810—*Washington Ed.*, V, 525–526.
40. *Cabell*, xxxiii.
41. To Colonel Charles Yancey, January 6, 1816—*Library Ed.*, XIV, 383–384.
42. *Library Ed.*, XIX, 211–221; *Cabell*, 384 ff.
43. *Cabell*, 36–37, 43–44, 48, 390.
44. To J. C. Cabell, January 24, 1816—*Cabell*, 48.
45. Cabell to Jefferson, February 21, 1816—*Cabell*, 57.
46. To J. C. Cabell, September 9, 1817—*Cabell*, 79–80.
47. To J. C. Cabell, September 10, 1817—*Cabell*, 80.
48. To James Madison, November 15, 1817—*Ms., L. C.*, Vol. 211.
49. Maddox—*op. cit.*, 66.
50. Ibid., 55.

51. Cabell to Jefferson, January 24, 1816—*Cabell*, 50–51.
52. To Governor Wilson C. Nicholas, April 2, 1816—*Library Ed.*, XIV, 446–456.
53. Maddox—*op. cit.*, 64.
54. Ibid., 66–68.
55. *Ford Ed.*, II, 220, Sections 2, 4, 5, 7; *Library Ed.*, XVII, 418, Sections 1, 4, 5, 11, 13.
56. Ibid., Sections 1, 6, 10.
57. To J. C. Cabell, October 24, 1817—*Cabell*, 84.
58. Cabell to Jefferson, December 29, 1817—*Cabell*, 93–94.
59. To J. C. Cabell, January 14, 1818—*Cabell*, 102–106.
60. *Cabell*, 94–98.
61. Cabell to Jefferson, January 22, 1818—*Cabell*, 108–110.
62. Cabell to Jefferson, January 23, 1818—*Cabell*, 111.
63. Cabell to Jefferson, February 1, 1818—*Cabell*, 112.
64. Cabell to Jefferson, February 6, 1818—*Cabell*, 117.
65. Cabell to Jefferson, February 13, 1818—*Cabell*, 122.
66. To Albert Gallatin, February 15, 1818—*Library Ed.*, XIX, 258–259.
67. To J. C. Cabell, February 16, 1818—*Cabell*, 124.
68. Cabell to Jefferson, February 20, 1818—*Cabell*, 125–126.
69. Maddox—*op. cit.*, 74–75; *Cabell*, 427–432.
70. To J. C. Cabell, November 28, 1820—*Cabell*, 185–187.
71. To General James Breckenridge, February 15, 1821—*Library Ed.*, XV, 314–318.
72. To William J. Barry, July 2, 1822—*Library Ed.*, XV, 388–390.
73. To J. C. Cabell, February 3, 1825—*Cabell*, 340.
74. To J. C. Cabell, February 4, 1826—*Cabell*, 364.
75. Adams, Herbert B.—*Thomas Jefferson and the University of Virginia*, 32.
76. Barnard—*op. cit.*, XXVII, 550.
77. Nathaniel Burwell to Jefferson, February 17, 1818—*Ms.*, M. H. S.
78. To Nathaniel Burwell, March 14, 1818—*Library Ed.*, XV, 166.
79. Maddox—*op. cit.*, 12.
80. To Benjamin Banneker, August 30, 1791—*Ford Ed.*, V, 377.
81. To John Wyche, May 19, 1809—*Library Ed.*, XII, 283.
82. John Wyche to Jefferson, September 7, 1809—*Thomas Jefferson Correspondence, Ford Ed.*, 183.

CHAPTER III

1. To John Adams, October 28, 1813—*Library Ed.*, XIII, 394–403.
2. To J. C. Cabell, February 2, 1816—*Cabell*, 53–54.
3. To J. C. Cabell, January 14, 1818—*Cabell*, 102–106.
4. Madison to Jefferson, February 15, 1787—*Writings of James Madison*, II, 308.

5. Cabell to Jefferson, December 3, 1817—*Cabell*, 86.
6. Adams, Herbert B.—*Thomas Jefferson and the University of Virginia*, 39.
7. "A Bill for the More General Diffusion of Knowledge."
8. Sections VII, XIV, XVI.
9. To John Adams, October 28, 1813—*Library Ed.*, XIII, 394–403; to Major John Cartwright, June 5, 1824—Adams, *op. cit.*, 31, Note.
10. "An Act for Establishing Elementary Schools."
11. To J. C. Cabell, February 2, 1816—*Cabell*, 54.
12. To J. C. Cabell, September 9, 1817—*Cabell*, 79.
13. To J. C. Cabell, November 28, 1820—*Cabell*, 187.
14. To Governor Tyler, May 26, 1810—*Washington Ed.*, V, 525; to J. C. Cabell, February 2, 1816—*Cabell*, 52–56.
15. To J. C. Cabell, February 4, 1826—*Cabell*, 364.
16. "A Bill for the More General Diffusion of Knowledge," Section VIII.
17. Ibid., Sections XII, XVII, XIX.
18. "A Bill to Amend the Constitution of William and Mary College," Section II.
19. To the trustees for the lottery of East Tennessee College, May 6, 1810—*Library Ed.*, XII, 386.
20. To Colonel Charles Yancey, January 6, 1816—*Library Ed.*, XIV, 383–384.
21. Sections 4, 5, 9, 10.
22. To J. Correa de Serra, November 25, 1817—*Library Ed.*, XV, 153–157.
23. Sections 22 and 42.
24. "An Act for Establishing Elementary Schools," Section 5, Note 1— *Library Ed.*, XVII, 422–423.
25. Cabell to Jefferson, December 29, 1817—*Cabell*, 93–94.
26. To J. C. Cabell, January 14, 1818—*Cabell*, 102–106.
27. To J. C. Cabell, November 28, 1820—*Cabell*, 186.
28. To J. C. Cabell, February 2, 1816—*Cabell*, 53.
29. Cubberley, Ellwood P.—*Public Education in the United States*, 88.
30. Dexter, Edwin G.—*A History of Education in the United States*, 75.
31. Ibid.
32. "An Act for Establishing Elementary Schools"—*Library Ed.*, XVII, 424.
33. Ibid., Note.
34. To Chevalier de Onis, 1814—*Washington Ed.*, VI, 342.
35. To Dupont de Nemours, April 24, 1816—*Library Ed.*, XIV, 491–492.
36. "A Bill for the More General Diffusion of Knowledge," Section VI —*Ford Ed.*, II, 220 ff.
37. "An Act for Establishing Elementary Schools," Section 5—*Library Ed.*, XVII, 422–423.

CHAPTER IV

1. "A Bill for the More General Diffusion of Knowledge," Section IX —*Ford Ed.*, II, 223–224.
2. Section X—Ibid., 224–225.
3. Section XI—Ibid., 225.
4. Section XII—Ibid.
5. Section XIII—Ibid.
6. Section XIV—Ibid., 225–226.
7. Section XV—Ibid., 226.
8. Sections XVI and XVII—Ibid.
9. Section XVIII—Ibid.
10. Section XIX—Ibid., 227–228.
11. To a friend in Albemarle, December 31, 1783—*Cabell*, xxii–xxiii.
12. To Dugald Stewart, April 26, 1824—*Library Ed.*, XVIII, 331–334.
13. To John Adams, July 5, 1814—*Library Ed.*, XIV, 144–151.
14. Adams to Jefferson, July 16, 1814—quoted in *Library Ed.*, XIV, 152–161.
15. "A Bill for the More General Diffusion of Knowledge," Section XIII; "An Act for Establishing Elementary Schools," Section 21.
16. "A Bill to Amend the Constitution of William and Mary College"— *Ford Ed.*, II, 223.
17. *Library Ed.*, I, 70–72.
18. To J. C. Cabell, January 5, 1815—*Cabell*, 36–37.
19. To Dr. Thomas Cooper, August 25, 1814—*Library Ed.*, XIV, 173–175.
20. To Dr. Joseph Priestley, August 25, 1814—*Library Ed.*, X, 140.
21. To M. Pictet, February 5, 1803—*Library Ed.*, X, 355.
22. Cabell to Jefferson, January 24, 1816—*Cabell*, 51.
23. To J. C. Cabell, September 10, 1817—*Cabell*, 80–81.
24. "Report of the Commissioners Appointed to Fix the Site of the University of Virginia"—*Cabell*, 439–440.
25. Cabell to Jefferson, January 24, 1816, and February 26, 1816—*Cabell*, 51, 61.
26. Cabell to Jefferson, October 14, 1817, December 3, 1817, December 29, 1817, January 22, 1818, and others—*Cabell*, 82, 86, 90–92, 109.
27. Cabell to Jefferson, May 5, 1824—*Cabell*, 305.
28. Cabell to Jefferson, December 24, 1818—*Cabell*, 142–143.
29. Cabell to Jefferson, December 29, 1817, and February 6, 1818— *Cabell*, 92, 117.
30. To J. C. Cabell, October 24, 1817—*Cabell*, 84.
31. "A Bill for the More General Diffusion of Knowledge," Section XI —*Ford Ed.*, II, 225.
32. "An Act for Establishing Elementary Schools," Section 18—*Library Ed.*, XVII, 418 ff.

33. To J. C. Cabell, February 4, 1826—*Cabell*, 364.
34. To J. C. Cabell, January 13, 1823—*Cabell*, 267.
35. *Cabell*, 362.
36. To J. C. Cabell, February 4, 1826—*Cabell*, 364.
37. *Cabell*, 439.
38. To J. C. Cabell, December 22, 1824—*Cabell*, 321.
39. To Ralph Izard, July 17, 1788—*Washington Ed.*, II, 428.
40. "Report of the Commissioners Appointed to Fix the Site of the University of Virginia"—*Cabell*, 440.
41. *Cabell*, 305–307.
42. To J. C. Cabell, May 16, 1824—*Cabell*, 309.
43. Ibid., 312.
44. Cabell to Jefferson, June 13, 1824, and December 17, 1824—*Cabell*, 315, 317.
45. To J. C. Cabell, December 22, 1824—*Cabell*, 320–323.
46. Cabell to Jefferson, January 6, 1825—*Cabell*, 329.
47. Cabell to Jefferson, January 16, 1825—*Cabell*, 333.
48. To J. C. Cabell, January 22, 1825—*Cabell*, 335.
49. Cabell to Jefferson, February 7, 1825—*Cabell*, 341.
50. To J. C. Cabell, February 4, 1826—*Cabell*, 364.
51. Cabell to Jefferson, February 8, 1826—*Cabell*, 367.
52. To J. C. Cabell, February 14, 1826—*Cabell*, 373.
53. Cabell to Jefferson, February 15, 1826—*Cabell*, 374–375.
54. *Cabell*, 376–377, Note.
55. Bruce, Philip A.—*History of the University of Virginia*, I, 93.

CHAPTER V

1. "A Bill to Amend the Constitution of William and Mary College," Section II—*Ford Ed.*, II, 232.
2. Section I—Ibid., 231.
3. Section II—Ibid., 233.
4. *Autobiography*, 75–76.
5. To J. C. Cabell, February 22, 1821—*Cabell*, 207.
6. Bruce, Philip A.—*History of the University of Virginia*, I, 52.
7. *Notes on the State of Virginia*, Query XV, cited by Adams—*Thomas Jefferson and the University of Virginia*, 42.
8. Barnard, Henry—*Journal of Education*, XXVII, 535.
9. Adams—*op. cit.*, 21–26.
10. Heatwole, Cornelius J.—*Education in Virginia*, 91–92; Cf. Tyler, Lyon J.—*History of William and Mary College*, 66.
11. Adams—*op. cit.*, 21–26.
12. To Quesney de Beaurepaire, January 6, 1788—*Library Ed.*, VI, 413.
13. Adams—*op. cit.*, 28–30.
14. Bruce—*op. cit.*, I, 59–60, 64–65.
15. To J. Bannister, Jr., December 22, 1791—*Library Ed.*, V, 185.
16. To Mr. M'Alister, December 22, 1791—*Library Ed.*, VIII, 274–275.

17. Adams—*op. cit.*, 27.
18. To George Washington, February 23, 1795—*Library Ed.*, XIX, 108.
19. Adams—*op. cit.*, 27; also *Library Ed.*, X, 355.
20. To George Washington, February 23, 1795—*Library Ed.*, XIX, 109–110.
21. To Wilson C. Nicholas, November 22, 1794—*Library Ed.*, IX, 291.
22. To M. D'Ivernois, February 6, 1795—*Ford Ed.*, VIII, 163–164.
23. To John Adams, February 6, 1795—*Works of John Adams*, VIII, 516.
24. Richardson, James D.—*Messages and Papers of the Presidents*, I, 66, 202.
25. To George Washington, January 4, 1786—*Library Ed.*, XIX, 23–25.
26. To George Washington, February 23, 1795—*Library Ed.*, XIX, 108–113.
27. Washington to Jefferson, March 15, 1795—*Writings of George Washington*, W. C. Ford, Ed., XIII, 48–51.
28. Washington to Governor Brooke, March 16, 1795—cited by Barnard—*op. cit.*, XVII, 47.
29. Barnard—*op. cit.*, XVII, 48.
30. To M. Pictet, February 5, 1803—*Library Ed.*, X, 355.
31. Curtis, W. E.—*The True Thomas Jefferson*, 258.
32. Bruce—*op. cit.*, I, 64.
33. Todd, Charles Burr—*Life and Letters of Joel Barlow*, 208–209.
34. Barlow, Joel—*Prospectus of a National Institution*.
35. Todd—*op. cit.*, 208–209.
36. To Joel Barlow, February 24, 1806—*Federal Ed.*, X, 232.
37. Richardson—*op. cit.*, I, 409–410.
38. To Joel Barlow, December 10, 1807—*Ford Ed.*, IX, 168.
39. Bruce—*op. cit.*, I, 98.
40. To Dr. Joseph Priestley, January 18, 1800—*Library Ed.*, X, 140.
41. To M. Pictet, February 5, 1803—*Library Ed.*, X, 355.
42. Isaac A. Coles to J. C. Cabell, 1807—*Cabell*, xxx.
43. Maddox, William A.—*The Free School Idea in Virginia*, 46–47.
44. Bruce—*op. cit.*, I, 85.
45. To Governor Wilson C. Nicholas, April 2, 1816—*Library Ed.*, XIV, 446–456.
46. Cabell to Jefferson, February 13, 1818—*Cabell*, 122.
47. To J. C. Cabell, February 16, 1818—*Cabell*, 124.
48. Cabell to Jefferson, February 20, 1818—*Cabell*, 125–126.
49. Cabell to Jefferson, February 22, 1818—*Cabell*, 127.

CHAPTER VI

1. To Patrick Gibson, August 1, 1818—*Ms., M. H. S.;* Gibson to Jefferson, July 27, 1818—*Ms., M. H. S.*
2. *The University of Virginia Record*, March 15, 1927, 11.

3. Tucker, George—*Life of Thomas Jefferson*, II, 431.
4. Bruce, Philip A., *History of the University of Virginia*, I, 285–286, 181–182.
5. Minutes of the Board of Visitors—*Library Ed.*, XIX, 365.
6. Bruce—*op. cit.*, I, 201–202, quoting Cocke to Cabell, March 1, 1819.
7. Minutes of the Board of Visitors, April 3–4, 1826—*Library Ed.*, XIX, 492–493.
8. Bruce—*op. cit.*, II, 31, Note; Cf. Kennedy—*Life of William Wirt*, II, 180–181.
9. *Cabell*, 174, Note.
10. Bruce—*op. cit.*, I, 144.
11. Quoted by Bruce—*op. cit.*, I, 248.
12. Ibid.
13. *Cabell*, xxvii–xxxvi.
14. To J. C. Cabell, January 5, 1815—*Cabell*, 37.
15. Cabell to Jefferson, January 25, 1821—*Cabell*, 198.
16. To J. C. Cabell, January 31, 1821—*Cabell*, 202–203.
17. Cabell to Jefferson, February 8, 1821—*Cabell*, 203.
18. *Cabell*, xxxv, Note.
19. Bruce—*op. cit.*, I, 98, and Note.
20. To Elizabeth Trist, November 23, 1816—*Ms., M. H. S.*
21. To Dr. Thomas Cooper, January 16, 1814, quoted by Adams— *Thomas Jefferson and the University of Virginia*, 59.
22. To J. C. Cabell, January 22 and December 25, 1820, January 31, 1821, and December 28, 1822—*Cabell*, 178, 193, 201–202, 260; also to John Taylor, February 14, 1821—*Library Ed.*, XVIII, 312–313.
23. To M. D'Ivernois, February 6, 1795—*Ms., L. C.*, Vol. 98.
24. Section 8—*Cabell*, 430–431.
25. Cabell to Jefferson, February 22, 1818—*Cabell*, 127.
26. Cabell to Jefferson, February 20, 1818—*Cabell*, 126.
27. To J. C. Cabell, February 26, 1818—*Ms., L. C.*, Vol. 212, also *Cabell*, 128–129.
28. Cabell to Jefferson, March 11, 1818—*Cabell*, 129.
29. Archibald Stuart to Jefferson, May 30, 1818—*Ms., M. H. S.*
30. Probably to Judge Archibald Stuart, May 20, 1818—*Virginia Historical Magazine*, October, 1900, 124–125.
31. "Report of the Commissioners Appointed to Fix the Site of the University of Virginia"—*Cabell*, 447; Cabell to Jefferson, July 30, 1818—*Cabell*, 132–133.
32. Bruce—*op. cit.*, I, 218, 220.
33. Adams—*Thomas Jefferson and the University of Virginia*, 67.
34. Cabell to Jefferson, February 26, 1816—*Cabell*, 61.
35. Cabell to Jefferson, January 12, 1817—*Cabell*, 72–73.
36. Cabell to Jefferson, March 15, 1818—*Cabell*, 130; also "Report of Commissioners Appointed to Fix the Site of the University of Virginia"—*Cabell*, 445–446.

37. "Report of the Commissioners Appointed to Fix the Site of the University of Virginia"—*Cabell*, 446–447.
38. Bruce—*op. cit.*, I, 219–220.
39. Cabell to Jefferson, December 14, 17, and 24, 1818—*Cabell*, 139, 140, 143.
40. To J. C. Cabell, January 1, 1819—*Cabell*, 145–146.
41. To Littleton W. Tasewell, June 28, 1818—*Ms., M. H. S.*
42. To Judge Roane, June 28, 1818—*Ms., L. C.*, Vol. 213.
43. Tucker—*op. cit.*, II, 401.
44. Bruce—*op. cit.*, I, 218.
45. Ibid., 220, 226.
46. Archibald Stuart to Jefferson, May 30, 1818—*Ms., M. H. S.*
47. To Judge Roane, June 28, 1818—*Ms., L. C.*, Vol. 213.
48. To James Madison, June 28, 1818—*Ms., L. C.*, Vol. 213.
49. Cabell to Jefferson, December 8, 1818—*Cabell*, 137.
50. Cabell to Jefferson, December 14, 1818—*Cabell*, 138.
51. Cabell to Jefferson, December 14, 17, 24, 1818—*Cabell*, 139, 140, 143–144; January 18, 1819—*Cabell*, 151.
52. Cabell to Jefferson, December 24, 1818—*Cabell*, 142.
53. Cabell to Jefferson, December 14 and 17, 1818—*Cabell*, 138, 139.
54. Cabell to Jefferson, January 7, 1819—*Cabell*, 146–149.
55. Cabell to Jefferson, January 18, 21, 25, 1819—*Cabell*, 149–151, 152, 153.
56. To J. C. Cabell, January 28, 1819—*Cabell*, 154.
57. Bruce—*op. cit.*, I, 184.
58. To Hugh L. White, Thomas M'Corry, James Campbell, Robert Craighead, John N. Gamble, May 6, 1810—*Library Ed.*, XII, 386.
59. To Governor Wilson C. Nicholas, April 2, 1816—*Ms., L. C.*, Vol. 206, also *Library Ed.*, XIV, 453.
60. To Latrobe, cited by Bruce—*op. cit.*, I, 179.
61. Bruce—*op. cit.*, I, 179.
62. Ibid., 184.
63. Lambeth, William A.—*Thomas Jefferson as an Architect*, 3–11.
64. Bruce—*op. cit.*, I, 186–189.
65. Ibid., 273.
66. Ibid., 249.
67. Adams—*op. cit.*, 18 and Note.
68. Bruce—*op. cit.*, I, 245.
69. Tucker—*op. cit.*, II, 431.
70. Adams—*op. cit.*, 100.
71. Jefferson's Pocket Notebook, 1, cited by Lambeth—*Thomas Jefferson as an Architect*, Plate XIII.
72. Bruce—*op. cit.*, II, 387–388.
73. Minutes of the Board of Visitors—*Library Ed.*, XIX, 365.
74. Ibid., 379.
75. To J. C. Cabell, October 24, 1817—*Cabell*, 84–85.

76. To J. C. Cabell, December 19, 1817—*Cabell,* 88–89; cf. Cabell to Jefferson, January 5, 1818—*Cabell,* 101.
77. *Cabell,* 469.
78. To J. C. Cabell, April 15, 1825—*Cabell,* 348–349.
79. Bruce—*op. cit.,* II, 389.
80. "Report of the Commissioners Appointed to Fix the Site of the University of Virginia"—*Cabell,* 446–447.
81. Minutes of the Board of Visitors, October 7, 1822—*Library Ed.,* XIX, 409.
82. Ibid., 423.
83. Ibid., 427–428.
84. Report to the President and Directors of the Literary Fund—*Library Ed.,* XIX, 458.
85. "An Act Appropriating a Part of the Revenue of the Literary Fund" —*Cabell,* 431.
86. To J. C. Cabell, January 31, 1821—*Cabell,* 201.
87. To General James Breckenridge, April 9, 1822—*Library Ed.,* XV, 363, 365; Cf. Minutes of the Board of Visitors, February 26, 1818 —*Library Ed.,* XIX, 371–372; To William Short, June 22, 1819 —*Library Ed.,* XVIII, 303; To General Robert Taylor, May 16, 1820—*Library Ed.,* XV, 253–254.
88. Bruce—*op. cit.,* I, 307.
89. Cabell to Jefferson, August 5, 1821, and January 14, 1822—*Cabell,* 215, 233–237.
90. Cabell to Jefferson, February 25, 1821, February 3, 1823, January 26, 1824—*Cabell,* 209, 273, 288.
91. To J. C. Cabell, September 30, 1821, January 3 and 25, 1822, December 28, 1822, January 13 and 28 and March 12, 1823—*Cabell,* 219, 228, 239, 260, 266, 270, 278, and others.
92. To J. C. Cabell, November 28, 1820—*Cabell,* 184.
93. *Cabell,* 188–189.
94. To Governor Randolph, November 9, 1820—*Cabell,* 193–194.
95. Bruce—*op. cit.,* I, 287.
96. To J. C. Cabell, January 31, 1821—*Cabell,* 201.
97. To Nicholas P. Trist, June 14, 1822—*Correspondence of Thomas Jefferson,* W. C. Ford, Ed., 273.
98. To Joseph G. Swift, May 22, 1824—Ibid., 285.
99. To James Madison, September 24, 1824—*Library Ed.,* XIX, 278–279.
100. Jefferson's will—*Library Ed.,* XVII, 469.
101. Bruce—*op. cit.,* II, 192.
102. Ibid., 187.
103. By Librarian Wertenbaker, cited by Bruce—*op. cit.,* II, 186, Note.
104. Ibid., 201–202.

CHAPTER VII

1. To William Short, June 22, 1819—*Library Ed.*, XVIII, 304–305.
2. To William Short, October 31, 1819—*Library Ed.*, XV, 222–223.
3. To J. C. Cabell, February 3, 1824—*Cabell*, 291–292.
4. To Dugald Stewart, April 26, 1824—*Library Ed.*, XVIII, 331.
5. To J. C. Cabell, February 3, 1824—*Library Ed.*, XVI, 4–8; *Cabell*, 291–292.
6. To Mr. M'Alister, December 22, 1791—*Library Ed.*, VIII, 274–275.
7. To W. C. Nicholas, November 22, 1794—*Library Ed.*, IX, 291.
8. To James Madison, February 17, 1826—*Library Ed.*, XVI, 156.
9. Bruce, Philip A.—*History of the University of Virginia*, I, 195.
10. *Cabell*, 396.
11. Mellen, George F.—"Thomas Jefferson and Higher Education"—*New England Magazine*, July, 1902, 613.
12. To J. C. Cabell, September 10, 1817—*Cabell*, 81.
13. *Cabell*, 397.
14. Mellen—*op. cit.*, 613.
15. *Cabell*, 233 and 236, Note.
16. Ibid., 234, Note.
17. To J. C. Cabell, June 27, 1810—*Cabell*, 1–2.
18. To Dr. Thomas Cooper, August 25, 1814, November 2, 1822—*Library Ed.*, XIV, 173–175, XV, 403–406; Cf. *Cabell*, 397.
19. *Cabell*, 397.
20. To J. C. Cabell, December 18, 1817—*Cabell*, 88.
21. To J. C. Cabell, February 19, 1819—*Cabell*, 164–165.
22. Cabell to Jefferson, February 22, 1819—*Cabell*, 165.
23. To J. C. Cabell, March 1, 1819—*Cabell*, 167–169.
24. William Short to Jefferson, May 25, 1819—*Ms., M. H. S.*
25. To J. C. Cabell, March 1, 1819—*Cabell*, 167–169.
26. Cabell to Jefferson, February 22 and March 8, 1819—*Cabell*, 166, 172.
27. Cocke to Cabell, March 1, 1819, cited by Bruce—*op. cit*, I, 201.
28. *Cabell*, 454.
29. Ibid., 460, 469.
30. To James Madison, January 7, 1824—*Ms., L. C.*, Vol. 225; Cf. Madison to Jefferson—*Writings of James Madison*, IX, 174.
31. Adams—*Thomas Jefferson and the University of Virginia*, 143.
32. To J. C. Cabell, June 27, 1810—*Cabell*, 1.
33. Malone, Dumas—*The Public Life of Thomas Cooper.*
34. To Benjamin Waterhouse, January 8, 1825—*Ms., L. C.*, Vol. 228; also *Federal Ed.*, XII, 398.
35. Randall, Henry S.—*Life of Thomas Jefferson*—III, 467–468.
36. To Dr. Rush, January 3, 1808—*Ms., L. C.*, Vol. 174; also *Washington Ed.*, V, 226.
37. To a friend in Albemarle, December 31, 1783—*Cabell*, xxii–xxiii.

38. To Mr. M'Alister, December 22, 1791—*Library Ed.*, VIII, 274–275.
39. Curtis, W. E.—*The True Thomas Jefferson*, 258.
40. To Dr. Joseph Priestley, January 18, 1800—*Library Ed.*, X, 140; *Ford Ed.*, VII, 406.
41. To J. C. Cabell, January 5, 1815—*Cabell*, 36–37.
42. Cabell to Jefferson, November 29, 1813—*Cabell*, 11–12; To J. C. Cabell, January 31, 1814—*Cabell*, 19.
43. To Jean Batiste [*sic*] Say, March 2, 1815—*Ms.*, *M. H. S.*
44. To Nathaniel Bowditch, October 26, 1818—*Library Ed.*, XIX, 264.
45. October 3, 1820—*Cabell*, 460.
46. To John Adams, July 9, 1819—*Library Ed.*, XV, 207.
47. To William Roscoe, December 27, 1820—*Library Ed.*, XV, 302.
48. To J. C. Cabell, December 28, 1822—*Cabell*, 206.
49. Cabell to Jefferson, October 27, 1823—*Cabell* 283 and Note.
50. To Richard Rush, Dugald Stuart, and Samuel Carr, April 26, 1824. —*Library Ed.*, XVI, 31–35, XVIII, 331–334, 329.
51. To Samuel Carr, April 26, 1824—*Library Ed.*, XVIII, 329.
52. Bruce—*op. cit.*, II, 90–91.
53. To Edward Everett, July 21, 1825—*Library Ed.*, XIX, 284–285.
54. Minutes of the Board of Visitors, April 7, 1824—*Library Ed.*, XIX, 433.
55. Cabell to Jefferson, April 16, 1824—*Cabell* 303–304.
56. To J. C. Cabell, February 3, 1825—*Cabell*, 339.
57. To James Madison, February 1, 1825—*Ms.*, *L. C.*, Vol. 228.
58. To James Madison, February 12, 1825—*Ms.*, *L. C.*, Vol. 228.
59. Minutes of the Board of Visitors, March 4, 1825—*Library Ed.*, XIX, 460–461.
60. Minutes of the Board of Visitors, March 5, 1825—*Library Ed.*, XIX, 465.
61. Cabell to Jefferson, January 29, 1821—*Cabell*, 289–290.
62. To J. C. Cabell (circular), August 4, 1825—*Cabell*, 355.
63. Minutes of the Board of Visitors, October 3, 1825—*Library Ed.*, XIX, 468.
64. To Ellen W. Coolidge, August 27, 1825—*Library Ed.*, XVIII, 342.
65. Patton, John S.—*Jefferson, Cabell, and the University of Virginia*, 109.
66. Minutes of the Board of Visitors, April 3–4, 1826—*Library Ed.*, XIX, 492, 494.
67. To J. C. Cabell, April 21, 1826—*Cabell*, 377.
68. To Nathaniel Bowditch, October 26, 1826—*Library Ed.*, XIX, 266–267.
69. Francis W. Gilmer to George Long, August 21, 1824, quoted by Adams—*op. cit.*, 114–115, Note 2.
70. To J. C. Cabell, December 22, 1824—*Cabell*, 324.
71. To William Roscoe, December 27, 1820—*Library Ed.*, XV, 303.
72. Tucker, George—*Life of Thomas Jefferson*—II, 479.

73. Garnett, James M.—"The Elective System of the University of Virginia"—*Andover Review,* April, 1886.

74. *Cabell,* 519.

75. Garnett—*loc. cit.*

76. Tucker—*op. cit.,* II, 479.

77. Bruce—*op. cit.,* V, 6.

78. Chapman Johnson to Jefferson, April 23, 1825—*Collections of the Massachusetts Historical Society,* Seventh Series, Vol. I, 346.

79. Bruce—*op. cit.,* II, 29–30.

80. Minutes of the Board of Visitors, April 3–4, 1826—*Library Ed.,* XIX, 492–493.

81. Ibid.

82. Bruce—*op. cit.,* II, 31, Note; Kennedy—*Life of William Wirt,* II, 180–181.

83. To J. C. Cabell, April 21, 1826—*Cabell,* 377.

84. Bruce—*op. cit.,* II, 31.

85. Ibid., 180.

86. Ibid.

87. *Cabell,* 484.

88. Minutes of the Board of Visitors—*Library Ed.,* XIX, 264, 365–367, 375, 377, 390, 431–436.

89. To Dr. Joseph Priestley, January 18, 1800—*Library Ed.,* X, 140.

90. Minutes of the Board of Visitors, April 7, 1824—*Library Ed.,* XIX, 433–436.

91. To Dr. Thomas Cooper, January 16, 1814—*Library Ed.,* XIV, 59.

92. Cabell to Jefferson, February 3, 1825—*Cabell,* 338.

93. Minutes of the Board of Visitors, March 5, 1825—*Library Ed.,* XIX, 465.

94. Minutes of the Board of Visitors, October 3, 1825—*Library Ed.,* XIX, 470–471.

CHAPTER VIII

1. Minutes of the Board of Visitors—*Library Ed.,* XIX, 433–436.

2. Ibid.

3. Bruce, Philip A.—*History of the University of Virginia,* II, 135–136.

4. Adams—*Thomas Jefferson and the University of Virginia,* 41–42.

5. Heatwole, Cornelius J.—*History of Education in Virginia,* 90.

6. To J. C. Cabell, February 22, 1821—*Cabell,* 207.

7. Madison to Jefferson, October 17, 1788—*Writings of James Madison,* V, 269.

8. Bruce—*op. cit.,* I, 63–64.

9. *Old Dominion Magazine,* Vol. IV, March 15, 1870.

10. Adams—*op. cit.,* 51.

11. Bruce—*op. cit.,* I, 64.

12. *Cabell,* 481.

13. Minutes of the Board of Visitors—*Library Ed.,* XIX, 433.

14. To Dr. Thomas Cooper, January 16 and August 25, 1814—*Library Ed.*, XIV, 59, 173.
15. To Dr. Joseph Priestley, January 18 and 27, 1800—*Library Ed.*, X, 140–142, 146–147.
16. To M. Pictet, February 5, 1803—*Library Ed.*, X, 355.
17. To John Adams, July 5, 1814—*Library Ed.*, XIV, 144–151.
18. To Dr. Thomas Cooper, August 25, 1814—*Library Ed.*, XIV, 173–175.
19. Adams—*op. cit.*, 61.
20. To J. C. Cabell, February 22, 1821—*Cabell*, 207.
21. To Dr. Joseph Priestley, January 27, 1800—*Library Ed.*, X, 146–149; to John Adams, July 5, 1814—*Library Ed.*, XIV, 144–151.
22. To Elizabeth Trist, November 23, 1816—*Ms., M. H. S.*
23. "A Bill to Amend the Constitution of William and Mary College"—*Ford Ed.*, 220 ff.
24. Adams—*op. cit.*, 42.
25. Heatwole—*op. cit.*, 90.
26. "A Bill to Amend the Constitution of William and Mary College"—*Ford Ed.*, 220 ff.
27. "Notes on the State of Virginia"—*Library Ed.*, II, 206; to J. W. Eppes, July 28, 1787—*Library Ed.*, II, 189–190.
28. To Dr. Joseph Priestley, January 27, 1800—*Ms., L. C.*, Vol. 106, *Library Ed.*, X, 146–147.
29. Bruce—*op. cit.*, II, 90.
30. To Dr. Ezra Stiles, July 17, 1785—*Library Ed.*, V, 35–39.
31. To J. W. Eppes, July 28, 1787—*Library Ed.*, II, 189–190.
32. To Peter Carr, August 10, 1787—*Library Ed.*, II, 256.
33. Adams—*op. cit.*, 42–43; Cf. *Library Ed.*, XVIII, 360, Note.
34. *Library Ed.*, XVIII, 359–385.
35. Ibid., 385–411.
36. Ibid., 413–451.
37. Sheppard—"Thomas Jefferson as a Philologist"—*American Journal of Philology*, III, 213–214, quoted by Adams—*op. cit.*, 92, Note.
38. Quoted by Adams—*op. cit.*, 92, Note.
39. Bruce—*op. cit.*, I, 30, II, 92.
40. To Colonel T. M. Randolph, August 11, 1787—*Library Ed.*, VI, 266–269.
41. Minutes of the Board of Visitors, October 7, 1817—*Library Ed.*, XIX, 366–367.
42. "A Bill for the More General Diffusion of Knowledge," Sections VI and XIII—*Appendix A.*
43. To Ralph Izard, July 17, 1788—*Washington Ed.*, II, 428.
44. Minutes of the Board of Visitors, April 7, 1824—*Library Ed.*, XIX, 433.
45. Minutes of the Board of Visitors, October 4, 1824—*Library Ed.*, XIX, 439–440.
46. To Dr. John P. Emmett, May 2, 1826—*Library Ed.*, XVI, 168–172.

47. Quoted by Bruce—*op. cit.*, I, 34.
48. To Dr. Ezra Stiles, July 17, 1785—*Library Ed.*, V, 35–39.
49. Bruce—*op. cit.*, II, 96.
50. Ibid., 99.
51. Quoted by Bruce—*op. cit.*, I, 34.
52. To Dr. John P. Emmett, May 2, 1826—*Library Ed.*, XVI, 168–172.
53. To George Washington, February 23, 1795—*Library Ed.*, XIX, 108.
54. To David Williams, November 14, 1803—*Ms.*, *L. C.*, Vol. 136, *Randolph Ed.*, IV, 9–10.
55. To J. C. Cabell, January 5, 1815—*Cabell*, 37.
56. To Dr. John P. Emmett, April 27, 1826—*Library Ed.*, XVI, 163–167.
57. *Ford Ed.*, II, 220.
58. *Cabell*, 446.
59. Bruce—*op. cit.*, I, 271.
60. Jefferson's Notebook, quoted by Bruce,—*op. cit.*, I, 270.
61. Minutes of the Board of Visitors, October 3, 1825—*Library Ed.*, XIX, 470–471.
62. Minutes of the Board of Visitors, April 3–4, 1826—*Library Ed.*, XIX, 489–490.
63. To J. C. Cabell, May 16, 1824—*Cabell*, 310.
64. Heatwole—*op. cit.*, 91.
65. To J. Bannister, Jr., October 15, 1785—*Library Ed.*, V, 186; Cf. To Colonel T. M. Randolph, August 11, 1787—*Library Ed.*, VI, 266–269.
66. To John Adams, July 5, 1814—*Library Ed.*, XIV, 144–151.
67. To Major John Cartwright, June 5, 1824—*Library Ed.*, XVI, 51.
68. Cabell to Jefferson, January 23 and August 4, 1816, and Jefferson to Cabell, February 2, 1816—*Cabell*, 47, 69, 53.
69. To Dupont de Nemours, February 28, 1815—*Ms.*, *M. H. S.*
70. To J. C. Cabell, February 2, 1816—*Cabell*, 53.
71. To J. C. Cabell, February 5, 1815—*Cabell*, 36.
72. To J. C. Cabell, February 3, 1825—*Cabell*, 103–104.
73. Minutes of the Board of Visitors, March 4, 1825—*Library Ed.*, XIX, 460–461.
74. Adams—*op. cit.*, 140–142.
75. Ibid., 138–139.
76. To James Madison, February 17, 1826—*Library Ed.*, XVI, 156–157.
77. "A Bill for the More General Diffusion of Knowledge," Section VI —*Ford Ed.*, II, 220.
78. "Notes on the State of Virginia"—*Library Ed.*, II, 206.
79. To Peter Carr, September 7, 1814—*Cabell*, 384.
80. Bruce—*op. cit.*, II, 84.
81. Adams—*op. cit.*, 140.
82. To a professor, October 25, 1825—*Library Ed.*, XVI, 124–129.
83. To Peter Carr, August 10, 1787—*Library Ed.*, VI, 256–262.

84. To Dr. Thomas Cooper, August 14, 1820—*Library Ed.*, XV, 265.
85. To Peter Carr, August 10, 1787—*Library Ed.*, VI, 256-262.
86. To J. C. Cabell, February 22, 1821—*Cabell*, 207.
87. Adams—*op. cit.*, 61.
88. Minutes of the Board of Visitors, October 7, 1822—*Library Ed.*, XIX, 413–416; *Cabell*, 473–475.
89. To Dr. Thomas Cooper, November 2, 1822—*Library Ed.*, XV, 403.
90. Cabell to Jefferson, February 3, 1823—*Cabell*, 273.
91. Bruce—*op. cit.*, I, 242.
92. To William C. Rives, quoted by Bruce—*op. cit.*, I, 242–243.
93. To James Madison, January 2, 1826—*Ford Ed.*, X, 360.
94. Bruce—*op. cit.*, II, 126.
95. Minutes of the Board of Visitors, October 4, 1824—*Library Ed.*, XIX, 439–451.
96. To James Monroe, June 18, 1813—*Washington Ed.*, VI, 131.
97. To Peter Carr, September 7, 1814—*Cabell*, 384.
98. To Judge Brooke, November 7, 1817—*Ms. L. C.*, Vol. 211.
99. Minutes of the Board of Visitors, October 4, 1824—*Library Ed.*, XIX 439–451.
100. Bruce—*op. cit.*, II, 117, 120.
101. To Peter Carr, September 7, 1814—*Cabell*, 384.
102. Minutes of the Board of Visitors, October 4, 1824—*Library Ed.*, XIX, 439–451.
103. Bruce—*op. cit.*, II, 125–126.
104. To George Ticknor, July 16, 1823—*Library Ed.*, XV, 455.
105. "Report of the Commissioners Appointed to Fix the Site of the University of Virginia"—*Cabell*, 439.
106. Ibid.
107. Minutes of the Board of Visitors, October 4, 1824—*Library Ed.*, XIX, 439.
108. To Dr. Joseph Priestley, January 27, 1800—*Library Ed.*, X, 146.
109. Bruce—*op. cit.*, II, 81.
110. Ibid.
111. Dr. Cooper to Governor Nicholas, May 30, 1816, quoted by Adams—*op. cit.*, 74–76.
112. To William B. Giles, December 26, 1825—*Library Ed.*, XVI, 150.
113. Bruce—*op. cit.*, III, 233.
114. Ibid., II, 137; Garnett, J. M.—"The Elective System of the University of Virginia"—*Andover Review*, April, 1886.
115. To George Ticknor, July 16, 1823—*Library Ed.*, XV, 455.
116. *Cabell*, 460.
117. Quoted by Adams—*op. cit.*, 124.
118. Ibid., 126.
119. *President Eliot's Report*, 1883–84.
120. Ticknor to Jefferson, December 8, 1821—*Collections of the Massachusetts Historical Society*, Seventh Series, Vol. I, 310.
121. Bronson, Walter C.—*History of Brown University*, 273.

122. Bruce—*op. cit.*, III, 254.
123. Baird, William—"The University of Virginia"—*Educational Review*, December, 1896, 433.
124. Bruce—*op. cit.*, III, 245, 248–250.
125. Ibid., II, 137.
126. Minutes of the Board of Visitors, October 4, 1824—*Library Ed.*, XIX, 439–451.
127. Minutes of the Board of Visitors, October 3, 1825—*Library Ed.*, XIX, 470.
128. Bruce—*op. cit.*, II, 128–129.

CHAPTER IX

1. "Report of the Commissioners Appointed to Fix the Site of the University of Virginia"—*Cabell*, 443.
2. To Dr. Thomas Cooper, November 2, 1822—*Library Ed.*, XV, 406.
3. To George Ticknor, July 16, 1823—*Library Ed.*, XV, 455.
4. Minutes of the Board of Visitors, October, 1824—*Library Ed.*, XIX, 439–451.
5. To J. C. Cabell, April 15, 1825—*Cabell*, 350.
6. To Ellen W. Coolidge, August 27, 1825—*Library Ed.*, XVIII, 341.
7. John H. Cocke to J. C. Cabell, September, 1825. quoted by Bruce —*op. cit.*, II, 264.
8. To J. C. Cabell (circular), September 10, 1825—*Cabell*, 356–357.
9. To Joseph Coolidge, Jr., October 13, 1825—*Library Ed.*, XVIII, 342–346.
10. Minutes of the Board of Visitors, October 3, 1825—*Library Ed.*, XIX, 468–470.
11. Patton, John C.—*Jefferson, Cabell, and the University of Virginia.*
12. To Joseph Coolidge, Jr., October 13, 1825—*Library Ed.*, XVIII, 342–346.
13. Minutes of the Board of Visitors, October 6, 1825—*Library Ed.*, XIX, 478–479.
14. Tucker—*Life of Jefferson*, II, 481.
15. Minutes of the Board of Visitors, October 3, 5, 7, 1825—*Library Ed.*, XIX, 472–480.
16. Minutes of the Board of Visitors, October 7, 1825—*Library Ed.*, XIX, 483–484.
17. To Ellen W. Coolidge, November 14, 1825—*Library Ed.*, XVIII, 356.
18. To Joseph Coolidge, Jr., June 4, 1826—*Library Ed.*, XVIII, 356.
19. To George Ticknor, July 16, 1823—*Library Ed.*, XV, 455.
20. Patton—*op. cit.*, 129–130.
21. *Laws of Harvard College*—22, 13; *Enactments of the Rector and Visitors of the University of Virginia*—10, 7.
22. Ibid., 19, 39; 9, 12.
23. Bruce—*op. cit.*, II, 260–261.

24. Patton—*op. cit.*, 130.
25. Minutes of the Board of Visitors, October 3, 1825—*Library Ed.*, XIX, 472.
26. Ibid.
27. To Ellen W. Coolidge, November 14, 1825—*Library Ed.*, XVIII, 346–352.
28. Cabell to Jefferson, January 16, 1816—*Cabell*, 44.
29. Cabell to Jefferson, January 23, 1816—*Cabell*, 47–48.
30. To J. C. Cabell, January 24, 1816—*Ms.*, *L. C.*, Vol. 205; *Cabell*, 45.
31. *Board Minutes, Hampden-Sidney College*, 62–63.
32. Minutes of the Board of Visitors—*Library Ed.*, XIX, 439–451.
33. Ibid., 460.
34. Ibid., 468–470.
35. Ibid., 480.
36. Ibid., 481.
37. To Ellen W. Coolidge, November 14, 1825—*Library Ed.*, XVIII, 346–352.
38. Patton—*op. cit.*, *29; Cabell*, 44, Note.
39. Minutes of the Board of Visitors, October 6, 1825—*Library Ed.*, XIX, 477.
40. Patton—*op. cit.*, 137.
41. Ibid., 137–140.
42. Cabell to Jefferson, December 7, 1825—*Cabell*, 358.
43. *University of Virginia Record*, March 15, 1927, 12–13.

CHAPTER X

1. To Dr. Thomas Cooper, August 25, 1814—*Library Ed.*, XIV, 173–175; to Dr. Joseph Priestley, January 18, 1800—*Library Ed.*, X, 140.
2. Bruce, Philip A.—*History of the University of Virginia*, I, 34.
3. To General Kosciusko, 1810—*Washington Ed.*, V, 509.
4. To George Ticknor, November 15, 1817—*Ms.*, *L. C.*, Vol. 211.
5. To M. D'Ivernois, February 6, 1795—*Ms.*, *L. C.*; *Ford Ed.* VII, 3.
6. Maddox, William A.—*Free School Idea in Virginia*, 21.
7. To George Wythe, August 13, 1786—*Ms.*, *L. C.*, Vol. 23; *Library Ed.*, V, 396.
8. To Thomas Law, June 13, 1814—*Ms.*, *L. C.*, Vol. 201; *Library Ed.*, XIV, 142–143.
9. To M. Jullien, July 23, 1818—*Washington Ed.*, VII, 106.
10. To C. C. Blatchly, October 21, 1822—*Washington Ed.*, VII, 263.
11. To J. C. Cabell, November 28, 1820—*Ford Ed.*, X, 166.
12. To M. Correa, November 25, 1817—*Washington Ed.*, VII, 94.
13. To James Madison, December 20, 1787—*Washington Ed.*, II, 332.
14. First Inaugural Address, 1801—*Ford Ed.*, VIII, 5.

15. To Governor Nicholas, April 2, 1816—*Library Ed.*, XIV, 446.
16. To Governor Tyler, May 26, 1810—*Ms., L. C.*, Vol. 190; *Washington Ed.*, V, 525–526.
17. To J. C. Cabell, January 17, 1814 and February 2, 1816—*Cabell*, 15–16, 55–56.
18. *Cabell*, 19, Note.
19. Adams, Herbert B.—*Thomas Jefferson and the University of Virginia*, 39.
20. "Notes on the State of Virginia"—*Library Ed.*, II, 206–207.
21. To Colonel William Duane, September 16, 1810—*Library Ed.*, XII, 416–417.
22. "McCulloch v. Maryland"—IV, *Wheaton*, 316.
23. To William Charles Jarvis, September 28, 1820—*Library Ed.*, XV, 278.
24. To John Taylor, February 14, 1821—*Library Ed.*, XVIII, 312.
25. To General James Breckenridge, February 15, 1821—*Library Ed.*, XV, 314–318.
26. To J. C. Cabell, January 31, 1821—*Cabell*, 201–202.
27. To J. C. Cabell, January 22, 1820—*Cabell*, 178.
28. To J. C. Cabell, November 28, 1820—*Cabell*, 185.
29. To J. C. Cabell, December 25, 1820—*Cabell*, 193.
30. To J. C. Cabell, December 28, 1822—*Cabell*, 260.
31. To J. C. Cabell, February 3, 1825—*Cabell*, 339.
32. To J. C. Cabell, January 25, 1822—*Cabell*, 239.
33. To William B. Giles, December 26, 1825—*Library Ed.*, XVI, 151.
34. "Thoughts on Lotteries," February, 1826—*Library Ed.*, XVII. 462–463; Cf. To James Madison, February 17, 1826—*Library Ed.*, XVI, 156.
35. To Dr. Thomas Cooper, August 14, 1820—*Washington Ed.*, VII, 172.
36. Report of the Rector and Visitors, 1857, quoted by Morrison—*The Beginning of Public Education in Virginia*, 80–81.
37. Fitz-Hugh, Thomas—*The University of Virginia in Texas and the Southwest*, 4.
38. Bruce—*op. cit.*, III, 235.
39. "Autobiography"—*Library Ed.*, I, 70–72.
40. To General Robert Taylor, May 16, 1820—*Library Ed.*, XV, 254.
41. To Dr. Thomas Cooper, August 14, 1820—*Library Ed.*, XV, 267.
42. To William Short, April 13, 1820—*Library Ed.*, 245–246.
43. Maddox—*op. cit.*, 30–34.
44. To T. M. Randolph, Jr., July 6, 1787—*Library Ed.*, VI, 165.
45. Quoted in the Introduction—*Library Ed.*, IV, vi.
46. To David Williams, November 14, 1803—*Ms., L. C.*, Vol. 136; *Randolph Ed.*, IV, 8–10.
47. To Dr. Wistar, June 21, 1807—*Ford Ed.*, IX, 78.
48. To George Washington, February 23, 1795—*Library Ed.*, XIX, 108.
49. Minutes of the Board of Visitors, August 19, 1814—*Cabell*, 382.
50. *Cabell*, xxiv, Note.

51. Minutes of the Board of Visitors, May 5, 1817—*Library Ed.,* XIX, 393–394.
52. To John Adams, October 28, 1813—*Library Ed.,* XIII, 394–403.
53. Minutes of the Board of Visitors, April 15, 1814—*Cabell,* 380.
54. Cabell to Jefferson, February 15, 1819—*Cabell,* 162.
55. To J. C. Cabell, December 18, 1817—*Ms., L. C.,* Vol. 211; *Cabell,* 88.
56. To Judge Spencer Roane, March 9, 1821—*Library Ed.,* XV, 326.

CHAPTER XI

1. To Governor Tyler, May 26, 1810—*Ms., L. C.,* Vol. 190; *Washington Ed.,* V, 525–526; to John Adams, October 28, 1813—*Ms., L. C.,* Vol. 199; *Library Ed.,* XIII, 399–400; to J. C. Cabell, February 2, 1816—*Cabell,* 55–56.
2. *Autobiography,* 93; Cf. Madison to Jefferson, August 20, 1784—*Writings of James Madison,* II, 64.
3. Bronson, Walter C.—*History of Brown University,* 1764–1914, 88–89.
4. To Ellen W. Coolidge, August 27, 1825—*Library Ed.,* XVIII, 340–342.
5. To Major John Cartwright, June 5, 1824, quoted by Adams—*Thomas Jefferson and the University of Virginia,* 31, Note 1.
6. To William Roscoe, December 27, 1820—*Library Ed.,* XV, 302–304.
7. To Joseph Coolidge, Jr., January 15, 1825—*Collections of the Massachusetts Historical Society,* Seventh Series, I, 340.
8. Cabell to Jefferson, March 17, 1824—*Cabell,* 297.
9. Russel, Michael—*View of the System of Education at present pursued in the Schools and Universities of Scotland,* 110, 115.
10. Minutes of the Board of Visitors, October 3, 1825—*Library Ed.,* XIX, 470.
11. Russel—*op. cit.,* 154, vii.
12. "Report of the Commissioners to Fix the Site of the University of Virginia"—Appendix X.
13. Russel—*op. cit.,* 110.
14. Minutes of the Board of Visitors, October 4, 1824—*Library Ed.,* XIX, 439–451.
15. Russel—*op. cit.,* 121, 165.
16. Minutes of the Board of Visitors, October 4, 1824—*Library Ed.,* XIX, 439–451.
17. Russel—*op. cit.,* 135.
18. Minutes of the Board of Visitors, October 4, 1824—*Library Ed.,* XIX, 439.
19. Russel—*op. cit.,* 137, 141.
20. To Dr. John P. Emmett, May 2, 1826—*Library Ed.,* XVI, 168–172.
21. Russel—*op. cit.,* 102–103, 120.

22. To Mr. M'Alister, December 22, 1791—*Library Ed.*, VIII, 274–275.

23. To J. C. Cabell, February 3, 1824—*Cabell*, 291–292.

24. To Thomas Ritchie, September 27, 1814—*Ms., M. H. S.;* also Chinard, Gilbert—*Jefferson et les Idéologues,* passim.

25. To John Adams, October 14, 1816—*Ms., L. C.*, Vol. 208.

26. To John Adams, November 25, 1816—*Ms., L. C.*, Vol. 208.

27. To Destutt de Tracy, May 15, 1817, quoted by Chinard,—*op. cit.*, 169–170.

28. Manuscript *Catalog, M. H. S.; Catalogue of President Jefferson's Library,* 5.

29. To Peter Carr, September, 7, 1814—*Ms., L. C.*, Vol. 202; also *Cabell,* 384.

30. Destutt de Tracy—*Observations sur Le Système Actuel D'instruction Publique,* 332–334.

31. To Peter Carr, September 7, 1814—*Cabell,* 384.

32. Destutt—*op. cit.*, 336.

33. *Ibid.*, 338.

34. To Peter Carr, September 7, 1814—*Cabell,* 384.

35. Destutt, *op. cit.*, 361, 364–365.

36. *Ibid.*, 385; Cf. *Tableau Du Plan D'Études Des Écoles Centrales, Ibid.*, 324.

37. To Peter Carr, September 7, 1814, sub-title "General Schools."

38. Destutt, *op. cit.*, 387.

39. To M. A. Jullien, July 23, 1818—*Library Ed.*, XV, 171.

40. To M. Jullien, l'ainè, July 15, 1810—*Ms., L. C.*, Vol. 190.

41. To Peter Carr, September 7, 1814—*Cabell,* 384.

42. Cf. "Report of the Commissioners Appointed to Fix the Site of the University of Virginia" and "Enactments of the Board of Visitors," 1824—Appendix, X, XIII.

43. Jullien, M. A.—*Essai General D'Education,* 420.

44. *Catalogue of President Jefferson's Library,* 5.

45. To E. J. Dupont, September 9, 1817—*Ms., L. C.*, Vol. 211.

46. To Dupont de Nemours, April 12, 1800—*Ms., L. C.*, Vol. 106.

47. *Ibid,* December 12, 1800—*Ms., L. C.*, Vol. 108.

48. *Ibid.*, December 31, 1815—*Library Ed.*, XIV, 369–373.

49. Dupont de Nemours—*National Education in the United States of America,* Translated by B. G. Dupont, 1923.

50. Adams—*op cit.*, 51.

51. Bruce—*op. cit.*, I, 63–64.

52. To Colonel William Duane, September 16, 1810—*Ms., L. C.*, Vol. 191; also *Library Ed.*, XII, 416–417.

53. Manuscript *Catalog*—*M. H. S.;* Cf. *Catalogue of President Jefferson's Library,* 5.

54. To John Preston, August 19, 1816—*Ms., M. H. S.*

55. Ogilvie, James—*Cursory Reflexions on Government, Philosophy, and Education,* 16–17, 21, 22, 37.

56. *Early Proceedings of the American Philosophical Society*, 226–229.
57. Ibid.
58. Ibid., 246.
59. Ibid., *passim.*
60. Ibid., 265.
61. Ibid., 269.
62. Manuscript *Catalog—M. H. S.*
63. *Cabell,* 396.
64. To S. H. Smith, September 21, 1814—*Ford Ed.,* IX, 485–488.
65. *Early Proceedings,* 265.
66. Ibid., 274.
67. Knox, Samuel—*Essay on Education,* 77.
68. Ibid., 78–80.
69. Ibid., 61.
70. Ibid., 64.
71. Ibid., 128–129.
72. Ibid., 135.
73. Ibid., 161.
74. Ibid., 143.
75. Steiner, Bernard C.—"Reverend Samuel Knox," from the *Report of the Commissioner of Education for the year 1898–99,* I, 577–604; Cf. Bruce—*op. cit.,* I, 179, Note.
76. Knox—*op. cit.,* 152–155.
77. Smith, Samuel H.—*Remarks on Education,* 41.
78. Ibid., 46.
79. Ibid., 80, 82.
80. Ibid., 69.
81. To John Adams, July 5, 1814—*Library Ed.,* XIV, 144–151.
82. John Adams to Jefferson, July 16, 1814—quoted in *Library Ed.,* XIV, 159–160.
83. To Dr. Wistar, August, 25, 1814—*Ms., L. C.,* Vol. 202.
84. To Thomas Cooper, September 10, 1814—*Ms., L. C.,* Vol. 202.
85. Cooper to Jefferson, September 15, 1814—*Ms., M. H. S.* (in 1815 volume).
86. Ibid., September 21, 1814—*Ms., M. H. S.* (in 1815 volume).
87. H. G. Spofford to Jefferson, January 9, 1816—*Ms., M. H. S.*
88. Ibid., November 23, 1816—*Ms., M. H. S.*
89. Ibid., January 21, 1817—*Ms., M. H. S.*
90. To Thomas Cooper, April 12, 1823—*Ms., L. C.,* Vol. 224.
91. To George Ticknor, July 16, 1823—*Library Ed.,* XV, 455.
92. Manuscript *Catalog, M. H. S.;* McKee, George H.—*Th. Jefferson, Ami de la Révolution Française,* 18.
93. Adamson—*The Educational Writings of John Locke,* Section 94, p. 73.
94. Ibid., Section 162, pp. 124–125; Section 163, p. 125.
95. Ibid., Section 178, 146; Section 184, p. 151.
96. Ibid., Section 164, p. 125.

97. Ibid., Section 94, p. 77.

98. Ibid., Section 185, p. 151.

99. Ibid., Section 186, pp. 151–152.

100. To Dr. Joseph Priestley, January 18, 1800—*Ms., L. C.,* Vol. 106.

101. Manuscript *Catalog, M. H. S.*

102. Priestley—*Miscellaneous Observations,* 42.

103. Priestley—*Lectures on History,* Lectures 20–24, I, 283–285, 294, 303, 315; Cf. To a Member of the Faculty, October 25, 1825—*Ms., L. C.,* Vol. 230; Appendix XVI.

104. Priestley—*Lectures on History,* 3, 323.

105. To a Member of the Faculty, October 25, 1825—*Ms., L. C.,* Vol. 230.

106. Priestley—*Lectures on History,* I, 357.

107. To a Member of the Faculty, October 25, 1825—*Ms., L. C.,* Vol. 230.

108. Priestley—*Lectures on History,* I, 358–359; To a Member of the Faculty, October 25, 1825—*Ms., L. C.,* Vol. 230.

109. Priestley—*Lectures on History,* I, 19.

110. To Dr. Joseph Priestley, January 27, 1800—*Ms., L. C.,* Vol. 106.

111. Priestley—*Lectures on History,* Lecture 28, I, 361 ff.

APPENDICES

THE following documents are reproduced because of a peculiar interest possessed by each as illustrating some phase of Jefferson's plans or methods. As some of them deal with several subjects, they cannot be classified consistently, so are merely arranged in chronological order.

APPENDIX A

BILLS ON EDUCATION DRAFTED BY JEFFERSON AND REPORTED TO THE VIRGINIA ASSEMBLY FOR THE COMMITTEE OF REVISORS BY T. JEFFERSON AND G. WYTHE, JUNE 18, 1779.

(Writings of Thomas Jefferson, Ford edition, II, 220–237.)

A BILL FOR THE MORE GENERAL DIFFUSION OF KNOWLEDGE

SECTION I. Whereas it appeareth that however certain forms of government are better calculated than others to protect individuals in the free exercise of their natural rights, and are at the same time themselves better guarded against degeneracy, yet experience hath shown, that even under the best forms, those entrusted with power have, in time, and by slow operations, perverted it into tyranny; and it is believed that the most effectual means of preventing this would be, to illuminate, as far as practicable, the minds of the people at large, and more especially to give them knowledge of those facts, which history exhibiteth, that, possessed thereby of the experience of other ages and countries, they may be enabled to know ambition under all its shapes, and prompt to exert their natural powers to defeat its purposes; And whereas it is generally true that that people will be happiest whose laws are best, and are best administered, and that laws will be wisely formed, and honestly administered, in proportion as those who form and administer them are wise and honest; whence it becomes expedient for promoting the publick happiness that those persons, whom nature hath endowed with genius and virtue, should be rendered by liberal education worthy to receive, and able to guard the sacred deposit of the rights and liberties of their fellow citizens, and that they should be called to that charge without regard to wealth, birth or other accidental condition or circumstance; but the indigence of the greater number disabling them from so educating, at their own expense, those of their children whom nature hath fitly formed and disposed to become useful instruments for the public, it is better that such should be sought for and educated at the common expense of all, than that the happiness of all should be confined to the weak or wicked:

SECT. II. Be it therefore enacted by the General Assembly, that in every county within this commonwealth, there shall be chosen annually, by the electors qualified to vote for Delegates, three of the most honest and able men of their county, to be called the Aldermen of the county; and that the election of the said Aldermen shall be held at the same time and place, before the same persons, and notified and conducted in the same manner as by law is directed, for the annual election of Delegates for the county.

SECT. III. The person before whom such election is holden shall certify to the court of the said county the names of the Aldermen chosen, in order that the same may be entered of record, and shall give notice of their election to the said Aldermen within a fortnight after such election.

SECT. IV. The said Aldermen on the first Monday in October, if it be fair, and if not, then on the next fair day, excluding Sunday, shall meet at the court-house of their county, and proceed to divide their said county into hundreds, bounding the same by water courses, mountains, or limits, to be run and marked, if they think necessary, by the county surveyor, and at the county expence, regulating the size of the said hundreds, according to the best of their discretion, so as that they may contain a convenient number of children to make up a school, and be of such convenient size that all the children within each hundred may daily attend the school to be established therein, and distinguishing each hundred by a particular name; which division, with the names of the several hundreds, shall be returned to the court of the county and be entered of record, and shall remain unaltered until the increase or decrease of inhabitants shall render an alteration necessary, in the opinion of any succeeding Alderman, and also in the opinion of the court of the county.

SECT. V. The electors aforesaid residing within every hundred shall meet on the third Monday in October after the first election of Aldermen, at such place, within their hundred, as the said Aldermen shall direct, notice thereof being previously given to them by such person residing within the hundred as the said Aldermen shall require who is hereby enjoined to obey such requisition, on pain of being punished by amercement and imprisonment. The electors being so assembled shall choose the most convenient place within their hundred for building a school-house. If two or more places, having a greater number of votes than any others, shall yet be equal between themselves, the Aldermen, or such of them as are not of the same hundred, on information thereof, shall decide between them. The said Aldermen shall forthwith proceed to have a school-house built at the said place, and shall see that the same shall be kept in repair, and, when necessary, that it be rebuilt; but whenever they shall think necessary that it be rebuilt, they shall give notice as before directed, to the electors of the hundred to meet at the said school-house, on such a day as they shall appoint, to determine by vote, in the manner before directed, whether it shall be rebuilt at the same, or what other place in the hundred.

SECT. VI. At every of those schools shall be taught reading, writing, and common arithmetick, and the books which shall be used therein for instructing the children to read shall be such as will at the same time make them acquainted with Graecian, Roman, English, and American history. At these schools all the free children, male and female, resident within the respective hundred, shall be intitled to receive tuition gratis, for the term of three years, and as much longer, at their private expense, as their parents, guardians, or friends shall think proper.

SECT. VII. Over every ten of these schools (or such other number nearest thereto, as the number of hundreds in the county will admit, without fractional divisions) an overseer shall be appointed annually by the aldermen at their first meeting, eminent for his learning, integrity, and fidelity to the commonwealth, whose business and duty it shall be, from time to time, to appoint a teacher to each school, who shall give assurance of fidelity to the commonwealth, and to remove him as he shall see cause; to visit every school once in every half year at the least; to examine the scholars; see that any general plan of reading and instruction recommended by the visiters of William and Mary College shall be observed; and to superintend the conduct of the teacher in everything relative to his school.

SECT. VIII. Every teacher shall receive a salary of —— by the year, which, with the expences of building and repairing the school-houses, shall be provided in such manner as other county expences are by law directed to be provided and shall also have his diet, lodging, and washing found him, to be levied in like manner, save only that such levy shall be on the inhabitants of each hundred for the board of their own teacher only.

SECT. IX. And in order that grammer schools may be rendered convenient to the youth in every part of the commonwealth, be it therefore enacted, that on the first Monday in November, after the first appointment of overseers for the hundred schools, if fair, and if not, then on the next fair day, excluding Sunday, after the hour of one in the afternoon, the said overseers appointed for the schools in the counties of Princess Ann, Norfolk, Nansemond, and Isle-of-Wight, shall meet at Nansemond court-house; those for the counties of Southampton, Sussex, Surry and Prince George, shall meet at Sussex court-house; those for the counties of Brunswick, Mecklenburg and Lunenburg, shall meet at Lunenburg court-house; those for the counties of Dinwiddie, Amelia and Chesterfield, shall meet at Chesterfield court-house; those for the counties of Powhatan, Cumberland, Goochland, Henrico and Hanover, shall meet at Henrico court-house; those for the counties of Prince Edward, Charlotte and Halifax, shall meet at Charlotte court-house; those for the counties of Henry, Pittsylvania and Bedford, shall meet at Pittsylvania court-house; those for the counties of Buckingham, Amherst, Albemarle and Fluvanna, shall meet at Albemarle court-house; those for the counties of Botetourt, Rockbridge, Montgomery, Washington and Kentucky, shall meet at Botetourt court-house; those for the counties of Augusta, Rockingham and Greenbriar, shall meet at Augusta court-house; those for the counties of Accomack and Northampton, shall meet at Accomack court-house; those for the counties of Elizabeth City, Warwick, York, Gloucester, James City, Charles City and New-Kent, shall meet at James City court-house; those for the counties of Middlesex, Essex, King and Queen, King William and Caroline, shall meet at King and Queen court-house; those for the counties of Lancaster, Northumberland, Richmond and Westmoreland, shall meet at Richmond court-house; those for the counties of King George, Stafford, Spotsylvania, Prince William and Fairfax, shall meet at Spotsylvania court-house; those for the counties of Loudoun and Fauquier, shall meet at Loudoun court-house; those for the counties of Culpeper, Orange and Louisa, shall meet at Orange court-house; those for the county of Shenandoah and Frederick, shall meet at Frederick court-house; those for the counties of Hampshire and Berkeley, shall meet at Berkeley court-house; and those for the counties of Yohogania, Monongalia, and Ohio, shall meet at the Monongalia court-house; and shall fix on such place in some one of the counties in their district as shall be most proper for situating a grammar school-house, endeavoring that the situation be as central as may be to the inhabitants of the said counties, that it be furnished with good water, convenient to plentiful supplies of provision and fuel, and more than all things that it be healthy.   And if a majority of the overseers present should not concur in their choice of any one place proposed, the method of determining shall be as follows: If two places only were proposed, and the votes be divided, they shall decide between them by fair and equal lot; if more than two places were proposed, the question shall be put on those two which on the first division had the greater number of votes; or if no two places had a greater number of votes than the others, then it shall be decided by fair and equal lot (unless it can be agreed by a majority of votes) which of the places having equal numbers shall be thrown out of the competition, so that the question shall be put on the remaining two, and if on this ultimate question the votes shall be equally divided, it shall then be decided finally by lot.

Sect. X. The said overseers having determined the place at which the grammer school for their district shall be built, shall forthwith (unless they can otherwise agree with the proprietors of the circumjacent lands as to location and price) make application to the clerk of the county in which the said house is to be situated, who shall thereupon issue a writ, in the nature of a writ of ad quod damnum, directed to the sheriff of the said county commanding him to summon and impannel twelve fit persons to meet at the place, so destined for the grammer school-house, on a certain day, to be named in the said writ, not less than five, nor more than ten, days from the date thereof; and also to give notice of the same to the proprietors and tenants of the lands to be viewed if they be found within the county, and if not, then to their agents therein if any they have. Which freeholders shall be charged by the said sheriff impartially, and to the best of their skill and judgment to view the lands round about the said place, and to locate and circumscribe, by certain meets and bounds, one hundred acres thereof, having regard therein principally to the benefit and convenience of the said school, but respecting in some measure also the convenience of the said proprietors, and to value and appraise the same in so many several and distinct parcels as shall be owned or held by several and distinct owners or tenants, and according to their respective interests and estates therein. And after such location and appraisement so made, the said sheriff shall forthwith return the same under the hands and seals of the said jurors, together with the writ, to the clerk's office of the said county and the right and property of the said proprietors and tenants in the said lands so circumscribed shall be immediately devested and be transferred to the commonwealth for the use of the said grammer school, in full and absolute dominion, any want of consent or disability to consent in the said owners or tenants notwithstanding. But it shall not be lawful for the said overseers so to situate the grammer school-house, nor to the said jurors so to locate the said lands, as to include the mansion-house of the proprietor of the lands, nor the offices, curtilage, or garden, thereunto immediately belonging.

SECT. XI. The said overseers shall forthwith proceed to have a house of brick or stone, for the said grammer school, with necessary offices, built on the said lands, which grammer school-house shall contain a room for the school, a hall to dine in, four rooms for a master and usher, and ten or twelve lodging rooms for the scholars.

SECT. XII. To each of the said grammer schools shall be allowed out of the public treasury, the sum of —— pounds, out of which shall be paid by the Treasurer, on warrant from the Auditors, to the proprietors or tenants of the lands located, the value of their several interests as fixed by the jury, and the balance thereof shall be delivered to the said overseers to defray the expense of the said buildings.

SECT. XIII. In either of these grammer schools shall be taught the Latin and Greek languages, English Grammer, geography, and the higher part of numerical arithmetick, to wit, vulgar and decimal fractions, and the extrication of the square and cube roots.

SECT. XIV. A visiter from each county constituting the district shall be appointed, by the overseers, for the county, in the month of October annually, either from their own body or from their county at large, which visiters, or the greater part of them, meeting together at the first grammer school on the first Monday in November, if fair, and if not, then on the next fair day, excluding Sunday, shall have power to choose their own Rector, who shall call and preside at future meetings, to employ from time to time a master, and if necessary, an usher, for the said school, to remove them at their will, and to settle the price of tuition to be paid by the scholars. They shall also visit the school twice in every year at the least, either together or separately at their discretion, examine the scholars, and see that any general plan of instruction recommended by the visiters, of William and Mary College shall be observed. The said masters and ushers, before they enter on the execution of their office, shall give assurance of fidelity to the commonwealth.

SECT. XV. A steward shall be employed, and removed at will by the master, on such wages as the visiters shall direct; which steward shall see to the procuring provisions, fuel, servants for cooking, waiting, house cleaning, washing, mending, and gardening on the most reasonable terms; the expence of which, together with the steward's wages, shall be divided equally among all the scholars boarding either on the public or private expence. And the part of those who are on private expence, and also the price of their tuitions due to the master or usher, shall be paid quarterly by the respective scholars, their parents, or guardians, and shall be recoverable, if withheld, together with costs, on motion in any Court of Record, ten days notice thereof being previously given to the party, and a jury impannelled to try the issue joined, or enquire of the damages. The said steward shall also, under the direction of the visiters, see that the houses be kept in repair, and necessary enclosures be made and repaired, the accounts for which, shall, from time to time, be submitted to the Auditors, and on their warrant paid by the Treasurer.

SECT. XVI. Every overseer of the hundred schools shall, in the month of September annually, after the most diligent and impartial examination and inquiry, appoint from among the boys who shall have been two years at the least at some one of the schools under his superintendance, and whose parents are too poor to give them farther education, some one of the best and most promising genius and disposition, to proceed to the grammer school of his district; which appointment shall be made in the court-house of the county, and on the court day for that month if fair, and if not, then on the next fair day, excluding Sunday, in the presence of the Aldermen, or two of them at the least, assembled on the bench for that purpose, the said overseer being previously sworn by them to make such appointment, without favor or affection, according to the best of his skill and judgment, and being interrogated by the said Aldermen, either on their own motion, or on suggestions from the parents, guardians, friends, or teachers of the children, competitors for such appointment; which teachers the parents shall attend for the information of the Aldermen. On which interrogatories the said Aldermen, if they be not satisfied with the appointment proposed, shall have right to negative it; whereupon the said visiter may proceed to make a new appointment, and the said Aldermen again to interrogate and negative, and so toties quoties until an appointment be approved.

SECT. XVII. Every boy so appointed shall be authorized to proceed to the grammer school of his district, there to be educated and boarded during such time as is hereafter limited; and his quota of the expences of the house together with a compensation to the master or usher for this tuition, at the rate of twenty dollars by the year, shall be paid by the Treasurer quarterly on warrant from the Auditors.

SECT. XVIII. A visitation shall be held, for the purpose of probation, annually at the said grammer school on the last Monday in September, if fair, and if not, then on the next fair day, excluding Sunday, at which one third of the boys sent thither by appointment of the said overseers, and who shall have been there one year only, shall be discontinued as public foundationers, being those who, on the most diligent examination and enquiry, shall be thought to be the least promising genius and disposition; and of those who shall have been there two years, all shall be discontinued save one only the best in genius and disposition, who shall be at liberty to continue there four years longer on the public foundation, and shall thence forward be deemed a senior.

SECT. XIX. The visiters for the districts which, or any part of which, be southward and westward of James river, as known by that name, or by the names of Fluvanna and Jackson's river, in every other year, to wit, at the probation meetings held in the years, distinguished in the Christian computation by odd numbers, and the visiters for all the other districts at their said meetings to be held in those years, distinguished by even numbers, after diligent examination and enquiry as before directed, shall chuse one among the said seniors, of the best learning and most hopeful genius and disposition, who shall be authorized by them to proceed to William and Mary College; there to be educated, boarded, and clothed, three years; the expence of which annually shall be paid by the Treasurer on warrant from the Auditors.

A BILL FOR THE AMENDING OF THE CONSTITUTION OF THE COLLEGE OF WILLIAM AND MARY

SECTION I. Whereas a scheme for cultivating and disseminating useful knowledge in this country, which had been proposed by some of its liberal minded inhabitants, before the year 1690 of the Christian epocha, was approved, adopted, and cherished, by the General Assembly, upon whose petition King William and Queen Mary of England, to the crown whereof the people here at that time acknowledged themselves, as a colony, to be subject, by their charter bearing date the seventh day of February, in the fourth year of their reign, gave license, in due form, to Francis Nicholson, Esquire, Lieutenant Governor of the colony, and seventeen other trustees, particularly named, to found a place of universal study, or perpetual college, in such part of the country as the General Assembly should think fit, consisting of a President, six Professors, and an hundred scholars, more or less; enabled the trustees, and their survivors, to take and hold lands, tenements, and hereditaments, to the yearly value of two thousand pounds, with intention, and in confidence, that, after application of the profits thereof, with such donations as by themselves and others might be made for that purpose, to the erecting, founding, and adorning the college, they should transfer the same to the President and Professors; appointed James Blair, clerk, the first President, and empowered the trustees, and their successors, to elect the succeeding President, and the Professors; willed the college after it should be founded, to be called the College of William and Mary in Virginia; and incorporated the President and masters, enabling them and their successors to take and hold lands, tenements, hereditaments, goods and chattels, to the yearly value of two thousand pounds, of lawful money of England; appointed the trustees and their successors, to be elected in the manner therein prescribed, so as not to be less than eighteen, visiters of the College, with power to nominate one of themselves a rector annually and to ordain statutes for the government of the College, not contrary to the royal prerogative, the laws of England or Virginia, or the canons of the Church of England; willed that the President and Professors should have a Chancellor, to be nominated, every seventh year, in the manner therein prescribed; granted to the trustees a sum of money, then in the hands of William Byrd, Esquire, the Auditor, received for quitrents, to be applied towards erecting, founding and adorning the College; and also granted to the trustees, to be transferred to the President and Professors, in like manner as before directed, part of the then royal revenue, arising from the duty on tobacco exported; and also granted to the said trustees the office of surveyor general of Virginia, with intention, and in confidence, that they and their successors, or the longest livers of them, should receive the profits thereof, until the foundation of the College, and when that should be affected, account for and pay the same or the surplus above what should have been expended in that work, to the President and Professors; and that thereafter the said office should be held by the said President and Professors. And the said King and Queen, by their said charter, granted to the said trustees ten thousand acres of land, on the south side of the Blackwater swamp, and also other ten thousand acres of land in Pamunkey neck, between the forks or branches of the York river, with this intention, and in confidence, that the said trustees, or the longest livers of them, should transfer the said twenty thousand acres of land, after the foundation of the College, to the President and Professors; as by the said charter, among other things, relation being thereupon had, may more fully appear. And whereas voluntary contributions towards forwarding this beneficial scheme, the sum whereof exceeded two thousand pounds, sterling, was received by the said trustees, with one thousand pounds, sterling, out of the money arising from the quitrents granted to the use of said College by Queen Anne, part whereof was applied to the purchase of three hundred and thirty acres of land at the middle plantation, being the same place where the General Assembly, by their act, passed in the year 1693, had directed the said College to be built, and whereon the same was accordingly built, and the General Assembly, by one other act, passed in the same year 1693, intitled an Act for laying an imposition upon skins and furs, for the better support of the College of William and Mary in Virginia, endowed the said College with certain duties on skins and furs therein specified, which duties were afterwards enlarged and confirmed to the use of the said College, and made payable to the President and Professors by divers other acts of General Assembly. And by one other act passed in the year 1718, the said College was further endowed by the General Assembly with the sum of one thousand pounds, out of the public funds, in the hands of the Treasurer, which was directed to

be laid out for the maintaining and educating scholars, and to be accounted
for to the General Assembly, from time to time, when required: Which
sum was accordingly paid to the said visiters and by them invested in the
purchase of two thousand one hundred and nineteen acres of land, on
both sides of the Nottoway river, in the counties of Prince George, Surrey,
and Brunswick, and seventeen negro slaves, to be employed in tilling and
manuring the same, and certain scholarships were accordingly established
on the said funds: and the General Assembly, by their act, passed in the
year 1726, and entitled an Act for laying a duty on liquors, further endowed the said College with an annual revenue of two hundred pounds,
for twenty-one years, to be paid out of certain duties thereon imposed on
liquors, and by one other act, passed in the year 1734, endowed it with
the whole of the said duties, during the residue of the said term then un-
expired, a part or the whole thereof to be expended in purchasing a library
for the said College: And by divers other acts, passed at subsequent times,
the Assemblies, for the time being, having continued to the said College
the whole of the annual revenues, arising from the said duties, until the
first of June, which shall be in the year 1780, to be applied to the funding
scholarships, and other good uses, for the support of the said College, and to
be accounted for to the General Assembly; and the General Assembly by
          of   in the year gave a further donation to the
said College of   to be laid out in purchasing a mathematical
apparatus for the said College, which was accordingly purchased.   And
the said trustees, in pursuance of the trust reposed in them, proceeded to
erect the said College, and established one school of sacred theology, with
two professorships therein, to wit, one for teaching the Hebrew tongue,
and expounding the holy scriptures; and the other for explaining the common places of divinity, and controversies with heretics; one other school
for philosophy, with two professorships therein, to wit, one for the study
of rhetoric, logic, and ethics, and the other of physics, metaphysics, and
mathematics; one other school for teaching the Latin and Greek tongues;
and one other for teaching Indian boys reading, writing, vulgar arithmetic,
the catechism and the principles of the Christian religion; which last school
was founded on the private donation of the honorable Robert Boyle, of
the kingdom of England, and, by authority from his executors, submitted
to the direction of the Earl of Burlington, one of the said executors, of the
bishop of London, for the time being, and in default thereof, to the said
trustees, and over the whole they appointed one president as supervisor.

SECT. II. And whereas the experience of near an hundred years hath
proved, that the said College, thus amply endowed by the public, hath not
answered their expectations, and there is reason to hope, that it would become more useful, if certain articles in its constitution were altered and
amended, which being fixed, as before recited, by the original charters,
cannot be reformed by the said trustees whose powers are created and circumscribed by the said charters, and the said College being erected and
constituted on the requisition of the General Assembly, by the Chief
Magistrate of the state, their legal fiduciary for such purposes, being

founded and endowed with the lands and revenues of the public, and intended for the sole use and improvement, and no wise in nature of a private grant, the same is of right subject to the public direction, and may by them be altered and amended, until such form be devised as will render the institution publicly advantageous, in proportion as it is publicly expensive; and the late change in the form of our government, as well as the contest of arms in which we are at present engaged, calling for extraordinary abilities both in council and field, it becomes the peculiar duty of the Legislature, at this time, to aid and improve that seminary, in which those who are to be the future guardians of the rights and liberties of their country may be endowed with science and virtue, to watch and preserve the sacred deposit; Be it therefore enacted by the General Assembly, that, instead of eighteen visiters or governors of the said College, there shall in future be five only, who shall be appointed by joint ballot of both houses of Assembly, annually, to enter on the duties of their office on the new year's day ensuing their appointment, having previously given assurance of fidelity to the commonwealth, before any Justice of the Peace; and to continue in office until those next appointed shall be qualified, but those who shall be first appointed, after the passing of this act, and all others appointed during the course of any year to fill up vacancies happening by death, resignation, or removal out of the commonwealth, shall enter on duty immediately on such appointment; any four of the said visiters may proceed to business; they shall chuse their own Rector, at their first meeting, in every year, and shall be deemed the lawful successors of the first trustees, and invested with all the rights, powers, and capacities given to them, save only so far as the same shall be abridged by this act, nor shall they be restrained in their legislation, by the royal prerogative, or the laws of the kingdom of England; of the canons or the constitution of the English Church, as enjoined in the said charter. There shall be three Chancellors, in like manner appointed by joint ballot of both houses, from among the Judges of the High Court of Chancery, or of the General Court, to enter on that office immediately on such appointment, and to continue therein so long as they remain in either of the said courts; any two of whom may proceed to business; to them shall belong solely the power of removing the Professors, for breach or neglect of duty, immorality, severity, contumacy, or other good cause, and the judiciary powers in all disputes, which shall arise on the statutes of the College, being called on for that purpose by the Rector, or by the corporation of President and Professors, a copy of their sentence of deprivation, being delivered to the sheriff of the county wherein the College is, he shall forthwith cause the Professor deprived to be ousted of his chambers, and other freehold appertaining to the said College, and the remaining Professors to be reseized thereof, in like manner and form, and subject, on failure to the like fines by the said Chancellors, as in cases of writs of habere facias seisinam issued from Courts of Record. But no person shall be capable of being both visiter and Chancellor at the same time; nor shall any Professor be capable of being at the same time either visiter or Chancellor. Instead of the President and six Professors, licensed by the said charter, and established by the former visitors, there shall be eight Professors, one of whom shall also be appointed President, with an additional salary of one hundred pounds a year, before they enter on the execution of their office, they shall give assurance of fidelity to the commonwealth, before some justice of the Peace. These shall be deemed the lawful successors of the President and Professors appointed under the said charter, and shall have all their rights, powers and capabilities, not otherwise disposed of by this act; to them shall belong the ordinary government of the College, and administration of its revenues, taking the advice of the visiters on all matters of great concern. There shall, in like manner, be eight Professorships, to wit, one of moral philosophy, and the laws of nature and of nations, and of the fine arts; one of law and police; one of history, civil and ecclesiastical; one of mathematics; one of anatomy and medicine; one of natural philosophy and natural history; one of the ancient languages, oriental and northern; and one of modern languages. The said Professors shall likewise appoint, from time to time, a missionary, of approved veracity, to the several tribes of Indians, whose business shall be to investigate their laws, customs, religions, traditions, and more particularly their languages, constructing grammers thereof, as well as may be, and copious vocabularies, and, on oath to communicate, from time to time, to the said President and Professors the materials he collects, to be by them laid up and preserved in their library; for which trouble the said missionary shall be allowed a salary at the discretion of the visiters, out of the revenues of the College. And forasmuch as the revenue, arising from the duties on skins and furs, and those on liquors, with which the said College was endowed, by several acts of General Assembly, is subject to great fluctuations, from circumstances unforeseen, insomuch that no calculation of foresight can enable the said visiters or Professors to square thereto the expenditures of the said College, which being regular and permanent should depend on stable funds; Be it therefore enacted, that the revenue arising from the said duties, shall be henceforth transferred to the use of the public, to be applied towards supporting the contingent charges of government, and that, in lieu thereof, the said College shall be endowed with an impost of five pounds of tobacco, on every hogshead of tobacco, to be exported from this commonwealth, by land or by water, to be paid to the inspectors accounted for, on oath, to the said President and Professors on or before the 10th day of October, in every year, with an allowance of six per centum for their trouble; and if the said tobacco be not carried to any public ware-house, then the said impost shall be paid, collected and accounted for to the said President and Professors, by the same persons, at the same times, in and under the like manner, penalties and conditions, as prescribed by the laws, which shall be in force at the time, for collecting the duties imposed on exported tobacco, towards raising supplies of money for the public exigencies. And that this commonwealth may not be without so great an ornament, nor its youth such an help towards attaining astronomical science, as the mechanical representation, or model of the solar system, conceived and executed by that greatest of astronomers, David Ryttenhouse; Be it further enacted, that the visiters, first appointed under this act, and their successors, shall be authorized to engage the said David Ryttenhouse, on the part of this commonwealth, to make and erect in the said College of William and Mary, and for its use, one of the said models, to be called by the name of the Ryttenhouse, the cost and expence of making, transporting and erecting whereof shall, according to the agreement or allowance of the said visiters, be paid by the Treasurer of this commonwealth, on warrant from the Auditors.

A Bill for Establishing a Public Library

Section I. Be it enacted by the General Assembly, that on the first day of January, in every year, there shall be paid out of the treasury the sum of two thousand pounds, to be laid out in such books and maps as may be proper to be preserved in a public library, and in defraying the expences necessary for the care and preservation thereof; which library shall be established at the town of Richmond.

Sect. II. The two houses of Assembly shall appoint three persons of learning and attention to literary matters, to be visiters of the said library, and shall remove them, and fill any vacancies, from time to time, as they shall think fit; which visiters shall have power to receive the annual sums beforementioned, and therewith to procure such books and maps as aforesaid, and shall superintend the preservation thereof. Whensoever a keeper shall be found necessary they shall appoint such keeper, from time to time, at their will, on such annual salary (not exceeding one hundred pounds) as they shall think reasonable.

Sect. III. If during the time of war the importation of books and maps shall be hazardous, or if the rate of exchange between this commonwealth and any state from which such articles are wanted, shall from any cause be such that they cannot be imported to such advantage as may be hoped at a future day, the visiters shall place the annual sums, as they become due, in the public loan office, if any there be, for the benefit of interest, or otherwise shall suffer them to remain in the treasury until fit occasions shall occur of employing them.

Sect. IV. It shall not be lawful for the said keeper, or the visiters themselves, or any other person to remove any book or map out of the said library, unless it be for the necessary repair thereof; but the same be made useful by indulging the researches of the learned and curious, within the said library, without fee or reward, and under such rules for preserving them safe and in good order and condition as the visiters shall constitute.

Sect. V. The visiters shall annually settle their accounts with the Auditors and leave with them the vouchers for the expenditure of the monies put into their hands.

APPENDIX B

JEFFERSON'S LIBRARY CLASSIFICATION

In 1802 Jefferson prepared a catalogue for the Library of Congress, and his classification seems to have been used for four years. (Johnston— *History of the Library of Congress,* I, 36–37). When the library was burned and Congress bought his private library to replace it, he arranged the books in forty-four classes, and this grouping was followed for nearly a century (*Johnston,* I, 142–146). When he bought books for the University of Virginia in 1825 he classified them in nearly the same way (Patton—*Jefferson, Cabell, and the University of Virginia,* 263–267). All of these plans show only minor modifications of the classification of his second library reproduced here. It seems to have been written before 1785, and is taken from the manuscript in the possession of the Massachusetts Historical Society. Italics are used to indicate items written where something in the first draft had been erased. (For the classification of the Library of Congress, see *Johnston,* I, 146–147. The university library classification was published by *Patton,* 263–267, and in the *Alumni Bulletin of the University of Virginia,* November, 1895, 79–80).

BOOKS may be classed from the Faculties of the mind, which being

I Memory	II Reason	III Imagination
	are applied respectively to	
I History	II Philosophy	III Fine Arts"

				CHAP.
I. HISTORY	Civil	Civil proper	Antient — Antient hist.	1
			Modern — Foreign	2
			Modern — British	3
			Modern — American	4
		Ecclesiastical	Ecclesiastical	5
	Natural	Physics	at'l Ahilos'	6
			Agriculture	7
			Chemistry	8
			Surgery	9
			Medicine	10
		Nat'l Hist' prop.	Animals — Anatomy	11
			Animals — Zoology	12
			Vegetables — Botany	13
			Minerals — Mineralogy	14
		Occupations of man	Technical arts	15

					CHAP.

II. PHILOSOPHY

- **Moral**
  - Ethics .... { *Moral Philos. / Law Nature & Nations } — 16
  - Jurisprudence
    - Religions .... Religion — 17
    - Equity — 18
    - Municipal { Domestic
      - Common Law — 19
      - L. Merchant — 20
      - L. Maritime — 21
      - L. Ecclesiast'l — 22
    - Foreign
      - Foreign Law — 23
    - Oeconomical .... Politics — 24
    - Commerce — 25
- **Mathematical**
  - Pure .... Arithmetic — 26
    - Geometry — 27
  - Physico Mathematical .... { Mechanics / *Statics* / *Dynamics* / Pneumatics / *Phonics* / Optics } — 28
    - Astronomy — 29
    - Geography — 30

---

* In classing a small library one may throw under this head books which attempt what may be called the Natural history of the mind or an analysis of it's operations. The term and division of Metaphysics is rejected as meaning nothing or something beyond our reach, or what should be called by some other name.

				CHAP.
III. FINE ARTS	Gardening		Gardening	31
	Architecture		Architecture	32
	Sculpture		Sculpture	33
	Painting		Painting	34
	Music	Theoretical	Music Theory	35
		Practical	{ Music Vocal	36
			{ Music Instrumental	37
	Poetry	Narrative	{ Epic	38
			{ Romance	39
		Dramatic	{ Tragedy	40
			{ Comedy	41
			Pastorals	
			Odes	42
			Elegies	
			Dialogue	
		Didactic	{ Satire	
			{ Epigram	43
			{ Epistles	
	Oratory		{ Logic	
			{ Rhetoric	44
			Oration	
	Criticism		Criticism	45
	Authors who have written in various branches		*Polygraphical*	46

APPENDIX C

FIRST PLAN FOR THE UNIVERSITY OF VIRGINIA

(From Jefferson's letter to Dr. Joseph Priestley, written at Philadelphia, January 18, 1800. *Library Ed.*, X, 140–142).

We have in that State a College (William and Mary) just well enough endowed to draw out the miserable existence to which a miserable constitution has doomed it. It is moreover eccentric in its position, exposed to all bilious diseases as all the lower country is, and therefore abandoned by the public care, as that part of the country itself is in a considerable degree by its inhabitants. We wish to establish in the upper country, and more centrally for the State, an University on a plan so broad and liberal and *modern*, as to be worth patronizing with the public support, and be a temptation to the youth of other States to come and drink of the cup of knowledge and fraternize with us. The first step is to obtain a good plan; that is, a judicious selection of the sciences, and a practicable grouping of some of them together, and ramifying of others, so as to adapt the professorships to our uses and our means. In an institution meant chiefly for use, some branches of science, formerly esteemed, may be now omitted; so may others now valued in Europe, but useless to us for ages to come. As an example of the former, the Oriental learning, and of the latter, almost the whole of the institution proposed to Congress by the Secretary of War's report of the 5th instant. Now there is no one to whom this subject is so familiar as yourself. There is no one in the world who, equally with yourself, unites this full possession of the subject with such a knowledge of the state of our existence, as enables you to fit the garment to him who is to *pay* for it and to *wear* it. To you therefore we address our solicitations, and to lessen to you as much as possible the ambiguities of our object, I will venture even to sketch the sciences which seem useful and practicable for us, as they occur to me while holding my pen. Botany, chemistry, zoölogy, anatomy, surgery, medicine, natural philosophy, agriculture, mathematics, astronomy, geography, politics, commerce, history, ethics, law, arts, fine arts. This list is imperfect because I make it hastily, and because I am unequal to the subject. It is evident that some of these articles are too much for one professor and must therefore be ramified; others may be ascribed in groups to a single professor. This is the difficult part of the work, and requires a head perfectly knowing the extent of each branch, and the limits within which it may be circumscribed, so as to bring the whole within the powers of the fewest professors possible, and

215

consequently within the degree of expense practicable for us. We should propose that the professors follow no other calling, so that their whole time may be given to their academical functions; and we should propose to draw from Europe the first characters in science, by considerable temptations, which would not need to be repeated after the first set should have prepared fit successors and given reputation to the institution. From some splendid characters I have received offers most perfectly reasonable and practicable.

I do not propose to give you all this trouble merely of my own head, that would be arrogance. It has been the subject of consultation among the ablest and highest characters of our State, who only wait for a plan to make a joint and I hope a successful effort to get the thing carried into effect. They will receive your ideas with the greatest deference and thankfulness. We shall be here certainly for two months to come; but should you not have leisure to think of it before Congress adjourns, it will come safely to me afterwards by post, the nearest post office being Milton.

APPENDIX D

A COURSE OF READING FOR A STUDENT OF LAW

[The following course of legal study was drawn up by Jefferson about 1765 for Bernard Moore and revised by him in 1814 for the use of his grandson. It is substantially the course which he prescribed for Madison, Monroe, and others. It is here reproduced from Barnard's *Journal of Education*, XXVII, 545–547.]

Before you enter on the study of the law a sufficient groundwork must be laid. For this purpose an acquaintance with the Latin and French languages is absolutely necessary. The former you have; the latter must now be acquired. Mathematics and Natural Philosophy are so useful in the most familiar occurrences of life, and are so peculiarly engaging and delightful as would induce every one to wish an acquaintance with them. Besides this, the faculties of the mind, like the members of the body, are strengthened and improved by exercise. Mathematical reasonings and deductions are therefore a fine preparation for investigating the abstruse speculations of the law. In these and the analogous branches of science the following books are recommended:—

Mathematics.—Beyzout, Cours de Mathématiques—the best for a student ever published; Montucla or Bossut, Histoire des Mathématiques.
Astronomy.—Ferguson, and le Monnier or de Lalande.
Geography.—Pinkerton.
Nat. Philosophy.—Joyce's Scientific Dialogues; Martin's Philosophia Britannica, Muschenbroek's Cours de Physique.

This foundation being laid, you may enter regularly on the study of the law, taking with it such of its kindred sciences as will contribute to eminence in its attainment. The principal of these are Physics, Ethics, Religion, Natural Law, Belles Lettres, Criticism, Rhetoric, and Oratory. The carrying on several studies at a time is attended with advantage. Variety relieves the mind as well as the eye, palled with too long attention to a single object, but, with both, transitions from one object to another may be so frequent and transitory as to leave no impression. The mean is therefore to be steered, and a competent space of time allotted to each branch of study. Again, a great inequality is observable in the vigor of the mind at different periods of the day. Its powers at these periods should therefore be attended to, in marshaling the business of the day. For these reasons I should recommend the following distribution of your time:—

Till Eight o'clock in the morning, employ yourself in Physical Studies

Ethics, Religion, natural and sectarian, and Natural Law, reading the following books:—

Agriculture.—Dickson's Husbandry of the Ancients; Tull's Horse-hoeing Husbandry; Lord Kames' Gentleman Farmer; Young's Rural Economy; Hale's Body of Husbandry; De Serres's Théâtre d'Agriculture.

Chemistry.—Lavoisier, Conversations in Chemistry.

Anatomy.—John and James Bell's Anatomy.

Zoölogy.—Abrégé du Système de la nature de Linné par Gillbert; Manual d'Histoire Naturelle by Blumenbach, Buffon, including Montbeiliard and La Cepède; Wilson's American Ornithology.

Botany.—Barton's Elements of Botany; Turton's Linneus; Persoon's Synopsis Plantarum.

Ethics and Natural Religion.—Locke's Essay; Locke's Conduct of the Mind in the Search after Truth; Stewart's Philosophy of the Human Mind; Enfield's History of Philosophy; Condorcet, Progrès de l'Esprit Humain; Cicero de Officiis, Tusculanae, de Senectute, Somnia Scipionis; Senecae Philosophica; Hutchinson's Introduction to Moral Philosophy; Lord Kames' Natural Religion; Traité Elémentaire de Morale et Bonheur; La Sagesse de Charron.

Religion Sectarian.—Bible; New Testament, Commentaries on them by Middleton in his Works, and by Priestley in his Corruptions of Christianity and Early Opinions of Christ; The Sermons of Sterne, Massillon and Bourdaloue.

Natural Law.—Vattel, Droit des Gens; Rayneval, Institutions du Droit de la Nature et des Gens.

From Eight to Twelve read Law

The general course of this reading may be formed on the following grounds. Lord Coke has given us the first views of the whole body of law worthy now of being studied; for so much of the admirable work of Bracton is now obsolete that the students should turn to it occasionally only, when tracing the history of particular portions of the law. Coke's Institutes are a perfect digest of the law in his day. After this, new laws were added by the Legislature, and new developments of the old law by the judges, until they had become so voluminous as to require a new digest. This was ably executed by Matthew Bacon, although unfortunately under an alphabetical instead of analytical arrangement of matter. The same process of new laws and new decisions on the old laws going on, called at length for the same operation again, and produced the inimitable Commentaries of Blackstone. In the department of the Chancery, a similar progress has taken place. Lord Kames has given us the first digest of the principles of that branch of our jurisprudence, more valuable for the arrangement of matter than for its exact conformity with the English decisions. The reporters from the early times of that branch to that of the same Matthew Bacon are well digested, but alphabetically also in the abridgment of the cases in equity, the second volume of which is said to be done by him. This was followed by a number of able reporters, of which Fonblanque has given us a summary digest by commentaries on the text of the earlier work, ascribed to Ballow, entitled 'A Treatise on Equity.' The course of reading recommended then in these two branches of the law is the following:—

Common Law.—Coke's Institutes; Select Cases from the Subsequent Reporters to the time of Matthew Bacon; Bacon's Abridgment; Select Cases from the Subsequent Reporters to the Present Day; Select Tracts on Law, among which those of Baron Gilbert are all of the first merit; the Virginia Laws; Reports on them.

Chancery.—Lord Kames' Principles of Equity, 3rd edition; Select Cases from the Chancery Reporters to the time of Matthew Bacon; the Abridgment of Cases in Equity; Select Cases from the Subsequent Reporters to the Present Day; Fonblanque's Treatise of Equity.

Blackstone's Commentaries (Tucker's edition) as the best perfect digest of both branches of law.

In reading the Reporters, enter into a common-place book every case of value, condensed into the narrowest compass possible, which will admit of presenting distinctly the principles of the case. This operation is doubly useful, insomuch as it obliges the student to seek out the pith of the case, and habituates him to a condensation of thought, and to an acquisition of the most valuable of all talents, that of never using two words where one will do. It fixes the case, too, more indelibly in the mind.

From Twelve to One read Politics

Politics, General.—Locke on Government, Sidney on Government, Priestley's First Principles of Government, Review of Montesquieu's Spirit of Laws. De Lolme sur le constitution d'Angleterre; De Burgh's Political Disquisitions; Hatsell's Precedents of the House of Commons; Select Parliamentary Debates of England and Ireland; Chipman's Sketches of the Principles of Government; The Federalist.

Political Economy.—Say's Economie Politique; Malthus on the Principles of Population; De Tracy's work on Polit. Econ., now about to be printed, 1814.

In the Afternoon read History

History, Ancient.—The Greek and Latin Originals; Select histories from the Universal History; Gibbon's Decline of the Roman Empire; Histoire ancienne de Millot.

Modern.—Histoire moderne de Millot; Russel's History of Modern Europe; Robertson's Charles V.

English.—The original historians, to wit: The History of Edward 2nd, by E. F.; Haddington's Edward 4th; More's Richard 3rd; Lord Bacon's Henry 7th; Lord Herbert's Henry 8th; Goodwin's Henry 8th, Edward 6th, Mary; Camden's Elizabeth, James, Ludlow; Macaulay (Catharine); Fox; Belsham; Baxter's History of England; Hume republicanized and abridged; Robertson's History of Scotland.

American.—Robertson's History of America; Gordon's History of the Independence of the U. S.; Ramsay's History of the American Revolution; Burk's History of Virginia; Continuation of do., by Jones and Girardin, nearly ready for the press.

From Dark to Bedtime

Belles Lettres; Criticism; Rhetoric; Oratory, to wit:

Belles Lettres.—Read the best of the poets, epic, didactic, dramatic, pastoral, lyric, etc.; but among these, Shakspeare must be singled out by one who wishes to learn the full powers of the English language. Of him we must declare as Horace did of the Grecian models, 'Vos exemplaria Graeca nocturnâ versate manu, versate diurna.'

Criticism.—Lord Kames' Elements of Criticism; Tooke's Diversions of Purley. Of Biographical criticism, the Edinburgh Review furnishes the finest models extant.

Rhetoric.—Blair's Rhetoric; Sheridan on Elocution; Mason on Poetic and Prosaic Numbers.

Oratory.—This portion of time (borrowing some of the afternoon when the days are long and the nights short) is to be applied also to acquiring the art of writing and speaking correctly by the following exercises: Criticise the style of any book whatsoever, committing the criticism to writing. Translate into the different styles, to wit, the elevated, the middling, and the familiar. Orators and poets will furnish subjects of the first, historians of the second, and epistolary and comic writers of the third. Undertake at first, short compositions, as themes, letters, etc., paying great attention to the elegance and correctness of your language. Read the orations of Demosthenes and Cicero; analyze these orations, and examine the correctness of the disposition, language, figures, state of the cases, arguments, etc.; read good samples also of English eloquence. Some of these may be found in Small's American Speaker, and some in Carey's Criminal Recorder; in which last the defense of Eugene Aram is distinguished as a model of logic, condensation of matter and classical purity of style. Exercise yourself afterward in preparing orations on feigned cases. In this, observe rigorously the disposition of Blair into introduction, narration, etc. Adapt your language to the several parts of the orations, and suit your arguments to the audience before which it is supposed to be delivered. This is your last and most important exercise. No trouble should therefore be spared. If you have any person in your neighborhood engaged in the same study, take each of you different sides of the same cause, and prepare pleadings according to the custom of the bar, where the plaintiff opens, the defendant answers, and the plaintiff replies. It will further be of great service to pronounce your oration (having before you only short notes to assist your memory) in the presence of some person who may be considered as your judge.

Note.—Under each of the preceding heads, the books are to be read in the order in which they are named. These by no means constitute the whole of what might be usefully read in each of these branches of science. The mass of excellent works going more into detail is great indeed. But those here noted will enable the student to select for himself such others of detail as may suit his particular views and dispositions. They will give him a respectable, an useful and satisfactory degree of knowledge in these branches, and will themselves form a valuable and sufficient library for a lawyer who is at the same time a lover of science.

APPENDIX E

LETTER TO PETER CARR
(*Cabell*, 384 ff.)

Monticello, September 7th, 1814.

Dear Sir,—On the subject of the academy or college proposed to be established in our neighborhood, I promised the trustees that I would prepare for them a plan, adapted, in the first instance, to our slender funds, but susceptible of being enlarged, either by their own growth or by accession from other quarters.

I have long entertained the hope that this, our native State, would take up the subject of education, and make an establishment, either with or without incorporation into that of William & Mary where every branch of science, deemed useful at this day and in our country, should be taught in its highest degree. With this view, I have lost no occasion of making myself acquainted with the organization of the best seminaries in other countries, and with the opinions of the most enlightened individuals, on the subject of the sciences worthy of a place in such an institution. In order to prepare what I have promised our trustees, I have lately revised these several plans with attention; and I am struck with the diversity of arrangement observable in them—no two being alike. Yet, I have no doubt that these several arrangements have been the subject of mature reflection, by wise and learned men, who, contemplating local circumstances, have adapted them to the condition of the section of society for which they have been framed. I am strengthened in this conclusion by an examination of each separately, and a conviction that no one of them, if adopted without change, would be suited to the circumstances and pursuit of our country. The example they have set, then, is authority for us to select from their different institutions the materials which are good for us, and, with them, to erect a structure, whose arrangement shall correspond with our own social condition, and shall admit of enlargement in proportion to the encouragement it may merit and receive. As I may not be able to attend the meetings of the trustees, I will make you the depository of my ideas on the subject, which may be corrected, as you proceed, by the better view of others, and adapted, from time to time, to the prospects which open upon us, and which cannot be specifically foreseen and provided for.

In the first place, we must ascertain with precision the object of our institution, by taking a survey of the general field of science, and marking out the portion we mean to occupy at first, and the ultimate extension of our views beyond that, should we be enabled to render it, in the end, as comprehensive as we would wish.

1. ELEMENTARY SCHOOLS

It is highly interesting to our country, and it is the duty of its functionaries, to provide that every citizen in it should receive an education proportioned to the condition and pursuits of his life. The mass of our citizens may be divided into two classes—the laboring and the learned. The laboring will need the first grade of education to qualify them for their pursuits and duties; the learned will need it as a foundation for further acquirements. A plan was formerly proposed to the Legislature of this State for laying off every county into hundreds or wards of five or six miles square, within each of which should be a school for the education of the children of the ward, wherein they should receive three years' instruction gratis, in reading, writing, arithmetic, as far as fractions, the roots and ratios, and geography. The Legislature, at one time, tried an ineffectual expedient for introducing this plan, which having failed, it is hoped they will some day resume it in a more promising form.

2. GENERAL SCHOOLS

At the discharging of the pupils from the elementary schools, the two classes separate—those destined for labor will engage in the business of agriculture, or enter into apprenticeships to such handicraft art as may be their choice; their companions, destined to the pursuits of science, will proceed to the college, which will consist, 1st, of General Schools; and 2d, of Professional Schools. The General Schools will constitute the second grade of education.

The learned class may still be subdivided into two sections; 1, Those who are destined for learned professions, as a means of livelihood; and 2, The wealthy, who, possessing independent fortunes, may aspire to share in conducting the affairs of the nation, or to live with usefulness and respect in the private ranks of life. Both of these sections will require instruction in all the higher branches of science; the wealthy to qualify them for either public or private life; the professional section will need those branches, especially, which are the basis of their future profession, and a general knowledge, of the others, as auxiliary to that, and necessary to their standing and associating with the scientific class. All the branches, then, of useful science, ought to be taught in the general schools, to a competent extent, in the first instance. These sciences may be arranged into three departments, not rigorously scientific, indeed, but sufficiently so for our purposes. These are, I. Language; II, Mathematics; III, Philosophy.

I. *Language.* In the first department, I would arrange a distinct science. 1. Languages and History, ancient and modern; 2. Grammar; 3. Belles Lettres; 4. Rhetoric and Oratory; 5. A school for the deaf, dumb and blind.

History is here associated with languages, not as a kindred subject, but on a principle of economy, because both may be attained by the same course of reading, if books are selected with that view.

II. *Mathematics.* In the department of mathematics, I should give place distinctly, 1. Mathematics pure; 2. Physico-Mathematics; 3. Physics; 4. Chemistry; 5. Natural History, *to wit*: Mineralogy; 6. Botany; and 7. Zoölogy; 8. Anatomy; 9. the Theory of Medicine.

III. *Philosophy.* In the Philosophical department, I should distinguish, 1. Ideology; 2. Ethics; 3. the Law of Nature and Nations; 4. Government; 5. Political Economy.

But, some of these terms being used by different writers, in different degrees of extension, I shall define exactly what I mean to comprehend in each of them.

I. 3. Within the term of Belles Lettres I include poetry and composition generally, and Criticism.

II. 1. I consider pure Mathematics as the science of, I. Numbers, and II. Measure in the abstract; that of numbers comprehending Arithmetic, Algebra and Fluxions; that of Measure (under the general appellation of Geometry) comprehending Trigonometry, plane and spherical, conic sections, and transcendental curves.

II. 2. Physico-Mathematics treat of physical subjects by the aid of mathematical calculation. These are Mechanics, Statics, Hydrostatics, Hydraulics, Hydrodynamics, Navigation, Astronomy, Geography, Optics, Pneumatics, Acoustics.

II. 3. Physics, or Natural Philosophy, (not entering the limits of Chemistry,) treat of natural substances, their properties, mutual relations and action. They particularly examine the subjects of motion, attraction, action, magnetism, electricity, galvanism, light, meteorology, with an &c. not easily enumerated. These definitions and specifications render immaterial the question whether I use the Generic terms in the exact degree of comprehension in which others use them; to be understood is all that is necessary to the present object.

3. PROFESSIONAL SCHOOLS

At the close of this course the students separate; the wealthy retiring, with sufficient stock of knowledge, to improve themselves to any degree which their views may lead them, and the professional section to the professional schools, constituting the third grade of education, and teaching the particular sciences which the individuals of this section mean to pursue, with more minuteness and detail than was within the scope of the general schools for the second grade of instruction. In these professional schools each science is to be taught in the highest degree it has yet attained. They are to be the

1st *Department,* the fine arts, to wit: Civil Architecture, Gardening, Painting, Sculpture, and the theory of Music; the

2d *Department,* Architecture, Military and Naval; Projectiles, Rural

Economy, (comprehending Agriculture, Horticulture and Veterinary,) Technical Philosophy, the practice of Medicine, Materia Medica, Pharmacy and Surgery. In the

3d *Department,* Theology and Ecclesiastical History; Law, Municipal and Foreign.

To these professional schools will come those who separated at the close of their first elementary course, to wit:

The lawyer to the school of law.

The ecclesiastic to that of theology and ecclesiastical history.

The physician to those of the practice of medicine, materia medica, pharmacy and surgery.

The military man to that of military and naval architecture and projectiles.

The agricultor to that of rural economy.

The gentleman, the architect, the pleasure gardener, painter and musician to the school of fine arts.

And to that of technical philosophy will come the mariner, carpenter, ship-wright, plough-wright, wheel-wright, mill-wright, pump maker, clock maker, machinist, optician, metallurgist, founder, cutler, druggist, brewer, vintner, distiller, dyer, painter, bleecher, soap maker, tanner, powder maker, salt maker, glass maker, to learn as much as shall be necessary to pursue their art understandingly, of the sciences of geometry, mechanics, statics, hydrostatics, hydraulics, hydrodynamics, navigation, astronomy, geography, optics, pneumatics, acoustics, physics, chemistry, natural history, botany, mineralogy and pharmacy.

The school of technical philosophy will differ essentially in its functions from the other professional schools. The others are instituted to ramify and dilate the particular sciences taught in the schools of the second grade on a general scale only. The technical school is to abridge those which were taught there too much *in extenso* for the limited wants of the artificer or practical man. These artificers must be grouped together, according to the particular branch of science in which they need elementary and practical instruction; and a special lecture or lectures must be prepared for each group—and these lectures should be given in the evening, so as not to interrupt the labors of the day. The school, particularly, should be maintained wholly at the public expense, on the same principles with that of the ward schools. Through the whole of the collegiate course, at the hours of recreation on certain days, all the students should be taught the manual exercise, military evolutions and manoeuvres, should be under a standing organization as a military corps, and with proper officers to train and command them.

A tabular statement of this distribution of the sciences will place the system of instruction more particularly in view:

1st or Elementary Grade in the Ward Schools.

Reading, Writing, Arithmetic, Geography.

2d or General Grade

1. Language and History, ancient and modern.
2. Mathematics, viz:
   Mathematics pure,
   Physico-Mathematics,
   Physics,
   Chemistry,
   Anatomy,
   Theory of Medicine,
   Zoölogy.
   Botany and Mineralogy.
3. Philosophy, viz:
   Ideology, and Ethics,
   Law of Nature and Nations,
   Government,
   Political Economy.

3d or Professional Grades.

Theology and Ecclesiastical History.
Law, Municipal and Foreign.
Practice of Medicine.
Materia Medica and Pharmacy.
Surgery.
Architecture, Military and Naval, and Projectiles.
Technical Philosophy.
Rural Economy.
Fine Arts.

On this survey of the field of science, I recur to the question, what portion of it we mark out for the occupation of our institution? With the first grade of education we shall have nothing to do. The sciences of the second grade are our first object; and, to adapt them to our slender beginnings, we must separate them into groups, comprehending many sciences each, and greatly more, in the first instance, than ought to be imposed on, or can be competently conducted by a single professor permanently. They must be subdivided from time to time, as our means increase, until each professor shall have no more under his care than he can attend to with advantage to his pupils and ease to himself. In the further advance of our resources, the professional schools must be introduced, and professorships established for them also. For the present, we may group the sciences into professorships, as follows, subject, however, to be changed, according to the qualifications of the persons we may be able to engage.

I. *Professorship.*

Language and History, ancient and modern.
Belles Lettres, Rhetoric and Oratory.

II. *Professorship.*

Mathematics pure—Physico-Mathematics.
Physics—Anatomy—Medicine—Theory.

III. *Professorship*

Chemistry—Zoölogy—Botany—Mineralogy.

IV. *Professorship.*

Philosophy.

The organization of the branch of the institution which respects its government, police and economy, depending on principles which have no affinity with those of its institution, may be the subject of separate and subsequent consideration.

With this tribute of duty to the Board of Trustees, accept the assurance of my great esteem and consideration.

TH: JEFFERSON.

APPENDIX F

JEFFERSON'S PLAN FOR THE ESTABLISHMENT
OF WARD SCHOOLS

(From a manuscript letter to Cabell, February 2, 1816,
L. C., Vol. 206; See *Cabell*, 53–56.)

My letter of the 24th ult. conveyed to you the grounds of the two articles
objected to in the College bill. your last presents one of them in a new
point of view, that of the commencement of the Ward schools as likely to
render the law unpopular to the county. it must be a very inconsiderate
and rough process of execution that would do this. my idea of the mode of
carrying it into execution would be this. Declare the counties *ipso facto*
divided into wards, for the present by the boundaries of the militia captaincies; somebody attend the ordinary muster of each company, having first
desired the Captain to call together a full one. there explain the object of
the law to the people of the company, put to their vote whether they will
have a school established, and the most central and convenient place for it;
get them to meet & build a log school house, have a roll taken of the children
who would attend it, and of those of them able to pay. these would probably
be sufficient to support a common teacher, instructing gratis the few unable
to pay. if there should be a deficiency, it would require too trifling a contribution from the county to be complained of; and especially as the whole
county would participate, where necessary, in the same resource. should
the company, by it's vote, decide that it would have no school, let them
remain without one. the advantages of this proceeding would be, that it
would become the duty of the aldermen elected by the county to take an
active part in pressing the introduction of schools and to look out for tutors.
if however it is intended that the State government shall take this business
into it's own hands, and provide schools for every county, then by all means
strike out this provision of our bill. I would never wish that it should be
placed on a worse footing than the rest of the state. but if it is believed
that these elementary schools will be better managed by the Governor &
council, the Commissioners of the literary fund, or any other general authority of the government, than by the parents within each ward, it is a belief
against all experience. try the principle one step further, and amend the
bill so as to commit to the Governor & Council the management of all our
farms, our mills, & merchants' stores. No, my friend, the way to have good
and safe government, is not to trust it all to one; but to divide it among the
many, distributing to every one exactly the functions he is competent to.
let the National government be entrusted with the defence of the nation
and it's foreign & federal relations; the State governments with the civil

rights, laws, police & administration of what concerns the State generally; the Counties with the local concerns of the counties; and each Ward direct the interests within itself. it is by dividing and subdividing these republics from the great National one down thro' all its subordinations, until it ends in the administration of every man's farm and affairs by himself; by placing under every one what his own eye may superintend, that all will be done for the best. what has destroyed liberty and the rights of man in every government which has ever existed under the sun? the generalizing & concentrating all cares and powers into one body, no matter whether of the autocrats of Russia or France, or the aristocrats of a Venetian Senate. and I do believe that if the Almighty has not decreed that Man shall never be free, (and it is blasphemy to believe it,) that the secret will be found to be in the making himself the depository of the powers respecting himself, so far as he is competent to them, and delegating only what is beyond his competence by a synthetical process, to higher & higher orders of functionaries, so as to trust fewer and fewer powers, in proportion as the trustees become more and more oligarchical. the elementary republics of the wards, the county republics, the State republics and the republic of the Union, would form a gradation of authorities, standing each on the basis of law, holding every one it's delegated share of powers, and constituting truly a system of fundamental balances and checks for the government. where every man is a sharer in the direction of his ward republic, or of some of the higher ones, and feels that he is a participator in the government of affairs not merely at an election, one day in the year, but every day; when there shall not be a man in the state who will not be a member of some one of it's councils, great or small, he will let the heart be torn out of his body, sooner than his power be wrested from him by a Caesar or a Bonaparte. how powerfully did we feel the energy of this organization in the case of the Embargo? I felt the foundations of the Government shaken under my feet by the New England townships. there was not an individual in their states whose body was not thrown, with all it's momentum, into action, and, altho' the whole of the other states were known to be in favor of the measure, yet the organization of this little selfish minority enabled it to overrule the Union. what could the unwieldy counties of the middle, the South and the West do? call a county meeting, and the drunken loungers at and about the Courthouses would have collected, the distances being too great for the good people and the industrious generally to attend. the character of those who really met would have been the measure of the weight they would have had in the scale of public opinion. as Cato then concluded every speech with the words *'Carthago delenda est'*, so do I every opinion with the injunction 'divide the counties into wards'. begin them only for a single purpose; they will soon shew for what others they are best instruments. God bless you, and all our rulers, and give them the wisdom, as I am sure they have the will, to fortify us against the degeneracy of our government, and the concentration of all it's powers in the hands of the one, the few, the well-born, or but the many.

TH: JEFFERSON.

APPENDIX G

LETTER TO GOVERNOR WILSON C. NICHOLAS *

This letter has a distinctive interest as it comes, in point of time, midway between the letter to Peter Carr and the Bill for Establishing a System of Public Education.

—Library Ed., XIV, 446–455.

Monticello, April 2, 1816.

Dear Sir,—Your favor of March 22d has been received. It finds me more laboriously and imperiously engaged than almost on any occasion of my life. It is not, therefore, in my power to take into immediate consideration all the subjects it proposes; they cover a broad surface, and will require some development. They respect,

I.   Defence.
II. Education.
III. The map of the State.
   This last will comprise,
   1. An astronomical survey, to wit, Longitudes and Latitudes.
   2. A geometrical survey of the external boundaries, the mountains and rivers.
   3. A topographical survey of the counties.
   4. A mineralogical survey.

Each of these heads requires distinct consideration. I will take them up one at a time, and communicate my ideas as leisure will permit.

*   *   *   *   *   *   *   *   *   *

II. Education.—The President and Directors of the literary fund are desired to digest and report a system of public education, comprehending the establishment of an university, additional colleges or academies, and

* Wilson Cary Nicholas was a lifelong friend of Jefferson. He had supported the educational plan of 1779. It was to him that Jefferson confided the proposal of the Geneva faculty to remove to America in 1794, asking him to ascertain the feeling of the Virginia legislature toward that project. His discouraging reply, early in 1795, put an end to that plan. As president of the directors of the Literary Fund he asked of Jefferson the suggestions contained in this letter and included them in part in the report to the next legislature. During the legislative session of 1817–18 and those of succeeding years he was a constant adviser to Cabell and a friend of the University. He had declined to be a trustee of Albemarle Academy in 1814 but was one of the twelve chief contributors to Central College in 1818. His financial disasters in 1819 brought upon Jefferson, his indorser, a debt of $20,000, which he carried until his death by paying an annual interest of $1200. This burden upon his already depleted fortune led to his plan to dispose of Monticello by a lottery and made necessary its sale by his executor, but his friendship for Colonel Nicholas remained unimpaired until his death.

schools. The resolution does not define the portions of science to be taught in each of these institutions, but the first and last admit no doubt. The university must be intended for all useful sciences, and the schools mean elementary ones, for the instruction of the people, answering to our present English schools; the middle term, colleges or academies, may be more conjectural. But we must understand from it some middle grade of education. Now, when we advert that the ancient classical languages are considered as the foundation preparatory for all the sciences; that we have always had schools scattered over the country for teaching these languages, which often were the ultimate term of education; that these languages are entered on at the age of nine or ten years, at which age parents would be unwilling to send their children from every part of the State to a central and distant university, and when we observe that the resolution supposes there are to be a plurality of them, we may well conclude that the Greek and Latin are the objects of these colleges. It is probable, also, that the legislature might have under their eye the bill for the more general diffusion of knowledge, printed in the revised code of 1779, which proposed these three grades of institution, to wit: an university, district colleges, or grammar schools, and county or ward schools. I think, therefore, we may say that the object of these colleges is the classical languages, and that they are intended as the portico of entry to the university. As to their numbers, I know no better rule to be assumed than to place one within a day's ride of every man's door, in consideration of the infancy of the pledges he has at it. This would require one for every eighty miles square.

Supposing this the object of the colleges, the report will have to present the plan of an university, analyzing the sciences, selecting those which are useful, grouping them into professorships, commensurate each with the time and faculties of one man, and prescribing the regimen and all other necessary details. On this subject I can offer nothing new. A letter of mine to Peter Carr, which was published during the last session of Assembly, is a digest of all the information I possess on the subject, from which the Board will judge whether they can extract anything useful; the professorship of the classical languages being of course to be expunged, as more effectually supplied by the establishment of the colleges.

As the buildings to be erected will also enter into their report, I would strongly recommend to their consideration, instead of one immense building, to have a small one for every professorship, arranged at proper distances around a square, or rather three sides of a square, to admit extension, connected by a piazza, so that they may go dry from one school to another. This village form is preferable to a single great building for many reasons, particularly on account of fire, health, economy, peace and quiet. Such a plan had been approved in the case of the Albemarle College, which was the subject of the letter above mentioned; and should the idea be approved by the Board, more may be said hereafter on the opportunity these small buildings will afford, of exhibiting models in architecture of the purest forms of antiquity, furnishing to the student examples of the precepts he will be taught in that art.

The Elementary or Ward schools are the last branch of this subject; on this, too, my ideas have been long deposited in the bill for the diffusion of knowledge, before mentioned, and time and reflection have continued to strengthen them as to the general principle, that of a division of every county into wards, with a school in each ward. The details of the bill will of course be varied as the difference of present circumstances from those of that day will require.

My partiality for that division is not founded in views of education solely, but infinitely more as the means of a better administration of our government, and the eternal preservation of its republican principles. The example of this most admirable of all human contrivances in government, is to be seen in our Eastern States; and its powerful effect in the order and economy of their internal affairs, and the momentum it gives them as a nation, is the single circumstance which distinguishes them so remarkably from every other national association. In a letter to Mr. Adams a few years ago, I had occasion to explain to him the structure of our scheme of education as proposed in the bill for the diffusion of knowledge, and the views of this particular section of it; and in another lately to Mr. Cabell, on the occasion of the bill for the Albemarle College, I also took a view of the political effects of the proposed division into wards, which being more easily copied than thrown into new form here, I take the liberty of enclosing extracts from them. Should the Board of Directors approve of the plan, and make ward divisions the substratum of their elementary schools, their report may furnish a happy occasion of introducing them, leaving all their other uses to be adapted from time to time hereafter as occasions shall occur.

APPENDIX H

JEFFERSON'S SCHOOL BILL OF 1817

On September 9, 1817, Jefferson sent to Cabell the draft of a bill for the establishment of elementary schools. Soon afterward he prepared bills for district colleges and a university. These he combined into *A Bill for Establishing A System of Public Education* which he sent to Cabell on October 24. The first thirteen sections of this bill are almost identical with the earlier bill. It is here reproduced from *Cabell* (413 ff.), but with the restoration of passages omitted from that version by J. C. Cabell (see *Cabell*, 96–98). A confused blending of the two bills appears in the *Library Edition*, XVII, 418 ff.

A Bill for Establishing A System of Public Education

1. For establishing schools at which the children of all the citizens of this Commonwealth may receive a primary grade of education at the common expense.

Be it enacted by the General Assembly of Virginia as follows: At the first session of the Superior Court in every county within this Commonwealth, next ensuing the passage of this act, the Judge thereof shall appoint three discreet and well-informed persons, residents of the county, and not being ministers of the gospel, to serve as Visitors of the primary schools in the said county, of which appointment the sheriff shall, within fifteen days thereafter, deliver a certificate, under the hand of the clerk of said court, to each of the persons so appointed.

2. The said Visitors shall meet at the court-house of their county on the first county court day after they shall have received notice of their appointment, and afterwards at such times and places as they, or any two of them, with reasonable notice to the third, shall have agreed; and shall proceed to divide their county into wards, by metes and bounds so designated as to comprehend each, about the number of militia sufficient for a company, and so also as not to divide, and place in different wards the lands of any one person held in one body; which division into wards, shall, within six months from the date of their appointment, be completely designated, published, and reported, by their metes and bounds, to the office of the clerk of the Superior Court, there to be recorded, subject, however, to such alterations, from time to time afterwards, as changes of circumstances shall, in the opinion of the said Visitors or their successors, with the approbation of the said court, render expedient.

3. The said original division into wards being made, the Visitors shall appoint days for the first meeting of every ward, at such place as they shall name within the same, of which appointment notice shall be given at least two weeks before the day of meeting, by advertisement at some place within the ward, requiring every free, white male citizen, of full age, resident within the ward, to meet at the place, and by the hour of twelve of the day so appointed, at which meeting some one of the Visitors shall also attend, and a majority of the said warders being in attendance, the Visitor present shall propose to them to decide by a majority of their votes,— The location of a school-house for the ward, and a dwelling-house for the teacher, (the owner of the ground consenting thereto). The size and structure of the said houses; and Whether the same shall be built by the joint labor of the warders, or by their pecuniary contributions; and also to elect by a plurality of their votes a warden, resident, who shall direct and superintend the said buildings, and be charged with their future care.

4. And if they decide that the said buildings shall be erected by the joint labor of the warders, then all persons within the said ward liable to work in the highways, shall attend at the order of the said warden, and, under his direction, shall labor thereon until completed, under the same penalties as provided by law to enforce labor on the highways. And if they decide on erection by pecuniary contributions, the residents and owners of property within the ward shall contribute towards the cost, each in proportion to the taxes they last paid to the State for their persons and for the same property: of which the sheriff shall furnish a statement to the warden, who, according to the ratio of that statement, shall apportion and assess the quota of contribution for each, and be authorized to demand, receive, and apply the same to the purposes of the contribution, and to render account thereof, as in all other his pecuniary transactions for the school, to the Visitors; and on failure of payment by any contributor, the sheriff, on the order of the warden, shall collect and render the same under like powers and regulations as provided for the collection of the public taxes. And in every case it shall be the duty of the warden to have the buildings completed within six months from the date of his election.

5. It shall be the duty of the said Visitors to seek and to employ for every ward, whenever the number and ages of its children require it, a person of good moral character, qualified to teach reading, writing, numeral arithmetic and the elements of geography, whose subsistence shall be furnished by the residents and proprietors of the ward, either in money or in kind, at the choice of each contributor, and in the ratio of their public taxes, to be apportioned and levied as on the failures before provided for. The teacher shall also have the use of the house and accommodations provided for him, and shall moreover receive annually such standing wages as the Visitors shall have determined to be proportioned on the residents and proprietors of the ward, and to be paid, levied and applied as before provided in other cases of pecuniary contribution.

6. At this school shall be received and instructed gratis, every infant in the ward of competent age who has not already had three years' schooling.

And it is declared and enacted, that no person unborn or under the age of twelve years at the passing of this act, and who is compos mentis, shall, after the age of fifteen years, be a citizen of this commonwealth until he or she can read readily in some tongue, native or acquired.

7. To keep up a constant succession of Visitors, the judge of the Superior Court of every county shall at his first session in every bissextile year, appoint Visitors as before characterized, either the same or others, at his discretion. And in case of the death or resignation of any Visitor during the term of his appointment, or of his removal from the county, or by the said judge for good cause, moral or physical, he shall appoint another to serve until the next bissextile appointment. Which Visitors shall have their first meeting at their court-house on the county court day next ensuing their appointment, and afterwards at such times and places as themselves or any two of them with reasonable notice to the third shall agree. But the election of wardens shall be annually, at the first meeting of the ward after the month of March, until which election the warden last elected shall continue in office.

8. All ward meetings shall be at their schoolhouse, and on a failure of the meeting of a majority of the warders on the call of a Visitor, or of their warden, such Visitor or warden may call another meeting.

9. At all times when repairs or alterations of the buildings before provided for shall be wanting, it shall be the duty of the warden or of a Visitor, to call a ward meeting and to take the same measures towards such repairs or alterations as are herein before authorized for the original buildings.

10. When, on the application of any warden, authorized thereto by the vote of his ward, the judge of the Superior Court shall be of opinion that the contributors of any particular ward are disproportionably and oppressively overburdened with an unusual number of children of non-contributors of their ward, he may direct an order to the county court to assess in their next county levy the whole or such part of the extra burden as he shall think excessive and unreasonable, to be paid to the warden for its proper use, to which order the said county court is required to conform.

11. The said teachers shall, in all things relating to the education and government of their pupils, be under the direction and control of the Visitors; but no religious reading, instruction or exercise, shall be prescribed or practiced inconsistent with the tenets of any religious sect or denomination.

12. Some one of the Visitors, once in every year at least, shall visit the school, shall inquire into the proceedings and practices thereat: shall examine the progress of the pupils, and give to those who excel in reading, in writing, in arithmetic, or in geography, such honorary marks and testimonies of approbation, as may encourage and excite to industry and emulation.

13. All decisions and proceedings of the Visitors relative to the original designation of wards at any time before the buildings are begun, or changes of wards at any time after, to the quantum of subsistence, or wages allowed to the teacher, and to the rules prescribed to him for the education and government of his pupils, shall be subject to be controlled and corrected

by the judge of the Superior Court of the county, on the complaint of any individual aggrieved or interested.

And for the establishment of colleges whereat the youth of the commonwealth may, within convenient distances from their homes, receive a higher grade of education.

14. Be it further enacted as follows: The several counties of this commonwealth shall be distributed into nine collegiate districts, whereof one shall be composed of the counties of Accomac, Northampton, Northumberland, Lancaster, Richmond, Westmoreland, Middlesex, Essex, Matthews, Gloucester, King and Queen, King William, Elizabeth City, Warwick, York, James City, New Kent, and Charles City; one other of the counties of Princess Anne, Norfolk borough, Nansemond, Isle of Wight, Southampton, Surry, Prince George, Sussex, and Greeneville; one other of the counties of Fairfax, Loudon, King George, Stafford, Prince William, Fauquier, Culpeper, Madison, Caroline, and Spotsylvania; one other of the counties of Hanover, City of Richmond, Goochland, Louisa, Fluvanna, Powhatan, Cumberland, Buckingham, Orange, Albemarle, Nelson, Amherst, Augusta, and Rockbridge; one other of the counties of Chesterfield, town of Petersburg, Dinwiddie, Brunswick, Amelia, Nottoway, Lunenburg, Mecklenburg, Prince Edward, Charlotte, and Halifax; one other of the counties of Campbell, Pittsylvania, Bedford, Franklin, Henry, Patrick, Botetourt, and Montgomery; one other of the counties of Frederick, Jefferson, Berkeley, Hampshire, Shenandoah, Hardy, Rockingham, and Pendleton; one other of the counties of Monongalia, Brooke, Ohio, Randolph, Harrison, Wood, and Mason; and one other of the counties of Bath, Greenbriar, Kanawha, Cabell, Giles, Monroe, Tazewell, Wythe, Grayson, Washington, Russell, and Lee.

15. Within three months after the passing of this act, the president and directors of the literary fund, who shall henceforth be called the Board of Public Instruction, shall appoint one fit person in every county, in each of the districts, who, with those appointed in the other counties in the same district, shall compose the Board of Visitors for the college of that district; and shall, within four months after passing this act, cause notice to be given to each individual so appointed, prescribing to them a day, within one month thereafter, and a place within their district, for their first meeting, with supplementary instructions for procuring a meeting subsequently, in the event of failure at the time first appointed.

16. The said Visitors, or so many of them as, being a majority, shall attend, shall appoint a rector, of their own body, who shall preside at their meetings, and a secretary to record and preserve their proceedings; and shall proceed to consider of the site for a college most convenient for their district, having regard to the extent, population and other circumstances, and within the term of six months from the passing of this act shall report the same to the Board of Public Instruction, with the reasons on which each site is preferred; and if any minority of two or more members prefer any other place, the same shall be reported, with the reasons for and against the same.

17. Within seven months after the passing of this act the said Board of

Public Instruction shall determine on such of the sites reported as they shall think most eligible for the college of each district, shall notify the same to the said Visitors, and shall charge them with the office of obtaining from the proprietor with his consent, the proper grounds for the building, and its appurtenances, either by donation or purchase; or if his consent, on reasonable terms, cannot be obtained, the clerk of the county, wherein the site is, shall, on their request, issue and direct to the sheriff of the same county a writ of ad quod damnum, to ascertain by a jury the value of the grounds selected, and to fix their extent by metes and bounds, so, however, as not to include the dwelling house, or buildings appurtenant, the curtilege, gardens or orchards of the owner; which writ shall be executed according to the ordinary forms prescribed by law in such cases; and shall be returned to the same clerk to be recorded: Provided, that in no case, either of purchase or valuation by a jury, more grounds be located than of the value of $500; which grounds, if by donation or purchase, by the deed of the owner, or if by valuation of a jury, shall, by their inquest, become vested in the said Board of Public Instruction, as trustees for the commonwealth, and for the uses and purposes of a college of instruction.

18. On each of the sites so located shall be erected one or more substantial buildings—the walls of which shall be of brick or stone, with two school rooms, and four rooms for the accommodation of the professors, and with sixteen dormitories in or adjacent to the same, each sufficient for two pupils, and in which no more than two shall be permitted to lodge, with a fire place in each, and the whole in a comfortable and decent style, suitable to their purpose.

19. The plan of the said buildings, and their appurtenances, shall be furnished or approved by the said Board of Public Instruction, and that of the dormitories shall be such as may conveniently receive additions from time to time. The Visitors shall have all the powers which are necessary and proper for carrying them into execution, and shall proceed in their execution accordingly. Provided, that in no case shall the whole cost of the said buildings and appurtenances of any one college exceed the sum of $7,500.

20. The college of the district first in this act described, to wit: of Accomac, etc., shall be called the Wythe College, or the College of the District of Wythe; that of the second description, to wit: Princess Anne, etc., shall be called the ....; that of the third description, to wit: Fairfax, etc., shall be called the ....; that of the fourth description, to wit: Hanover, etc., shall be called the ....; that of the fifth description, to wit: Chesterfield, etc., shall be called the ....; that of the sixth description, to wit: Campbell, etc., shall be called ....; that of the seventh description, to wit: Frederick, etc., shall be called the ....; that of the eighth description, to wit: Monongalia, etc., shall be called the ....; and that of the ninth description, to wit: Bath, etc., shall be called the ....

21. In the said colleges shall be taught the Greek, Latin, French, Spanish, Italian and German Languages, English grammar, geography, ancient and

modern, the higher branches of numerical arithmetic, the mensuration of land, the use of the globes, and the ordinary elements of navigation.

22. To each of the said colleges shall be appointed two professors, the one for teaching Greek, Latin, and such other branches of learning, before described, as he may be qualified to teach, and the other for the remaining branches thereof, who shall each be allowed the use of the apartments provided for him, and a standing salary of $500 yearly, to be drawn from the literary fund, with such tuition fee from each pupil as the Visitors shall establish.

23. The said Visitors shall be charged with the preservation and repair of the buildings, the care of the ground and appurtenances for which, and other necessary purposes, they may employ a steward and competent laborers; they shall have power to appoint and remove the professors, to prescribe their duties, and the course of education to be pursued; they shall establish rules for the government and discipline of the pupils, for their sustenance and board, if boarded in the college, and for their accommodations, and the charges to which they shall be subject for the same, as well as the rent for the dormitories they occupy. They may draw from the literary fund such moneys as are hereby charged on it for their institution. And, in general, they shall direct and do all matters and things which, not being inconsistent with the laws of the land, to them shall seem most expedient for promoting the purposes of the said institution; which several functions may be exercised by them in the form of by-laws, resolutions, orders, instructions, or otherwise, as they shall deem proper.

24. The rents of the dormitories, the profits of boarding the pupils, donations and other occasional resources shall constitute the fund, and shall be at their disposal for the necessary purposes of the said institution, and not otherwise provided for; and they shall have authority to draw on the said Board of Public Instruction for the purchase or valuation money of the site of their college, for the cost of the buildings and improvements authorized by law, and for the standing salaries of the professors herein allowed—for the administration of all which they may appoint a bursar.

25. They shall have two stated meetings in the year, at their college, on the first Mondays of April and October, and occasional meetings at the same place, and at such other times, as they shall appoint; giving due notice thereof to every individual of their board.

26. A majority of them shall constitute a quorum for business, and on the death or resignation of a member or on his removal by the Board of Public Instruction, or out of the county from which he was appointed, the said Board shall appoint a successor, resident in the same county.

27. The Visitors of every collegiate district shall be a body politic and corporate, to be called the Visitors of the College, by name, for which they are appointed, with capacity to plead, or be impleaded, in all courts of justice, and in all cases interesting to their college, which may be subject of legal cognizance and jurisdiction, which pleas shall not abate by the determination of their office of all or any of them, but shall stand revived in the name of their successors; and they shall be capable in law, and in trust for their

college, of receiving subscriptions and donations, real and personal, as well from bodies corporate, or persons associated, as from private individuals.

28. Some member, or members, of the Board of Visitors, to be nominated by the said Board, or such other persons as they shall nominate, shall, once in every year, at least, visit the college of their district, enquire into the proceedings and practices thereat, examine the progress of the pupils, and give to those who excel in any branch of learning prescribed for the college, such honorary marks and testimonies of approbation as may encourage or excite to industry and emulation.

29. The decisions and proceedings of the said Board of Visitors shall be subject to control and correction by the Board of Public Instruction, either on the complaint of any individual, aggrieved or interested, or on the proper motion of the said Board.

30. On every 29th day of February, or, if that be Sunday, then on the next or earliest day thereafter, on which a meeting can be effected, the Board of Public Instruction shall be in session, and shall appoint, in every county of each district, a Visitor, resident therein, either the same before appointed, or another, at their discretion, to serve until the next ensuing 29th day of February, duly and timely notifying to them their appointment, and prescribing a day for their first meeting at the college of their district, after which, their stated meetings shall be at their college, on the first Mondays of April and October, annually; and their occasional meetings at the same place, and at such times as themselves shall appoint, due notice thereof being given to every member of their board.

And for establishing in a central and healthy part of the State an University wherein all branches of useful science may be taught, Be it enacted as follows:

31. Within the limits of the county of .... there shall be established an University, to be called the University of Virginia; and so soon as may be after the passage of this act the board of public instruction shall appoint eight fit persons to constitute the Board of Visitors for the said University; and shall forthwith give notice to each individual so appointed, prescribing to them a day for their first meeting at the Court-house of the said county, with supplementary instructions for procuring a meeting subsequently in the event of failure at the time first appointed.

And for establishing in a central and healthy part of the State an University wherein all the branches of useful science may be taught, Be it further enacted as follows:

31. Whensoever the Visitors of the Central College in Albemarle, authorized thereto by the consent in writing of the subscribers of the major part of the amount subscribed to that institution, shall convey or cause to be conveyed to the Board of Public Instruction, for the use of this Commonwealth, all the lands, buildings, property and rights of the said College, in possession, in interest, or in action, (save only so much as may discharge their engagements then existing,) the same shall be thereupon vested in this Commonwealth, and shall be

appropriated to the institution of an University to be called the University of Virginia, which shall be established on the said lands. The said Board of Public Instruction shall thereupon forthwith appoint eight fit persons who shall compose the Board of Visitors for the government of the said University, notifying thereof the persons so appointed, and prescribing to them a day for their first meeting at Charlottesville, with supplementary instructions for procuring a meeting subsequently, in the event of failure at the time first appointed.*

32. The said Visitors, or so many of them as, being a majority, shall attend, shall appoint a Rector of their own body, who shall preside at their meetings, and a Secretary to record and preserve their proceedings, and shall proceed to enquire into and select the most elegible site for the University, and to obtain from the proprietor, with his consent, the proper grounds for the buildings and appurtenances, either by donation or purchase, or, if his consent on reasonable terms cannot be obtained, the clerk of the county shall, on their request, issue and direct to the sheriff of the county a writ of ad quod damnum to ascertain by a jury the value of the grounds selected, and to fix their extent by metes and bounds, so however as not to include the dwelling house or buildings appurtenant, the curtilage, gardens or orchards of the owner; which writ shall be executed according to the ordinary forms prescribed by the laws in such cases, and shall be returned to the same clerk to be recorded: *Provided,* That in no case, either of purchase or valuation by a jury, shall more grounds be located than of the value of $2,000: which grounds, if by donation or purchase, shall, by the deed of the owner, or if by valuation of a jury, shall, by their inquest, become vested in the Board of Public Instruction aforesaid, as trustees for the Commonwealth, for the uses and purposes of an University.

32. The said Visitors, or so many of them as, being a majority, shall attend, shall appoint a Rector of their own body to preside at their meetings, and a Secretary to record and preserve their proceedings, and shall proceed to examine into the state of the property conveyed as aforesaid, shall make an inventory of the same, specifying the items whereof it consists, shall notice the buildings and other improvements already made, and those which are in progress, shall take measures for their completion, shall consider what others may be necessary in addition, and of the best plan for effecting the same, with estimates of the probable cost, and shall make report of the whole to the said Board of Public Instruction, which is authorized to approve, negative or modify any of the measures so proposed by the said Visitors.

33. A plan of the buildings and appurtenances necessary and proper for an University being furnished or approved by the Board of Public Instruction, in which that of the dormitories shall be such as may conveniently

* The alternative paragraphs were to be substituted if there seemed a fair prospect of having Central College adopted as the University.

admit additions from time to time, the Visitors shall have all the powers which shall be necessary and proper for carrying them into execution, and shall proceed in their execution accordingly.

33. The said measures being approved or modified, the Visitors shall have all the powers relative thereto which shall be necessary or proper for carrying them into execution, and shall proceed in their execution accordingly.

34. In the said University shall be taught history and geography, ancient and modern; natural philosophy, agriculture, chemistry and the theories of medicine; anatomy, zoölogy, botany, mineralogy and geology; mathematics, pure and mixed; military and naval science; ideology, ethics, the law of nature and of nations; law, municipal and foreign; the science of civil government and political economy; languages, rhetoric, belles lettres, and the fine arts generally; which branches of science shall be so distributed and under so many professorships, not exceeding ten, as the Visitors shall think most proper.

35. Each professor shall be allowed the use of the apartments and accommodations provided for him, and such standing salary, not exceeding $1,000 yearly, as the Visitors shall think proper, to be drawn from the literary fund, with such tuition fees from the students as the Visitors shall establish.

36. The said Visitors shall be charged with the erection, preservation and repair of the buildings, the care of the grounds and appurtenances, and of the interests of the University generally; they shall have power to appoint a bursar, employ a steward and all other necessary agents; to appoint and remove professors; to prescribe their duties, and the course of education to be pursued; to establish rules for the government and discipline of the students, for their subsistence, board and accommodations, if boarded by the University, and the charges to which they shall be subject for the same, as well as for the dormitories they occupy; to provide and control the duties and proceedings of all officers, servants and others, with respect to the buildings, land, appurtenances, and other property and interests of the University; to draw from the literary fund such moneys as are hereby charged on it for this institution; and in general to direct and do all matters and things which, not being inconsistent with the laws of the land, to them shall seem most expedient for promoting the purposes of the said institution; which several functions may be exercised by them in the form of by-laws, rules, resolutions, orders, instructions, or otherwise, as they shall deem proper.

37. They shall have two stated meetings in the year, to wit: on the first Mondays in April and October, and occasional meetings at such other times as they shall appoint, due notice thereof being given to every individual of their Board, which meetings shall be held at the said University; and on the death or resignation of a member, or on his removal by the Board of Public Instruction, or change of habitation to a greater than his former distance from the University, the said Board shall appoint a successor.

38. The Visitors of the said University shall be a body politic and cor-

porate under the style and title of the Visitors of the University of Virginia with capacity to plead or be impleaded in all courts of justice, and in all cases interesting to their college, [*sic*] which may be the subjects of legal cognizance and jurisdiction, which pleas shall not abate by the determination of their office, but shall stand revived in the name of their successors; and they shall be capable in law, and in trust for their college, of receiving subscriptions and donations, real and personal, as well from bodies corporate or persons associated, as from private individuals.

39. Some member or members of the Board of Visitors, to be nominated by the said Board, or such other person as they shall nominate, shall, once in every year at least, visit the said University, enquire into the proceedings and practices thereat, examine the progress of the students, and give to those who excel in any branch of science there taught such honorary marks and testimonies of approbation as may encourage and excite to industry and emulation.

40. All decisions and proceedings of the Visitors shall be subject to control and direction by the Board of Public Instruction, either on the complaint of any individual aggrieved or interested, or on the proper motion of the said Board.

41. On every 29th day of February, or, if that be Sunday, then on the next or earliest day thereafter on which a meeting can be effected, the said Board of Public Instruction shall be in session, and shall appoint Visitors for the said University either the same or others, at their discretion, to serve until the 29th day of February next ensuing, duly and timely notifying to them their appointment, and prescribing a day for their first meeting at the University, after which their stated meetings shall be on the first Mondays of April and October annually, and their occasional meetings at the same place, and at such times as themselves shall appoint, due notice thereof being given to every member of their Board.

NOTE.—If the Central College be adopted for the University, the following section may be added: "Provided, that nothing in this act contained shall suspend the proceedings of the Visitors of the said Central College of Albemarle; but, for the purpose of expediting the objects of the said institution, they shall be authorized, under the control of the Board of Public Instruction, to continue the exercise of their functions until the first meeting of the Visitors of the University."

And to avail the commonwealth of those talents and virtues which nature has sown as liberally among the poor as rich, and which are lost to their country by the want of means for their cultivation. Be it further enacted as follows:

42. On the 29th day of February, or, if that be Sunday, then on the next day, the Visitors of the ward-schools in every county shall meet at the courthouse of their county, and after the most diligent and impartial observation and enquiry of the boys who have been three years at the ward-schools, and whose parents are too poor to give them a collegiate education, shall select from among them some one of the most promising and sound understanding, who shall be sent to the first meeting of the Visitors of their col-

legiate district, with such proofs as the case requires and admits, for the examination and information of that Board; who, from among the candidates so offered from the several counties of their district, shall select two of the most sound and promising understanding, who shall be admitted to their college, and there be maintained and educated five years at the public expense, under such rules and limitations as the Board of Public Instruction shall prescribe; and at the end of the said five years the said Collegiate Visitors shall select that one of the two who shall, on their most diligent and impartial enquiry and best information, be adjudged by them to be of the most sound and promising understanding and character, and most improved by their course of education, who shall be sent on immediately thereafter to the University, there to be maintained and educated in such branches of the sciences taught there as are most proper to qualify him for the calling to which his parents or guardians may destine him; and to continue at the said University three years at the public expense, under such rules and limitations as the Board of Public Instruction shall prescribe. And the expenses of the persons so to be publicly maintained and educated at the colleges and University shall be drawn by their respective Visitors from the literary fund.

APPENDIX I

THE COST OF WARD SCHOOLS

On December 29, 1817, Cabell had written to Jefferson: "Judge Roane, Col. Nicholas, and most of the persons with whom I have conferred, disapprove of your plan of an assessment on the wards; they think neither the people nor their representatives would agree to that mode of taxation; they advise that the money should come out of the literary fund, but that your mode of administration should be kept up." (*Cabell*, 93–4). The following letter to Cabell is Jefferson's answer (*Cabell*, 102–106).

Monticello, January 14, 1818.

Dear Sir,—When, on the 6th inst., I was answering yours of December 29, I was so overwhelmed with letters to be answered, that I could not take time to notice the objection stated, that it was apprehended that neither the people nor their representatives would agree to the plan of assessment on the wards for the expenses of the ward schools. I suppose that by this is meant the "pecuniary expense of wages to the tutor;" for, as to what the people are to do, or to contribute in kind, every one who knows the situation of our people in the country, knows it will not be felt. The building of the log-houses will employ the laborers of the ward three or four days in every twenty years. The contributions for subsistence, if averaged on the families, would be eight or nine pounds of pork, and half a bushel of corn, for a family of middling circumstances; not more than two days' subsistence of the family and its stock; and less in proportion as it could spare less. There is not a family in the country so poor as to feel this contribution. It must then be the assessment of the pecuniary contribution which is thought so formidable an addition to the property tax we now pay to the State, that neither the people nor their representatives would agree to. Now let us look this objection in the face, and bring it to the unerring test of figures; premising that this pecuniary tax is to be of $150 on a ward.

Not possessing the documents which would give me the numbers to be quoted, correctly to an unit, I shall use round numbers, so near the truth, that, with the further advantage of facilitating our calculations as we go along, they will make no sensible error in the result. I will proceed therefore on the following postulates, and on the ground that there are in the whole State one hundred counties and cities.

	In the whole State	In every co'ty on an average
The free white inhabitants of all ages and sexes, at the last census were	600,000	6,000
The number of militia was somewhere about .	80,000	800
The number of captain's companies, of 67 each, would be about	1,200	12
Free white inhabitants for every militia company, 600,000 ÷ 1,200	500	500
The tax on property paid to the State is nearly	500,000	5,000

Let us then proceed, on these data, to compare the expense of the proposed, and of the existing system of primary schools. I have always supposed that the wards should be so laid off as to comprehend the number of inhabitants necessary to furnish a captain's company of militia. This is before stated at 500 persons of all ages and sexes. From the tables of mortality (Buffon's) we find that where there are 500 persons of all ages and sexes, there will always be 14 in their 10th year, 13 and a fraction in their 11th, and 13 in their 12th year; so that the children of these three years (which are those that ought to be devoted to the elementary schools,) will be a constant number of 40; about enough to occupy one $150 on 67 heads of families (if levied equally) would be $2 24 on each. teacher constantly. His wages of $150, partitioned on these 40, make their teaching cost $3¾ a piece, annually. If we reckon as many heads of families in a ward as there are militia (as I think we may, the unmarried militia men balancing in numbers, the married and unmarried exempts,) At the same time the property tax on the ward being $5,000÷12, or $416, and that again subdivided on 67 heads of families (if it were levied equally) would be $6 20 on a family of middling circumstances, the tax which it now pays to the State. So that to $6 20, the present State tax, the school tax would add $2 24, which is about 36 cents to the dollar, or one-third to the present property tax; and to the whole State would be $150 x 1,200 wards, equal to $180,000 of tax added to the present $500,000.

Now let us see what the present primary schools cost us, on the supposition that all the children of 10, 11, and 12 years old are, as they ought to be at school; and, if they are not, so much the worse is the system; for they will be untaught, and their ignorance and vices will, in future life, cost us much dearer in their consequences, than it would have done, in their correction, by a good education.

I am here at a loss to say what is now paid to our English elementary schools, generally through the State. In my own neighborhood, those who formerly received from 20s. to 30s. a scholar, now have from 20 to 30 dollars; and having no other information to go on, I must use my own numbers: the result of which, however, will be easily corrected, and accommodated to the average price through the State, when ascertained;

and will yet, I am persuaded, leave abundance of difference between the two systems.

Taking a medium of $25, the 40 pupils in each ward, now cost $1,000 a year, instead of $150, or $15 on a family, instead of $2 24: and the 1,200 wards cost to the whole State $1,200,000 of tax, in addition to the present $500,000, instead of $180,000 only; producing a difference of $1,020,000 in favor of the ward system, more than doubling the present tax, instead of adding one-third only, and should the price of tuition, which I have adopted from that in my own neighborhood, be much above the average through the State, yet no probable correction will bring the two systems near a level.

But take into consideration, also, the important difference, that the $1,200,000 are now paid by the people, as a poll tax, the poor having as many children as the rich, and paying the whole tuition money themselves; whereas, on the proposed ward-levies the poor man would pay in proportion to his hut and peculium only, while the rich would pay on their palaces and principalities. It cannot, then, be that the "people" will not agree to have their tuition tax lightened by levies on the ward, rather than on themselves; and as I little believe that their "representatives" will disagree to it; for even the rich will pay less than they now do. The portion of the $180,000, which, on the ward system, they will pay for the education of the poor, as well as of their own children, will not be as much as they now pay for their own alone.

And will the wealthy individual have no retribution? and what will this be? 1. The peopling his neighborhood with honest, useful, and enlightened citizens, understanding their own rights, and firm in their perpetuation. 2. When his own descendants become poor, which they generally do within three generations, (no law of primogeniture now perpetuating wealth in the same families,) their children will be educated by the then rich; and the little advance he now makes to poverty, while rich himself, will be repaid by the then rich, to his descendants when become poor, and thus give them a chance of rising again. This is a solid consideration, and should go home to the bosom of every parent. This will be seed sown in fertile ground. It is a provision for his family looking to distant times, and far in duration beyond that he has now in hand for them. Let every man count backwards in his own family, and see how many generations he can go, before he comes to the ancestor who made the fortune he now holds. Most will be stopped at the first generation, many at the second, few will reach the third, and not one in the State go beyond the fifth.

I know that there is much prejudice, even among the body of the people, against the expense and even the practicability of a sufficient establishment of elementary schools, but I think it proceeds from vague ideas on a subject they have never brought to the test of facts and figures; but our representatives will fathom its depth, and the people could and would do the same, if the facts and considerations belonging to the subject were presented to their minds, and their subsequent as certainly as their previous approbation, would be secured.

But if the whole expense of the elementary schools, wages, subsistence, and buildings, are to come from the literary fund, and if we are to wait until that fund should be accumulated to the requisite amount, we may justly fear that some one unlucky Legislature will intervene within the time, change the whole appropriation to the lightening of taxes, and leave us where we now are.

There is, however, an intermediate measure which might bring the two plans together. If the literary fund be of one and a half million of dollars, take the half million for the colleges and university, it will establish them meagrely, and make a deposit of the remaining million. Its interest of $60,000 will $50 to each ward, towards the teacher's wages, and reduce that tax to 24 instead of 36 cents to the dollar; and as the literary fund continues to accumulate, give one-third of the increase to the colleges and university, and two-thirds to the ward-schools. The increasing interest of this last portion will be continually lessening the school tax, until it will extinguish it altogether; the subsistence and buildings remaining always to be furnished by the ward in kind.

A system of general instruction, which shall reach every description of our citizens, from the richest to the poorest, as it was the earliest, so will it be the latest, of all the public concerns in which I shall permit myself to take an interest. Nor am I tenacious of the form in which it shall be introduced. Be that what it may, our descendants will be as wise as we are, and will know how to amend and amend it until it shall suit their circumstances. Give it to us, then, in any shape, and receive for the inestimable boon the thanks of the young and the blessings of the old, who are past all other services but prayers for the prosperity of their country and blessings to those who promote it.

TH: JEFFERSON.

Joseph C. Cabell, Esq.

APPENDIX J

REPORT OF THE COMMISSIONERS APPOINTED TO FIX THE SITE OF THE UNIVERSITY OF VIRGINIA, &c.

(*Cabell*, 432 ff.)*

The Commissioners for the University of Virginia, having met, as by law required, at the tavern, in Rockfish Gap, on the Blue Ridge, on the first day of August, of this present year, 1818; and having formed a board, proceeded on that day to the discharge of the duties assigned to them by the act of the Legislature, entitled "An act, appropriating part of the revenue of the literary fund, and for other purposes;" and having continued their proceedings by adjournment, from day to day, to Tuesday, the 4th day of August, have agreed to a report on the several matters with which they were charged, which report they now respectfully address and submit to the Legislature of the State.

The first duty enjoined on them, was to enquire and report a site, in some convenient and proper part of the State, for an university, to be called the "University of Virginia." In this enquiry, they supposed that the governing considerations should be the healthiness of the site, the fertility of the neighboring country, and its centrality to the white population of the whole State. For, although the act authorized and required them to receive any voluntary contributions, whether conditional or absolute, which might be offered through them to the President and Directors of the Literary Fund, for the benefit of the University, yet they did not consider this as establishing an auction, or as pledging the location to the highest bidder.

Three places were proposed, to wit: Lexington, in the county of Rockbridge, Staunton, in the county of Augusta, and the Central College, in the county of Albemarle. Each of these was unexceptionable as to healthiness and fertility. It was the degree of centrality to the white population of the State which alone then constituted the important point of comparison between these places; and the Board, after full enquiry, and impartial and mature consideration, are of opinion, that the central point of the white population of the State is nearer to the Central College than to either Lexington or Staunton, by great and important differences; and all other circumstances of the place in general being favorable to it, as a position for an university, they do report the Central College, in Albemarle, to be a convenient and proper part of the State for the University of Virginia.

* This report was written by Jefferson before the meeting and was adopted by the commissioners with only minor changes.

2. The Board having thus agreed on a proper site for the University, to be reported to the Legislature, proceed to the second of the duties assigned to them—that of proposing a plan for its buildings—and they are of opinion that it should consist of distinct houses or pavilions, arranged at proper distances on each side of a lawn of a proper breadth, and of indefinite extent, in one direction, at least; in each of which should be a lecturing room, with from two to four apartments, for the accommodation of a professor and his family; that these pavilions should be united by a range of dormitories, sufficient each for the accommodation of two students only, this provision being deemed advantageous to morals, to order, and to uninterrupted study; and that a passage of some kind, under cover from the weather, should give a communication along the whole range. It is supposed that such pavilions, on an average of the larger and smaller, will cost each about $5,000; each dormitory about $350, and hotels of a single room, for a refectory, and two rooms for the tenant, necessary for dieting the students, will cost about $3500 each. The number of these pavilions will depend on the number of professors, and that of the dormitories and hotels on the number of students to be lodged and dieted. The advantages of this plan are: greater security against fire and infection; tranquillity and comfort to the professors and their families thus insulated; retirement to the students; and the admission of enlargement to any degree to which the institution may extend in future times. It is supposed probable, that a building of somewhat more size in the middle of the grounds may be called for in time, in which may be rooms for religious worship, under such impartial regulations as the Visitors shall prescribe, for public examinations, for a library, for the schools of music, drawing, and other associated purposes.

3, 4. In proceeding to the third and fourth duties prescribed by the Legislature, of reporting "the branches of learning, which should be taught in the University, and the number and description of the professorships they will require," the Commissioners were first to consider at what point it was understood that university education should commence? Certainly not with the alphabet, for reasons of expediency and impracticability, as well from the obvious sense of the Legislature, who, in the same act, make other provision for the primary instruction of the poor children, expecting, doubtless, that in other cases it would be provided by the parent, or become, perhaps, subject of future and further attention of the Legislature. The objects of this primary education determine its character and limits. These objects would be,

To give to every citizen the information he needs for the transaction of his own business;

To enable him to calculate for himself, and to express and preserve his ideas, his contracts and accounts, in writing;

To improve, by reading, his morals and faculties;

To understand his duties to his neighbors and country, and to discharge with competence the functions confided to him by either;

To know his rights; to exercise with order and justice those he retains;

to choose with discretion the fiduciary of those he delegates; and to notice their conduct with diligence, with candor, and judgment;

And, in general, to observe with intelligence and faithfulness all the social relations under which he shall be placed.

To instruct the mass of our citizens in these, their rights, interests and duties, as men and citizens, being then the objects of education in the primary schools, whether private or public, in them should be taught reading, writing and numerical arithmetic, the elements of mensuration (useful in so many callings,) and the outlines of geography and history. And this brings us to the point at which are to commence the higher branches of education, of which the Legislature require the development; those, for example, which are,

To form the statesmen, legislators and judges, on whom public prosperity and individual happiness are so much to depend;

To expound the principles and structure of government, the laws which regulate the intercourse of nations, those formed municipally for our own government, and a sound spirit of legislation, which, banishing all arbitrary and unnecessary restraint on individual action, shall leave us free to do whatever does not violate the equal rights of another;

To harmonize and promote the interests of agriculture, manufactures and commerce, and by well informed views of political economy to give a free scope to the public industry;

To develop the reasoning faculties of our youth, enlarge their minds, cultivate their morals, and instill into them the precepts of virtue and order;

To enlighten them with mathematical and physical sciences, which advance the arts, and administer to the health, the subsistence, and comforts of human life;

And, generally, to form them to habits of reflection and correct action, rendering them examples of virtue to others, and of happiness within themselves.

These are the objects of that higher grade of education, the benefits and blessings of which the Legislature now propose to provide for the good and ornament of their country, the gratification and happiness of their fellow-citizens, of the parent especially, and his progeny, on which all his affections are concentrated.

In entering on this field, the Commissioners are aware that they have to encounter much difference of opinion as to the extent which it is expedient that this institution should occupy. Some good men, and even of respectable information, consider the learned sciences as useless acquirements; some think that they do not better the condition of man; and others that education, like private and individual concerns, should be left to private individual effort; not reflecting that an establishment embracing all the sciences which may be useful and even necessary in the various vocations of life, with the buildings and apparatus belonging to each, are far beyond the reach of individual means, and must either derive existence from public patronage, or not exist at all. This would leave us, then, without those callings which depend on education, or send us to other countries to seek the instruction they require. But the Commissioners are happy in considering the statute under which they are assembled as proof that the Legislature is far from the abandonment of objects so interesting. They are sensible that the advantages of well-directed education, moral, political and economical, are truly above all estimate. Education generates habits of application, of order, and the love of virtue; and controls, by the force of habit, any innate obliquities in our moral organization. We should be far, too, from the discouraging persuasion that man is fixed, by the law of his nature, at a given point; that his improvement is a chimera, and the hope delusive of rendering ourselves wiser, happier or better than our forefathers were. As well might it be urged that the wild and uncultivated tree, hitherto yielding sour and bitter fruit only, can never be made to yield better; yet we know that the grafting art implants a new tree on the savage stock, producing what is most estimable both in kind and degree. Education, in like manner, engrafts a new man on the native stock, and improves what in his nature was vicious and perverse into qualities of virtue and social worth. And it cannot be but that each generation succeeding to the knowledge acquired by all those who preceded it, adding to it their own acquisitions and discoveries, and handing the mass down for successive and constant accumulation, must advance the knowledge and well-being of mankind, not *infinitely*, as some have said, but *indefinitely*, and to a term which no one can fix and foresee. Indeed, we need look back half a century, to times which many now living remember well, and see the wonderful advances in the sciences and arts which have been made within that period. Some of these have rendered the elements themselves subservient to the purposes of man, have harnessed them to the yoke of his labors, and effected the great blessings of moderating his own, of accomplishing what was beyond his feeble force, and extending the comforts of life to a much enlarged circle, to those who had before known its necessaries only. That these are not the vain dreams of sanguine hope, we have before our eyes real and living examples. What, but education, has advanced us beyond the condition of our indigenous neighbors? And what chains them to their present state of barbarism and wretchedness, but a bigotted veneration for the supposed superlative wisdom of their fathers, and the preposterous idea that they are to look backward for better things, and not forward, longing, as it should seem, to return to the days of eating acorns and roots, rather than indulge in the degeneracies of civilization? And how much more encouraging to the achievements of science and improvement is this, than the desponding view that the condition of man cannot be ameliorated, that what has been must ever be, and that to secure ourselves where we are, we must tread with awful reverence in the footsteps of our fathers. This doctrine is the genuine fruit of the alliance between Church and State; the tenants of which, finding themselves but too well in their present condition, oppose all advances which might unmask their usurpations, and monopolies of honors, wealth, and power, and fear every change, as endangering the comforts they now hold. Nor must we omit to mention, among the benefits of education, the incalculable advantage of training up able counsellors to administer the affairs of our country in all its departments, legislative, executive and judiciary, and to bear their proper share in the councils of our national government; nothing more than education advancing the prosperity, the power, and the happiness of a nation.

Encouraged, therefore, by the sentiments of the Legislature, manifested in this statute, we present the following tabular statements of the branches of learning which we think should be taught in the University, forming them into groups, each of which are within the powers of a single professor:

    I. Languages, ancient:

          Latin,
          Greek,
          Hebrew.

    II. Languages, modern:

          French,
          Spanish,
          Italian,
          German,
          Anglo-Saxon.

    III. Mathematics, pure:

          Algebra,
          Fluxions,
          Geometry, Elementary,
                        Transcendental.
          Architecture, Military,
                        Naval.

    IV. Physico-Mathematics:

          Mechanics,
          Statics,
          Dynamics,
          Pneumatics,
          Acoustics,
          Optics,
          Astronomy,
          Geography.

    V. Physics, or Natural Philosophy:

          Chemistry,
          Mineralogy.

    VI. Botany,
          Zoölogy.

VII. Anatomy,
  Medicine.

VIII. Government,
  Political Economy,
  Law of Nature and Nations,
  History, being interwoven with Politics and Law.

IX. Law, municipal.

X. Ideology,
  General Grammar,
  Ethics,
  Rhetoric,
  Belles Lettres, and the fine arts.

Some of the terms used in this table being subject to a difference of acceptation, it is proper to define the meaning and comprehension intended to be given them here:

Geometry, Elementary, is that of straight lines and of the circle.
  Transcendental, is that of all other curves; it includes, of course, *Projectiles,* a leading branch of the military art.
Military Architecture includes Fortification, another branch of that art.
Statics respect matter generally, in a state of rest, and include Hydrostatics, or the laws of fluids particularly, at rest or in equilibrio.
Dynamics, used as a general term, include Dynamics proper, or the laws of *solids* in motion; and Hydrodynamics, or Hydraulics, those of *fluids* in motion.
Pneumatics teach the theory of air, its weight, motion, condensation, rarefaction, &c.
Acoustics, or Phonics, the theory of sound.
Optics, the laws of light and vision.
Physics, or Physiology, in a general sense, mean the doctrine of the physical objects of our senses.
Chemistry is meant, with its other usual branches, to comprehend the theory of agriculture.
Mineralogy, in addition to its peculiar subjects, is here understood to embrace what is real in geology.
Ideology is the doctrine of thought.
General Grammar explains the construction of language.

Some articles in this distribution of sciences will need observation. A professor is proposed for ancient languages, the Latin, Greek, and Hebrew, particularly; but these languages being the foundation common to all the sciences, it is difficult to foresee what may be the extent of this school. At the same time, no greater obstruction to industrious study could be proposed than the presence, the intrusions and the noisy turbulence of a multitude of small boys; and if they are to be placed here for the rudiments of the languages, they may be so numerous that its character and value as an University will be merged in those of a Grammar school. It is, therefore, greatly to be wished, that preliminary schools, either on private or public establishment, could be distributed in districts through the State, as preparatory to the entrance of students into the University. The tender age at which this part of education commences, generally about the tenth year, would weigh heavily with parents in sending their sons to a school so distant as the central establishment would be from most of them. Districts of such extent as that every parent should be within a day's journey of his son at school, would be desirable in cases of sickness, and convenient for supplying their ordinary wants, and might be made to lessen sensibly the expense of this part of their education. And where a sparse population would not, within such a compass, furnish subjects sufficient to maintain a school, a competent enlargement of district must, of necessity, there be submitted to. At these district schools or colleges, boys should be rendered able to read the easier authors, Latin and Greek. This would be useful and sufficient for many not intended for an University education. At these, too, might be taught English grammar, the higher branches of numerical arithmetic, the geometry of straight lines and of the circle, the elements of navigation, and geography to a sufficient degree, and thus afford to greater numbers the means of being qualified for the various vocations of life, needing more instruction than merely menial or praedial labor, and the same advantages to youths whose education may have been neglected until too late to lay a foundation in the learned languages. These institutions, intermediate between the primary schools and University, might then be the passage of entrance for youths into the University, where their classical learning might be critically completed, by a study of the authors of highest degree; and it is at this stage only that they should be received at the University. Giving then a portion of their time to a finished knowledge of the Latin and Greek, the rest might be appropriated to the modern languages, or to the commencement of the course of science for which they should be destined. This would generally be about the fifteenth year of their age, when they might go with more safety and contentment to that distance from their parents. Until this preparatory provision shall be made, either the University will be overwhelmed with the grammar school, or a separate establishment, under one or more ushers, for its lower classes, will be advisable, at a mile or two distant from the general one; where, too, may be exercised the stricter government necessary for young boys, but unsuitable for youths arrived at years of discretion.

The considerations which have governed the specification of languages to be taught by the professor of modern languages were, that the French is the language of general intercourse among nations, and as a depository of human science, is unsurpassed by any other language, living or dead; that the Spanish is highly interesting to us, as the language spoken by so great a portion of the inhabitants of our continents, with whom we shall probably have great intercourse ere long, and is that also in which is written the greater part of the earlier history of America. The Italian abounds with works of very superior order, valuable for their matter, and still more distinguished as models of the finest taste in style and composition. And the German now stands in a line with that of the most learned nations in richness of erudition and advance in the sciences. It is too of common descent with the language of our own country, a branch of the same original Gothic stock, and furnishes valuable illustrations for us. But in this point of view, the Anglo-Saxon is of peculiar value. We have placed it among the modern languages, because it is in fact that which we speak, in the earliest form in which we have knowledge of it. It has been undergoing, with time, those gradual changes which all languages, ancient and modern, have experienced; and even now needs only to be printed in the modern character and orthography to be intelligible, in a considerable degree, to an English reader. It has this value, too, above the Greek and Latin, that while it gives the radix of the mass of our language, they explain its innovations only. Obvious proofs of this have been presented to the modern reader in the disquisitions of Horn Tooke; and Fortescue Aland has well explained the great instruction which may be derived from it to a full understanding of our ancient common law, on which, as a stock, our whole system of law is engrafted. It will form the first link in the chain of an historical review of our language through all its successive changes to the present day, will constitute the foundation of that critical instruction in it which ought to be found in a seminary of general learning, and thus reward amply the few weeks of attention which would alone be requisite for its attainment; a language already fraught with all the eminent science of our parent country, the future vehicle of whatever we may ourselves achieve, and destined to occupy so much space on the globe, claims distinguished attention in American education.

Medicine, where fully taught, is usually subdivided into several professorships, but this cannot well be without the accessory of an hospital, where the student can have the benefit of attending clinical lectures, and of assisting at operations of surgery. With this accessory, the seat of our University is not yet prepared, either by its population or by the numbers of poor who would leave their own houses, and accept of the charities of an hospital. For the present, therefore, we propose but a single professor for both medicine and anatomy. By him the medical science may be taught, with a history and explanations of all its successive theories from Hippocrates to the present day; and anatomy may be fully treated. Vegetable pharmacy will make a part of the botanical course, and mineral and chemical pharmacy of those of mineralogy and chemistry. This degree of medical information is such as the mass of scientific students would wish to possess, as enabling them in their course through life, to estimate with satisfaction the extent and limits of the aid to human life and health, which they may understandingly expect from that art; and it constitutes such a foundation for those intended for the profession, that the finishing course of practice at the bed-sides of the sick, and at the operations of surgery in a hospital, can neither be long nor expensive. To seek this finishing elsewhere, must therefore be submitted to for a while.

In conformity with the principles of our Constitution, which places all sects of religion on an equal footing, with the jealousies of the different sects in guarding that equality from encroachment and surprise, and with the sentiments of the Legislature in favor of freedom of religion, manifested on former occasions, we have proposed no professor of divinity; and the rather as the proofs of the being of a God, the creator, preserver, and supreme ruler of the universe, the author of all the relations of morality, and of the laws and obligations these infer, will be within the province of the professor of ethics; to which adding the developments of these moral obligations, of those in which all sects agree, with a knowledge of the languages, Hebrew, Greek, and Latin, a basis will be formed common to all sects. Proceeding thus far without offence to the Constitution, we have thought it proper at this point to leave every sect to provide, as they think fittest, the means of further instruction in their own peculiar tenets.

We are further of opinion, that after declaring by law that certain sciences shall be taught in the University, fixing the number of professors they require, which we think should, at present, be ten, limiting (except as to the professors who shall be first engaged in each branch,) a maximum for their salaries, (which should be a certain but moderate subsistence, to be made up by liberal tuition fees, as an excitement to assiduity), it will be best to leave to the discretion of the visitors, the grouping of these sciences together, according to the accidental qualifications of the professors; and the introduction also of other branches of science, when enabled by private donations, or by public provision, and called for by the increase of population, or other change of circumstances; to establish beginnings, in short, to be developed by time, as those who come after us shall find expedient. They will be more advanced than we are in science and in useful arts, and will know best what will suit the circumstances of their day.

We have proposed no formal provision for the gymnastics of the school, although a proper object of attention for every institution of youth. These exercises with ancient nations, constituted the principal part of the education of their youth. Their arms and mode of warfare rendered them severe in the extreme; ours, on the same correct principle, should be adapted to our arms and warfare; and the manual exercise, military manoeuvres, and tactics generally, should be the frequent exercise of the students, in their hours of recreation. It is at that age of aptness, docility, and emulation of the practices of manhood, that such things are soonest learnt and longest remembered. The use of tools too in the manual arts is worthy of encouragement, by facilitating to such as choose it, an admission into the neighboring workshops. To these should be added the arts which embellish life, dancing, music, and drawing; the last more especially, as an important part of military education. These innocent arts furnish amusement and happiness to those who, having time on their hands, might less inoffensively employ it. Needing, at the same time, no regular incorporation with the institution, they may be left to accessory teachers, who will be paid by the individuals employing them, the University only providing proper apartments for their exercise.

The fifth duty prescribed to the Commissioners, is to propose such general provisions as may be properly enacted by the Legislature, for the better organizing and governing the University.

In the education of youth, provision is to be made for, 1, tuition; 2, diet; 3, lodging; 4, government; and 5, honorary excitements. The first of these constitutes the proper functions of the professors; 2, the dieting of the students should be left to private boarding houses of their own choice, and at their own expense; to be regulated by the Visitors from time to time, the house only being provided by the University within its own precincts, and thereby of course subjected to the general regimen, moral or sumptuary, which they shall prescribe. 3. They should be lodged in dormitories, making a part of the general system of buildings. 4. The best mode of government for youth, in large collections, is certainly a desideratum not yet attained with us. It may be well questioned whether fear after a certain age, is a motive to which we should have ordinary recourse. The human character is susceptible of other incitements to correct conduct, more worthy of employ, and of better effect. Pride of character, laudable ambition, and moral dispositions are innate correctives of the indiscretions of that lively age; and when strengthened by habitual appeal and exercise, have a happier effect on future character than the degrading motive of fear. Hardening them to disgrace, to corporal punishments, and servile humiliations cannot be the best process for producing erect character. The affectionate deportment between father and son, offers in truth the best example for that of tutor and pupil; and the experience and practice of other countries, in this respect, may be worthy of enquiry and consideration with us. It will then be for the wisdom and discretion of the Visitors to devise and perfect a proper system of government, which, if it be founded in reason and comity, will be more likely to nourish in the minds of our youth the combined spirit of order and self-respect, so congenial with our political institutions, and so important to be woven into the American character. 5. What qualifications shall be required to entitle to entrance into the University, the arrangement of the days and hours of lecturing for the different schools, so as to facilitate to the students the circle of attendance on them; the establishment of periodical and public examinations, the premiums to be given for distinguished merit; whether honorary degrees shall be conferred, and by what appellations; whether the title to these shall depend on the time the candidate has been at the University, or, where nature has given a greater share of understanding, attention, and application; whether he shall not be allowed the advantages resulting from these endowments, with other minor items of government, we are of opinion should be entrusted to the Visitors; and the statute under which we act having provided for the appointment of these, we think they should moreover be charged with

The erection, preservation, and repair of the buildings, the care of the grounds and appurtenances, and of the interest of the University generally.

That they should have power to appoint a bursar, employ a proctor, and all other necessary agents.

To appoint and remove professors, two-thirds of the whole number of Visitors voting for the removal.

To prescribe their duties and the course of education, in conformity with the law.

To establish rules for the government and discipline of the students, not contrary to the laws of the land.

To regulate the tuition fees, and the rent of the dormitories they occupy.

To prescribe and control the duties and proceedings of all officers, servants, and others, with respect to the buildings, lands, appurtenances, and other property and interests of the University.

To draw from the literary fund such moneys as are by law charged on it for this institution; and in general

To direct and do all matters and things which, not being inconsistent with the laws of the land, to them shall seem most expedient for promoting the purposes of the said institution; which several functions they should be free to exercise in the form of by-laws, rules, resolutions, orders, instructions, or otherwise, as they should deem proper.

That they should have two stated meetings in the year, and occasional meetings at such times as they should appoint, or on a special call with such notice as themselves shall prescribe by a general rule; which meetings should be at the University, a majority of them constituting a quorum for business; and that on the death or resignation of a member, or on his removal by the President and Directors of the Literary Fund, or the Executive, or such other authority as the Legislature shall think best, such President and Directors, or the Executive, or other authority, shall appoint a successor.

That the said Visitors should appoint one of their own body to be Rector, and with him be a body corporate, under the style and title of the Rector and Visitors of the University of Virginia, with the right, as such, to use a common seal; that they should have capacity to plead and be impleaded in all courts of justice, and in all cases interesting to the University, which may be the subjects of legal cognizance and jurisdiction; which pleas should not abate by the determination of their office, but should stand revived in the name of their successors, and they should be capable in law and in trust for the University, of receiving subscriptions and donations, real and personal, as well from bodies corporate, or persons associated, as from private individuals.

And that the said Rector and Visitors should, at all times, conform to such laws as the Legislature may, from time to time, think proper to enact for their government; and the said University should, in all things, and at all times, be subject to the control of the Legislature.

And lastly, the Commissioners report to the Legislature the following conditional offers to the President and Directors of the Literary Fund, for the benefit of the University:

On the condition that Lexington, or its vicinity, shall be selected as the site of the University, and that the same be permanently established there within two years from the date, John Robinson, of Rockbridge county, has executed a deed to the President and Directors of the Literary Fund, to take effect at his death, for the following tracts of land, to wit:

400 acres on the North fork of James river, known by the name of Hart's bottom, purchased of the late Gen. Bowyer.

171 acres adjoining the same, purchased of James Griggsby.

203 acres joining the last mentioned tract, purchased of William Paxton.

112 acres lying on the North river, above the lands of Arthur Glasgow, conveyed to him by William Paxton's heirs.

500 acres adjoining the lands of Arthur Glasgow, Benjamin Camden and David Edmonson.

545 acres lying in Pryor's gap, conveyed to him by the heirs of William Paxton, deceased.

260 acres lying in Childer's gap, purchased of Wm. Mitchell.

300 acres lying, also, in Childer's gap, purchased of Nicholas Jones.

500 acres lying on Buffalo, joining the lands of Jas. Johnston.

340 acres on the Cowpasture river, conveyed to him by General James Breckenridge—reserving the right of selling the two last mentioned tracts, and converting them into other lands contiguous to Hart's bottom, for the benefit of the University; also, the whole of his slaves, amounting to 57 in number; one lot of 22 acres, joining the town of Lexington, to pass immediately on the establishment of the University, together with all the personal estate of every kind, subject only to the payment of his debts and fulfillment of his contracts.

It has not escaped the attention of the Commissioners, that the deed referred to is insufficient to pass the estate in the lands intended to be conveyed, and may be otherwise defective; but, if necessary, this defect may be remedied before the meeting of the Legislature, which the Commissioners are advised will be done.

The Board of Trustees of Washington College have also proposed to transfer the whole of their funds, viz: 100 shares in the funds of the James River Company, 31 acres of land upon which their buildings stand, their philosophical apparatus, their expected interest in the funds of the Cincinnati Society, the libraries of the Graham and Washington Societies, and $3,000 in cash, on condition that a reasonable provision be made for the present professors. A subscription has also been offered by the people of Lexington and its vicinity, amounting to $17,878, all which will appear from the deed and other documents, reference thereto being had.

In this case, also, it has not escaped the attention of the Commissioners, that questions may arise as to the power of the trustees to make the above transfers.

On the condition that the Central College shall be made the site of the University, its whole property, real and personal, in possession or in action, is offered. This consists of a parcel of land of 47 acres, whereon the buildings of the college are begun, one pavilion and its appendix of dormitories being already far advanced, and with one other pavilion, and equal annexation of dormitories, being expected to be completed during the present season—of another parcel of 153 acres, near the former, and including a considerable eminence very favorable for the erection of a future observatory; of the proceeds of the sales of two glebes, amounting to $3,280 86 cents; and of a subscription of $41,248, on papers in hand, besides what is on outstanding papers of unknown amount, not yet returned—out of these sums are to be taken, however, the cost of the lands, of the buildings, and other works done, and for existing contracts. For the conditional transfer of these to the President and Directors of the Literary Fund, a regular power, signed by the subscribers and founders of the Central College generally, has been given to its Visitors and Proctor, and a deed conveying the said property accordingly to the President and Directors of the Literary Fund, has been duly executed by the said Proctor, and acknowledged for record in the office of the clerk of the county court of Albemarle.

Signed and certified by the members present, each in his proper handwriting, this 4th day of August, 1818.

TH: JEFFERSON,
CREED TAYLOR,
PETER RANDOLPH,
WM. BROCKENBROUGH,
ARCH'D RUTHERFORD,
ARCH'D STUART,
JAMES BRECKENRIDGE,
HENRY E. WATKINS,
JAMES MADISON,
A. T. MASON,

HUGH HOLMES,
PHIL. C. PENDLETON,
SPENCER ROANE,
JOHN M. C. TAYLOR,
J. G. JACKSON,
PHIL. SLAUGHTER,
WM. H. CABELL,
NAT. H. CLAIBORNE,
WM. A. C. DADE,
WILLIAM JONES,

THOMAS WILSON.

APPENDIX K

LETTER TO GENERAL BRECKENRIDGE—
A CAMPAIGN DOCUMENT

This letter has a setting of exceptional interest. In Jefferson's letter to Cabell, January 31, 1821, urging him to remain in the Virginia Senate, occur three allusions to General Breckenridge—"As to what had better be done, ... I trust with entire confidence to what yourself, General Brecken-ridge, and Mr. Johnson shall think best;" "I have ever hoped that yourself, General Breckenridge, and Mr. Johnson, would stand at your posts in the Legislature until everything was effected, and the institution opened;" "But I will die in the last ditch. And so, I hope, you will, my friend, as well as our firm-breasted brothers and colleagues, Mr. Johnson and General Breckenridge." (*Cabell*, 201–202). On February 8 Cabell wrote:

"Your letter has kindled great zeal in Gen. Breckenridge. Yesterday Gen. Blackburn, in discussing Selden's resolutions, spoke of the University as 'a grand institution highly deserving our patronage'. We have great difficulties to contend with. Your name and hand-writing have great effect here. Let me entreat you, with the freedom of a friend, immediately to write to Gen. Breckenridge a letter on the subject of the University, such as may be shown generally, showing no preference and making no im-putations. He wishes it, and will make powerful use of it. You may rely on our discretion. I write you with his privity, and at his instance." (*Cabell*, 203–204).

The same day that he wrote the letter to General Breckenridge, Jefferson sent to Cabell the following comments and admonitions:

"I addressed this day to Gen. Breckenridge a letter as you desired; to be shown if it is thought expedient, within the circle of discretion. I doubt much, myself, whether its exhibition to members independent in their purposes, and jealous of that independence, may not do more harm than good. On this I put myself into the hands of my friends. I am sure you will see the propriety of letting no copy be taken, or possibility occur, of its getting beyond the limits of our own State; and even within these limits, some of its expressions should not go forth." (Cabell, 204).

At this time Jefferson was trying to obtain a loan of $60,000 from the Literary Fund with which to finish the university buildings and was resisted by the opponents of the institution and by some of the advocates of free schools for the poor.   On February 22 Cabell wrote:

"The University bill passed to a second reading in the House of Delegates, by a majority of one vote only.   It is now in its third reading, and will be read tomorrow.   Our friends, I think, are increasing.   General Blackburn will support it.   Mr. Garland came over and voted for it.   If we lose the bill in the Lower House, we shall hang on upon the Poor-school Bill. I hope we shall work it through, in one way or the other.   The enemies, seeing its decisive character, have done their best to destroy it" (*Cabell*, 206).

Three days later he reported that the bill had passed, with the following significant sidelight:

"Gen. Blackburn took the floor most zealously in favor of the measure, and is now fairly enlisted.   I wish you could see him on his way through Charlottesville, accompany him to the University, and invite him to return to the Assembly.   I am satisfied he is now very much disposed to support your literary views; but from the course of his past life [He had been a Federalist], and the pride of his character, he will be shy, and the first advances must come from yourself . . .   Our great friend in that House is Gen. Breckenridge.   He is, in truth, a powerful friend, and you must insist on his remaining in the Assembly" (*Cabell*, 208).

"My principal object, in writing you at this time," wrote Cabell on March 10, "is to apprise you that we are likely to lose our friend Gen. Breckenridge, and to ask you to use your influence to prevent it.   He told me he could not consent to come again; but at last said he would not commit himself till the meeting of the Board of Visitors.   I am told, however, that when he left town he said he should not offer, and would not serve again. He is the only man that can keep the Western delegation correct; and is worth more than all the rest of us put together.   If he quits us, I shall be in utter despair for years to come.   Therefore, I beseech you and Mr. Madison both, to write him earnestly and without delay" (*Cabell*, 211).

"I regret to find," he wrote on April 28, "that Gen. Breckenridge will not be in the next Assembly; as also to discover in Gen. Blackburn's speech on the University some remarks which I did not know it contained, till I saw it in the Enquirer" (*Cabell*, 213).

This conversion of General Blackburn to the "correct" attitude gains point from the fact that General Breckenridge also had been a Federalist and the recognized leader of that party in the Virginia Assembly before his election to Congress in 1809.   The letter, with its skilful appeal to sectional interest and local pride, and the entire story splendidly illustrate Jefferson's method of campaigning and the implicit faith of his supporters (*Ms., L. C.*, Vol. 219, also *Randolph Ed.*, IV, 341–343; *Library Ed.*, XV, 314–318).*

---

* James Breckenridge was born near Fincastle, Virginia, March 7, 1763, the grandson of a Scotch covenanter.   In 1781 he served in Colonel Preston's rifle regiment under

Monticello, Feb. 15, '21.

Dear Sir,

I learn with deep affliction, that nothing is likely to be done for our University this year. so near as it is to the shore that one shove more would land it there, I had hoped that would be given; and that we should open with the next year an institution on which the fortunes of our country depend more than may meet the general eye. the reflections that the boys of this age are to be the men of the next; that they should be prepared to receive the holy charge which we are cherishing to deliver over to them; that in establishing an institution of wisdom for them we secure it to all our future generations; that in fulfilling this duty we bring home to our own bosoms the sweet consolation of seeing our sons rising, under a luminous tuition, to destinies of high promise; these are considerations which will occur to all. but all, I fear, do not see the speck in our horizon which is to burst on us as a tornado, sooner or later. the line of division lately marked out between different portions of our confederacy, is such as will never, I fear, be obliterated, and we are now trusting to those who are against us in position and principle, to fashion to their own form the minds & affections of our youth. if, as has been estimated, we send 300,000. D a year to the Northern seminaries for the instruction of our own sons, then we must have there at all times 500. of our sons imbibing opinions and principles in discord with those of their own country. this canker is eating on the vitals of our existence, and if not arrested at once will be beyond remedy. we are now certainly furnishing recruits to their school. if it be asked what are we to do? or said that we cannot give the last lift to the University without stopping our primary schools and these we think the most important; I answer, I know their importance. Nobody can doubt my zeal for the general instruction of the people. Who first started that idea? I may surely say myself. turn to the bill in the revised code which I drew more than 40. years ago; and before which the idea of a plan for the education of the people generally had never been suggested in this state. there you will see developed the first rudiments of the whole system of general education we are now urging and acting on. and it is well known to those with whom I have acted on this subject, that I never have proposed a sacrifice of the primary to the ultimate grade of instruction. let us keep our eye steadily on the whole system. if we cannot do every thing at once, let us do one at a time. the primary schools need no preliminary expence. the ultimate grade requires a considerable expenditure in advance. a suspension of proceeding for a year or two on the primary schools, and an application of the whole income during that time, to the

General Greene. He graduated from William and Mary in 1785, was admitted to the bar in 1787, and practised in Fincastle. He served in the War of 1812, Chapman Johnson, afterward his associate on the Board of Visitors, being his aide. He was one of the Rockfish commissioners and voted to locate the University at Lexington. He was appointed a Visitor of the University, February 13, 1819, and held the office till after Jefferson's death. He was one of the promoters of the Chesapeake and Ohio canal. He died at Fincastle, August 9, 1846. He was a brother of John Breckenridge, author of the Kentucky Resolutions of 1799, who was the grandfather of Vice-President Breckenridge and of a number of brilliant officers of the Union and Confederate service.

completion of the buildings necessary for the University, would enable us then to start both institutions at the same time. the intermediate branch of colleges, academies, and private classical schools, for the middle grade, may hereafter receive any necessary aids when the funds shall have become competent. in the mean time they are going on sufficiently, as they have ever yet gone on, at the private expence of those who use them, and who in numbers and means are competent to their own exigencies. the experience of 3. years has, I presume, left no doubt that the present plan of primary schools, of putting money into the hands of 1200. persons acting for nothing, and under no responsibility, is entirely inefficient. some other must be thought of; and during this pause, if it be only for a year, the whole revenue of that year, with that of the last 3. years which has not been already thrown away, would place our University in readiness to start with a better organization of primary schools, and both may then go on, hand in hand, for ever. no diminution of the capital will in this way have been incurred; a principle which ought to be deemed sacred. a relinquishment of interest on the late loan of 60,000. D., would so far also forward the university, without lessening the capital. But what may be best done, I leave with entire confidence to yourself and your colleagues in legislation, who know better than I do the conditions of the literary fund, and its wisest application; and I shall acquiesce with perfect resignation to their will. I have brooded, perhaps with fondness, over this establishment, as it held up to me the hope of continuing to be useful while I continued to live. I had believed that the course and circumstances of my life had placed within my power some services favorable to the out-set of the institution. but this may be egoism; pardonable perhaps when I express a consciousness that my colleagues and successors will do as well, whatever the legislature shall enable them to do.

I have thus, my dear Sir, opened my bosom, with all it's anxieties, freely to you. I blame nobody, for seeing things in a different light. I am sure all act conscientiously, and that all will be done honestly and wisely which can be done. I yield the concerns of the world with cheerfulness to those who are appointed in the order of nature to succeed to them; and for yourself, for our colleagues, and for all in charge of our country's future fame and fortune, I offer up sincere prayers.

TH: JEFFERSON.

APPENDIX L

PROPOSED REMOVAL OF WILLIAM AND MARY— MEDICAL EDUCATION

Jefferson has been called a traitor to his alma mater for proposing to appropriate the endowments of William and Mary to the use of the University or to establish district colleges when the proposed removal of that institution to Richmond threatened, as he believed, the ruin of the University. His letter to Cabell on this subject, shows his attitude toward the old college, and gives a vivid picture of his conception of the methods of medical instruction. (*Cabell*, 308–312).

Monticello, May 16, 1824.

Dear Sir,—Your favor of the 5th from Williamsburg has been duly received, and presents to us a case of pregnant character, admitting important issues, and requiring serious consideration and conduct. Yet I am more inclined to view it with hope than dismay. It involves two questions. 1. Shall the college of William & Mary be removed? 2d. To what place? As to the first, I never doubted the lawful authority of the Legislature over the college, as being a public institution, endowed from the public property, by the public agents for that function, and for public purposes. Some have doubted this authority without a relinquishment of what they call a vested right, by the body corporate; but as their voluntary relinquishment is a circumstance of the case, it is relieved from that doubt. I certainly never wished that my venerable Alma Mater should be disturbed. I considered it as an actual possession of that ancient and earliest settlement of our forefathers, and was disposed to see it yielded as a courtesy, rather than taken as a right. They, however, are free to renounce a benefit, and we to receive it. Had we dissolved it on the principle of right, to give a direction to its funds more useful to the public, the professors, although their chartered tenure is during pleasure only, might have reasonably expected a vote of a year or two's salary, as an intermediate support until they could find other employment for their talents. And, notwithstanding that their abandonment is voluntary, this should still be given them. On this first question, I think we should be absolutely silent and passive, taking no part in it until the old institution is loosened from its foundation, and fairly placed on its wheels.

2. On the second question, to what place shall it be removed? we may take the field boldly. Richmond, it seems, claims it, but on what ground of advantage to the public? When the professors, their charter and funds shall be translated to Richmond, will they become more enlightened there than at the old place? Will they possess more science? be more capable of communicating it, or more competent to raise it from the dead, in a new seat, than to keep it alive in the ancient one? Or has Richmond any peculiarities more favorable for the communication of the sciences generally, than the place which the Legislature has preferred and fixed on for that purpose? This will not be pretended. But it seems they possess advantages for a medical school. Let us scan them. Anatomy may be as completely taught at the University as at Richmond. The only subjects of dissection which either place can count on, are equally acquirable at both. And as to medicine, whatever can be learnt from lectures or books, may be taught at the University of Virginia as well as at Richmond, or even at Baltimore, Philadelphia, New York, or Boston, with the inestimable additional advantage of acquiring at the same time the kindred sciences by attending the other schools. But Richmond thinks it can have a hospital which will furnish subjects for the clinical branch of medicine. The classes of people which furnish subjects for the hospitals of Baltimore, Philadelphia, New York, and Boston, do not exist at Richmond. The shipping constantly present at those places furnish many patients. Is there a ship at Richmond? The class of white servants in those cities, which is numerous and pennyless, and whose regular resource in sickness is always the hospital, constitutes the great body of their patients. This class does not exist at Richmond. The servants there are slaves, whose masters are, by law, obliged to take care of them in sickness, as in health, and who could not be admitted into a hospital. These resources then being null, the free inhabitants alone remain for a hospital at Richmond. And I will ask how many families in Richmond would send their husbands, wives, or children to a hospital, in sickness? to be attended by nurses hardened by habit against the feelings of pity, to lie in public rooms, harrassed by the cries and sufferings of disease under every form, alarmed by the groans of the dying, exposed as a corpse, to be lectured over by a clinical professor, to be crowded and handled by his students, to hear their case learnedly explained to them, its threatening symptoms developed, and its probable termination foreboded? In vindication of Richmond, I may surely answer, that there is not in the place a family so heartless, as relinquishing their own tender cares of a child or parent, to abandon them in sickness to this last resource of poverty. For it is poverty alone which peoples hospitals; and those alone who are on the charities of their parish would go to their hospital. Have they paupers enough to fill a hospital? and sickness enough among these? One reason alleged for the removal of the college to Richmond is, that Williamsburg is sickly and Richmond healthy. The latter then being little sickly, is happily little apt for the situation of a hospital. No, sir, Richmond is no place to furnish subjects for clinical lectures. I have always had Norfolk in view for this purpose. The climate and Pontine

country around Norfolk render it truly sickly in itself. It is moreover the rendezvous not only of the shipping of commerce, but of the vessels of the public navy. The United States have there a hospital already established, and supplied with subjects from these local circumstances. I had thought, and have mentioned to yourself and our colleagues, that when our medical school has got well under way, we should propose to the federal government the association with the establishment, and at our own expense, of the clinical branch of our medical school, so that our students after qualifying themselves with the other branches of the science here, might complete their course of preparation by attending clinical lectures for six or twelve months at Norfolk.

But that Richmond has a claim, as being the seat of government. The indisposition of Richmond towards our University has not been unfelt. But would it not be wiser in them to rest satisfied with the government and their local academy? Can they afford, on the question of a change of the seat of government, by hostilizing the middle counties, to transfer them from the Eastern to the Western interest? To make it their interest to withdraw from the former that ground of claim, if used for adversary purposes? With things as they are, let both parties remain content and united.

If, then, William & Mary is to be removed, and not to Richmond, can there be two opinions how its funds may be directed to the best advantage for the public? When it was found that that seminary was entirely ineffectual towards the object of public education, and that one on a better plan, and in a better situation, must be provided, what was so obvious as to employ for that purpose the funds of the one abandoned, with what more would be necessary to raise the new establishment? And what so obvious as to do now what might reasonably have been done then by consolidating together the institutions and their funds? The plan sanctioned by the Legislature required for our University ten professors; but the funds appropriated will maintain but eight, and some of these are consequently overburdened with duties. The hundred thousand dollars of principal which you say still remains to William & Mary, by its interest of $6,000, would give us the two deficient professors, with an annual surplus for the purchase of books. And certainly the Legislature will see no public interest, after the expense incurred on the new establishment, in setting up a rival in the city of Richmond; they cannot think it better to have two institutions crippling one another, than one of healthy powers, competent to that highest grade of instruction, which neither with a divided support could expect to attain.

Another argument may eventually arise in favor of consolidation. The contingent gift, at the late session, of $50,000 for books and apparatus, shews a sense in the Legislature that those objects are still to be provided. If we fail in obtaining that sum, they will feel an incumbency to provide it otherwise. What so ready as the derelict capital of William & Mary, and the large library they uselessly possess? Should that college, then, be removed, I cannot doubt that the Legislature, keeping in view its original object, will consolidate it with the University.

But it will not be removed. Richmond is doubtless in earnest; but that the Visitors should concur is impossible.

*　*　*　*　*　*　*　*　*　*　*　*　*　*

I will only add to this long letter an opinion that we had better say as little as we can on this whole subject. Give them no alarm. Let them petition for the removal; let them get the old structure completely on wheels, and not till then put in our claim to its reception. I shall communicate your letter, as you request, to Mr. Madison, and with it this answer. Why can you not call on us, on your way to Warminster, and make this a subject of conversation? With my devoted respects to Mrs. Cabell, assure her that she can no where be more cordially received than by the family at Monticello; and the deviation from your direct road is too small to merit consideration.

Ever and affectionately your friend and servant,

TH: JEFFERSON.

APPENDIX M

ORGANIZATION AND GOVERNMENT OF THE UNIVERSITY

ENACTMENT OF THE BOARD OF VISITORS OF THE UNIVERSITY OF VIRGINIA,
APRIL 7, 1824, JEFFERSON, MADISON, JOHNSON, COCKE,
AND CABELL BEING PRESENT
(*Library Ed.*, XIX, 433–436.)

In the University of Virginia shall be instituted eight professorships, to wit: 1st, of ancient languages; 2d, modern languages; 3d, mathematics; 4th, natural philosophy; 5th, natural history; 6th, anatomy and medicine; 7th, moral philosophy; 8th, law.

In the school of ancient languages shall be taught the higher grade of the Latin and Greek languages, the Hebrew, rhetoric, belles-lettres, ancient history and ancient geography.

In the school of modern languages shall be taught French, Spanish, Italian, German and the English language in its Anglo-Saxon form; also modern history and modern geography.

In the school of mathematics shall be taught mathematics generally including the high branches of numerical arithmetic, algebra, trigonometry, plane and spherical geometry, mensuration, navigation, conic sections, fluxions or differentials, military and civil architecture.

In the school of natural philosophy shall be taught the laws and properties of bodies generally, including mechanics, statics, hydrostatics, hydraulics, pneumatics, acoustics, optics and astronomy.

In the school of natural history shall be taught botany, zoölogy, mineralogy, chemistry, geology and rural economy.

In the school of anatomy and medicine shall be taught anatomy, surgery, the history of the progress and theories of medicine, physiology, pathology, materia medica and pharmacy.

In the school of moral philosophy shall be taught mental science generally, including ideology, general grammar, logic and ethics.

In the school of law shall be taught the common and statute law, that of the chancery, the laws feudal, civil, mercatorial, maritime and of nature and nations; and also the principles of government and political economy.

This arrangement, however, shall not be understood as forbidding occasional transpositions of a particular branch of science from one school to another in accommodation of the particular qualifications of different professors.

In each of these schools instruction shall be communicated by lessons or lectures, examinations and exercises, as shall be best adapted to the nature of the science, and number of the school; and exercises shall be prescribed to employ the vacant days and hours.

The professors shall be permitted to occupy, rent free, a pavilion each, with the grounds appropriated to it. They shall also receive from the funds of the University such compensation as shall have been stipulated by the agent or fixed by the Board; and from each student attending them tuition fees as hereinafter declared.

The professors shall permit no waste to be committed in their tenements, and shall maintain the internal of their pavilions, and also the windows, doors and locks external during their occupation, in as good repair and condition as they shall have received them.

The collegiate duties of a professor, if discharged conscientiously, with industry and zeal, being sufficient to engross all his hours of business, he shall engage in no other pursuits of emolument unconnected with the service of the University without the consent of the Visitors.

Every student shall pay to the professor whom he attends, if he attends but one, fifty dollars the session of ten months and a half; if two, thirty dollars each, if three or more, twenty-five dollars each—and these payments shall be made in advance, and before his admission into the school. And they shall maintain their dormitories in the condition in which they shall receive them in like manner as is required of the professors. The proctor shall in duty attend in both cases to the observance of this requisition.

REGULATIONS ADOPTED BY THE BOARD OF VISITORS OF THE UNIVERSITY OF VIRGINIA, OCTOBER 4, 1824, JEFFERSON, MADISON, BRECKENRIDGE, COCKE, LOYALL, AND CABELL BEING PRESENT

(Library Ed., XIX, 439–451.)

Each of the schools of the University shall be held two hours of every other day of the week; and that every student may be enabled to attend those of his choice, let their sessions be so arranged, as to days and hours, that no two of them shall be holden at the same time. Therefore,

The school of ancient languages shall occupy from 7:30 to 9:30 a.m., on Mondays, Wednesdays and Fridays.

That of modern languages shall occupy the same hours on Tuesdays, Thursdays, and Saturdays.

That of mathematics shall occupy from 9:30 to 11:30 a.m., on Mondays, Wednesdays and Fridays.

That of natural philosophy the same hours on Tuesdays, Thursdays, and Saturdays.

That of natural history shall occupy from 11:30 a.m. to 1:30 p.m., on Mondays, Wednesdays and Fridays.

That of anatomy and medicine the same hours on Tuesdays, Thursdays and Saturdays.

That of moral philosophy shall occupy from 1:30 to 3:30 p.m., on Mondays, Wednesdays and Fridays.

That of law the same hours on Tuesdays, Thursdays and Saturdays.

The Visitors of the University shall be free, severally or together, to attend occasionally any school, during its session, as inspectors and judges of the mode in which it is conducted.

Wherein the instruction is by lessons, and the class too numerous for a single instructor, assistant tutors may be employed, to be chosen by the professor, to have the use of two adjacent dormitories each, rent free, and to divide with the professor the tuition fees, as shall be agreed between them.

The professors, tutors and all officers of the University shall reside constantly in the apartments of the University, or of its precincts, assigned to them.

At a meeting of the faculty of professors, on matters within their functions, one of them shall preside, by rotation, for the term of one year each. A majority of the members shall make a quorum for business. They may appoint a secretary of their own body, or otherwise, who shall keep a journal of their proceedings, and lay the same before the Board of Visitors at their first ensuing meeting, and whenever else required. The compensation for such secretary shall be fifty dollars yearly, payable from the funds of the University.

Meetings of the faculty may be called by the presiding member of the year, or by any three of the professors, to be held in an apartment of the rotunda, and the object of the call shall be expressed in the written notification to be served by the janitor. But when assembled, other business also may be transacted.

The faculty may appoint a janitor, who shall attend its meetings, and the meetings of the Visitors, and shall perform necessary menial offices for them, for which he shall receive 150 dollars yearly from the funds of the University, and be furnished with a lodging room.

No student is to be received under sixteen years of age, rigorously proved. None to be admitted into the mathematical school, or that of natural philosophy, who is not an adept in all the branches of numerical arithmetic; and none into the school of ancient languages, unless qualified, in the judgment of the professor, to commence reading the higher Latin classics; nor to receive instruction in Greek, unless qualified in the same degree in that language.*

No one shall enter as a student of the University, either at the beginning or during the progress of the session, but as for the whole session, ending on the 15th day of December, and paying as for the whole.

The dormitories shall be occupied by two students each, and no more, at fifteen dollars yearly rent, to be paid to the proctor at or before the end of the session, one-half by each occupant, or the whole by one, if there be only one. And every student, within the same term, shall pay to the proctor, also, for the University, fifteen dollars annually for his participation in the use of the public apartments during the session.

The students shall be free to diet themselves in any of the hotels of the

* Cf. pp. 131–132.

University, at their choice, or elsewhere, other than in taverns, as shall suit themselves, but not more than fifty shall be allowed to diet at the same hotel.

No keeper of any of the hotels of the University shall require or receive more than 100 dollars for dieting any student and for performing the necessary offices of his dormitory, during the session of ten months and a half, nor shall suffer ardent spirits or wine, mixed or unmixed, to be drank within his tenement, on pain of an immediate determination of his lease, and removal by the Faculty; nor shall any person boarding elsewhere than with their parents, in any house, and using wine or ardent spirits, mixed or unmixed, within such house, or its tenement, or paying more than 120 dollars for diet, lodging, and other offices and accommodations of the house and tenement, during a like term, be admitted to any school of the University.

Every student shall be free to attend the schools of his choice, and no other than he chooses.

There will be one vacation only in the year, and that shall be from the 15th day of December to the last day of January.

Examination of the candidates for honorary distinctions shall be held in the presence of all the professors and students, in the week preceding the commencement of the vacation. At these examinations shall be given, to the highly meritorious only, and by the vote of a majority of the professors, diplomas, or premiums of medals or books, to be provided by the University, to wit: Diplomas to those of the highest qualifications, medals of more or less value to those of the second grade of acquisition, and books of more or less value to those of a third. These diplomas shall be of two degrees; the highest of doctor, the second of graduate. And the diploma of each shall express the particular school or schools in which the candidate shall have been declared eminent, and shall be subscribed by the particular professors approving it. But no diploma shall be given to any one who has not passed such an examination in the Latin language as shall have proved him able to read the highest classics in that language with ease, thorough understanding and just quantity; and if he be also a proficient in the Greek, let that, too, be stated in his diploma. The intention being that the reputation of the University shall not be committed but to those who, to an eminence in some one or more of the sciences taught in it, add a proficiency in these languages which constitute the basis of good education, and are indispensable to fill up the character of a "well-educated man."

Punishment for major offences shall be expulsion, temporary suspension, or interdiction of residence or appearance within the precincts of the University. The minor punishment shall be restraint [within those precincts, within their own chamber, or in diet], reproof by a professor, privately or in presence of the school of the offender, or of all the schools, [a seat of degradation in his school-room of longer or shorter duration, removal to a lower class,] dismission from the schoolroom for the day, [imposition of a task;] and insubordination to these sentences shall be deemed and punished as contumacy. (Bracketed words expunged, October 3, 1825. *Library Ed.*, XIX, 472.)

Contumacy shall be liable to any of the minor punishments. ("minor" changed to "major", October 3, 1825. *Library Ed.*, XIX, 472.)

The precincts of the University are to be understood as co-extensive with the lot or parcel of its own grounds on which it is situated.

The major punishments of expulsion from the University, temporary suspension of attendance and presence there, or interdiction of residence or appearance within its precincts, shall be decreed by the professors themselves. Minor cases may be referred to a board of six censors, to be named by the faculty, from the most discreet of the students, whose duty it shall be, sitting as a board, to inquire into the facts, propose the minor punishment which they think proportioned to the offence, and to make report thereof to the professors for their approbation, or their commutation of the penalty, if it be beyond the grade of the offence. The censors shall hold their offices until the end of the session of their appointment, if not sooner revoked by the faculty.

Inattendance on school, inattention to the exercises prescribed, and misbehavior or indecorum in school shall be subject to any of the minor punishments; and the professor of the school may singly reprove, [impose a task,] or dismiss from the room for the day.

(Bracketed words expunged, October 3, 1825. *Library Ed.*, XIX, 472.)

Habits of expense, of dissoluteness, dissipation, or of playing at games of chance, being obstructive to the acquisition of science by the student himself and injurious by example to others, shall be subject in the first instance to admonition and reproof to the offender, and to communication and warning to the parent or guardian, and, if not satisfactorily corrected, to a refusal of further continuance at the University.

No student shall make any festive entertainment within the precincts of the University, nor contribute or be present at them, there or elsewhere, but with the consent of each of the professors whose school he attends, on pain of a minor punishment.

No student shall admit any disturbing noises in his room, or make them anywhere within the precincts of the University, or fire a gun or pistol within the same, on pain of such minor sentence as the faculty shall decree or approve. But the proper use of musical instruments shall be freely allowed in their rooms, and in that appropriated for instruction in music.

Riotous, disorderly, intemperate or indecent conduct of any student within the precincts shall be punished by interdiction of a residence within the precincts; [and repetitions of such offences, by expulsion from the University.]

(Bracketed words expunged, "or any of the minor or major punishments at the discretion of the faculty" substituted, and "that every occupant of a dormitory permitting these offences therein, be subject to any of the minor punishments at the discretion of the faculty" added October 3, 1825, *Library Ed.*, XIX, 472.)

Fighting with weapons which may inflict death, or a challenge to such fight, given or accepted, shall be punished by instant expulsion from the University, not remissible by the Faculty; and it shall be the duty of the proctor to give information thereof to the civil magistrate, that the parties may be dealt with according to law.

Offences cognisable by the laws of the land shall be left to the cognisance of the civil magistrate, if claimed by him, or otherwise to the judgment of the faculty; all others to that of the faculty. And such of these as are not specially designated in enactments of the Visitors may be subjected by the faculty to any of the minor punishments permitted by these enactments.

Sentences of expulsion from the University (except in the case of challenge or combat with arms) * shall not be final until approved by the Board of Visitors or, when they are not in session, by a majority of them, separately consulted. But residence within the precincts, and attendance on the schools may be suspended in the meantime.

No student shall, within the precincts of the University, introduce, keep or use any spirituous or vinous liquors, keep or use weapons or arms of any kind, or gunpowder, keep a servant, horse or dog, appear in school with a stick, or any weapon, nor while in school, be covered without permission of the professor, nor use tobacco by smoking or chewing, on pain of any of the minor punishments at the discretion of the faculty, or of the board of censors, approved by the faculty.

All damages done to instruments, books, buildings or other property of the University by any student, shall be made good at his expense; and wilful injury to any tree, shrub or other plant within the precincts, shall be punished by fine, not exceeding ten dollars, at the discretion of the faculty.

When a professor knocks at the door of a student's room, any person being within, and announces himself, it shall be opened, on pain of minor punishment; and the professor may, if refused, have the door broken open; and the expenses of repair shall be levied on the student or students within.

At the hour appointed for the meeting of every school, the roll of the school shall be called over, the absentees and those appearing tardily, shall be noted, and if no sufficient cause be offered, at the rising of the school, to the satisfaction of the professor, the notation shall stand confirmed, and shall be given in to the faculty, the presiding member of which for the time being shall, on the 15th days of May, August and December, or as soon after each of these days as may be, transmit by mail a list of these notations to the parent or guardian of each delinquent.

When testimony is required from a student, it shall be voluntary, and not on oath. And [if unwilling to give it, let the moral obligation be explained and urged, under which every one is bound to bear witness, where wrong has been done, but finally let it] be left to his own sense of right.

(Bracketed words expunged and "the obligation to give it shall" substituted, March 4, 1825, *Library Ed.*, XIX, 460.)

Should the religious sects of this State, or any of them, according to the invitation held out to them, establish within, or adjacent to, the precincts of the University, schools for instruction in the religion of their sect, the students of the University will be free, and expected to attend religious

* Note Jefferson's extreme abhorrence of dueling.

worship at the establishment of their respective sects, in the morning, and in time to meet their school in the University at its stated hour.

The students of such religious school, if they attend any school of the University, shall be considered as students of the University, subject to the same regulations, and entitled to the same rights and privileges.

The room provided for a school-room in every pavilion shall be used for the school of its occupant professor, and shall be furnished by the University with necessary benches and tables.

The upper circular room of the rotunda * shall be reserved for a library.

One of its larger elliptical rooms on its middle floor shall be used for annual examinations, for lectures to such schools as are too numerous for their ordinary school room, and for religious worship, under the regulations allowed to be prescribed by law. The other rooms on the same floor may be used by schools of instruction in drawing, music, or any other of the innocent and ornamental accomplishments of life; but under such instructors only as shall be approved and licensed by the faculty.

The rooms in the basement story of the rotunda shall be, one of them for a chemical laboratory, and the others for any necessary purpose to which they may be adapted.

The two open apartments, adjacent to the same story of the rotunda, shall be appropriated to the gymnastic exercises and games of the students, among which shall be reckoned military exercises.

A military instructor shall be provided at the expense of the University, to be appointed by the faculty, who shall attend on every Saturday from half after one o'clock to half after three P. M., and shall instruct the students in the manual exercise, in field evolutions, manoeuvres and encampments. The students shall attend these exercises, and shall be obedient to the military orders of their instructor. The roll shall be regularly called over by him at the hour of meeting, absences and insubordinations shall be noted, and the list of the delinquents shall be delivered to the presiding member of the faculty for the time being to be animadverted on by the faculty, and such minor punishment imposed as each case shall, in their discretion, require. The school of modern languages shall be pretermitted on the days of actual military exercise.

Substitutes in the form of arms shall be provided by the proctor, at the expense of the University; they shall be distinguished by numbers, delivered out, received in and deposited under the care and responsibility of the instructor, in a proper depository to be furnished him; and all injuries to them by a student shall be repaired at the expense of such student.

Work-shops shall be provided, whenever convenient, at the expense of the University, wherein the students who choose, may exercise themselves in the use of tools, and such mechanical practices as it is convenient and useful for every person to understand, and occasionally to practice. These shops may be let, rent free, to such skillful and orderly mechanics as shall be approved by the faculty, on the condition that they will permit the use of their tools, instruments and implements, within the shop, to

* Not now separate from the room below.

such students as shall desire and use the permission discreetly, and under a liability for any injury they may do them; and on the further condition, if necessary, of such mechanics receiving instruction gratis in the mechanical and philosophical principles of his art, so far as taught in any of the schools.

ADDITIONAL REGULATIONS ADOPTED OCTOBER 3, 1825

(*Library Ed.*, XIX, 472–473.)

Resolved, that the faculty shall have the power, for offensive conduct, of removing the occupant from any dormitory.

Resolved, that if a student be irregular in all his classes for more than a month, after his parent or guardian has been informed, the faculty shall have the discretionary power to dismiss him from the University.

Resolved, that the faculty shall have power from time to time to prescribe regulations of police, not inconsistent with the laws of the land, or the enactments of this Board, which regulations shall be submitted to the Visitors at their next succeeding meeting and shall be in force till disapproved by the Visitors or repealed by the faculty.

ADDITIONAL REGULATIONS ADOPTED OCTOBER 5, 1825

(*Library Ed.*, XIX, 474–475.)

No student shall appear out of his dormitory masked or disguised in any manner whatever, which may render the recognition of his person more difficult, on pain of suspension or expulsion by the faculty of professors.

Intoxication shall, for the first offense, be liable to any of the minor punishments, and any repetition of the offence to any of the major punishments.

Resolved, that the 40th enactment * be amended, by inserting after the word "dissipation," the words "or profane swearing."

No person who has been a student at any other incorporated seminary of learning shall be received at this University, but on producing a certificate from such seminary or other satisfactory evidence to the faculty with respect to his general good conduct.

The professors being charged with the execution of the laws of the University, it becomes their duty to pursue proper means to discover and prevent offences. Respect from the student to the professor being at all times due, it is more especially so when the professor is engaged in his duty. Such respect, therefore, is solemnly enjoined on every student, and it is declared and enacted, that if any student refuse his name to a professor, or being required by him to stop, shall fail to do so, or shall be guilty of any other disrespect to a professor, he shall be liable to any of the punishments, minor or major.

* This appears as the fifth paragraph, p. 275, beginning "Habits of expense . . ."

ADDITIONAL REGULATION ADOPTED OCTOBER 7, 1825

(*Library Ed.*, XIX, 480.)

Resolved, that the proctor be charged with the duty at all times, as the attorney in fact of the rector and Visitors, of preventing trespasses and intrusions on the property of the University real and personal, and of recovering its possession from any person who shall improperly withhold the same, and, for this purpose, that he institute such legal proceeding as may be proper. It shall also be his duty to lay before the civil authorities, and to communicate to the proper law officer, such information as he may at any time have, and as may be calculated to prevent or punish breaches of the peace, trespasses and other misdemeanors within the precincts of the University, or committed by students elsewhere, and especially that he take the proper measures to bring the late offenses at the University before the civil authorities.

RESOLUTION OF THE BOARD OF VISITORS OF THE UNIVERSITY OF VIRGINIA, OCTOBER 3, 1825, JEFFERSON, MADISON, BRECKENRIDGE, CABELL, COCKE, JOHNSON, AND LOYALL BEING PRESENT

(*Library Ed.*, XIX, 468–470.)

Resolved, that it be communicated to the Faculty of the professors of the University, as the earnest request and recommendation of the rector and Visitors, that so far as can be effected by their exertions, they cause the statutes and rules enacted for the government of the University, to be exactly and strictly observed; that the roll of each school particularly be punctually called at the hour at which its students should attend; that the absent and the tardy, without reasonable cause, be noted, and a copy of these notations be communicated by mail or otherwise to the parent or guardian of each student respectively, on the first days of every month during the term (instead of the days prescribed in a former statute for such communications).

That it is requested of them to make known to the students that it is with great regret that some breaches of order, committed by the unworthy few who lurk among them unknown, render necessary the extension to all of processes afflicting to the feelings of those who are conscious of their own correctness, and who are above all participation in these vicious irregularities. While the offenders continue unknown the tarnish of their faults spreads itself over the worthy also, and confounds all in a common censure. But that it is within their power to relieve themselves from the imputations and painful proceedings to which they are thereby subjected, by lending their aid to the faculty, on all occasions toward detecting the real guilty. The Visitors are aware that a prejudice prevails too extensively among the young that it is dishonorable to bear witness one against another. While this prevails, and under the form of a matter of conscience, they have been unwilling to authorize constraint, and have therefore, in their regulations on this subject, indulged the error, however unfounded in reason or morality. But this loose principle in the ethics of school-boy combinations, is unworthy of mature and regulated minds, and is accordingly condemned by the laws of their country, which, in offences within their cognisance, compel those who have knowledge of a fact, to declare it for the purposes of justice, and of the general good and safety of society. And certainly, where wrong has been done, he who knows and conceals the doer of it, makes himself an accomplice, and justly censurable as such. It becomes then but an act of justice to themselves, that the innocent and the worthy should throw off with disdain all communion of character with such offenders, should determine no longer to screen the irregular and the vicious under the respect of their cloak, and to notify them, even by a solemn association for the purpose, that they will co-operate with the faculty in future, for preservation of order, the vindication of their own character, and the reputation and usefulness of an institution which their country has so liberally established for their improvement, and to place within their reach those acquirements in knowledge on which their future happiness and fortunes depend. Let the good and the virtuous of the alumni of the University do this, and the disorderly will then be singled out for observation, and deterred by punishment, or disabled by expulsion, from infecting with their inconsideration the institution itself, and the sound mass of those which it is preparing for virtue and usefulness.

APPENDIX N

A COMPARISON OF HARVARD, SOUTH CAROLINA, AND VIRGINIA RULES

When Jefferson drafted the rules for the University of Virginia he is supposed to have been considerably influenced by the rules then in force at Harvard. He possessed copies not only of these but of the contemporary rules of South Carolina College. A few of the laws of the three institutions which show the greatest similarity are here brought together for convenient comparison. Others show less similarity if any. These specimens are taken from the *Enactments of the Rector and Visitors of the University of Virginia,* 1825, the *Laws of Harvard College,* 1820, and Green's *History of the University of South Carolina,* 1916.

HARVARD — VI, pp. 20–21.

"IV. To prevent those tumults and disorders which are frequent at entertainments, and to guard against extravagance and needless expenses, no undergraduate shall make any festive entertainments in the College, the town of Cambridge, or the vicinity, except at Commencement and at public Exhibitions, with the permission of the President, under a penalty, for making or being present at such, not exceeding eight dollars."

SOUTH CAROLINA — *Green*, p. 221.

"No student shall make any festival [*sic*] entertainment in the college, or in the town of Columbia or take part in anything of the kind, without liberty previously obtained of the President."

VIRGINIA — p. 8.

"No student shall make any festive entertainment within the precincts of the University, nor contribute to, or be present at them there or elsewhere but with the consent of each of the Professors whose school he attends, on pain of a minor punishment."

HARVARD — VI, p. 22.

"VII. No student shall keep a gun or pistol, or any gunpowder in the College or town of Cambridge; nor shoot, fish, or scate over deep waters, without leave from the President, or one of the Tutors or Professors, under the penalty of fifty cents. And if any scholar shall fire a gun or pistol within the College walls, yard, or near the College, or near houses, or behind fences or inclosures, in the town, he shall be fined not exceeding one dollar, or suffer other college punishments."

SOUTH CAROLINA — *Green,* pp. 220–221.

"No student may keep in his room any kind of firearms or gun powder; nor fire any in or near the College, in any manner whatever; and any student who shall violate this law, shall be liable to admonition, suspension, or expulsion.

"All the students are strictly forbidden to play on any instrument of music in the hours of study, and also on Sundays; and shall abstain from their usual diversions and exercises on those days."

VIRGINIA — p. 9.

"No student shall admit any disturbing noises in his room, or make them anywhere within the precincts of the University, or fire a gun or pistol within the same, on pain of such minor sentences as the Faculty shall decree, or approve; but the proper use of musical instruments, shall be freely allowed in their rooms, and in that appropriated for the instruction in music."

HARVARD — VI, pp. 22–23.

"The students, when required, shall give evidence respecting the breach of any laws; shall admit into their chambers any of the officers, or, when sent for by them, shall immediately attend . . . or be punished by one of the high censures. . . . If entrance into a room be refused, an executive officer may break open any study or chamber door."

SOUTH CAROLINA — *Green,* p. 221.

"If any student shall refuse to open the door of his room, when required to do it by one of the Faculty, he shall be liable to public admonition; and the Faculty, when they shall think it necessary, may break open any room in the college at the expense of those by whom they are refused admittance."

VIRGINIA — pp. 9–10.

"When a Professor knocks at the door of a student's room, any person being within, and announces himself, it shall be opened on pain of a minor punishment; and the Professor may, if refused, have the door broken open; and the expenses of repair shall be levied on the student or students within."

APPENDIX O

QUALIFICATIONS OF PROFESSORS

On January 29, 1824, Cabell had written to Jefferson suggesting Chancellor Carr for Law Professor in the University. Jefferson's reply to this suggestion is taken from his letter of February 3, written from Monticello.

(*Library Ed.*, XVI 4–8; *Cabell*, 291–2)

Monticello, February 3, 1824.

*   *   *   *   *   *   *   *   *

I remark what you say on the subject of committing ourselves to any one for the Law appointment. Your caution is perfectly just. I hope, and am certain, that this will be the standing law of discretion and duty with every member of our Board in this and all cases. You know that we have all, from the beginning, considered the high qualifications of our professors as the only means by which we could give our institution splendor and pre-eminence over all its sister seminaries. The only question, therefore, we can ever ask ourselves, as to any candidate, will be, is he the most highly qualified? The College of Philadelphia has lost its character of primacy by indulging motives of favoritism and nepotism, and by conferring appointments as if the professorships were entrusted to them as provisions for their friends. And even that of Edinburgh, you know, is also much lowered from the same cause. We are next to observe, that a man is not qualified for a professor, knowing nothing but merely his own profession. He should be otherwise well educated as to the sciences generally; able to converse understandingly with the scientific men with whom he is associated, and to assist in the councils of the Faculty on any subject of science on which they may have occasion to deliberate. Without this, he will incur their contempt and bring disreputation on the institution. With respect to the professorship you mention, I scarcely know any of our judges personally; but I will name, for example, the late Judge ******, who, I believe, was generally admitted to be among the ablest of them. His knowledge was confined to the common law merely, which does not constitute one-half the qualification of a really learned lawyer, much less that of a Professor of Law for an University. And as to any other branches of science, he must have stood mute in the presence of his literary associates, or of any learned strangers or others visiting the University. Would this constitute the splendid stand we propose to take?

The individual named in your letter is one of the best, and to me the dearest of living men. From the death of his father, my most cherished friend, leaving him an infant in the arms of my sister, I have ever looked on him as a son. Yet these are considerations which can never enter into the question of his qualifications as a Professor of the University. Suppose all the chairs filled in similar degree, would that present the object which we have proposed to ourselves, and promised to the liberalities and expectations of our country? In the course of the trusts which I have exercised through life, with powers of appointment, I can say with truth, and unspeakable comfort, that I never did appoint a relation to office, and that merely because I never saw the case in which some one did not offer or occur, better qualified; and I have the most unlimited confidence that in the appointment of Professors to our nursling institution, every individual of my associates will look with a single eye to the sublimation of its character, and adopt as our sacred motto, *detur digniori.* In this way it will honor us, and bless our country.

I perceive that I have permitted my reflections to run into generalities beyond the scope of the particular intimation in your letter. I will let them go, however, as a general confession of faith, not belonging merely to the present case. Name me affectionately to our brethren with you, and be assured yourself of my constant friendship and respect.

TH: JEFFERSON.

Mr. Cabell

Jefferson's caution in selecting professors is further illustrated by his circular letter to the other visitors, sent to Cabell, May 13, 1825.

(*Cabell*, 351-2)

Monticello, May 13, 1825.

Dear Sir,—Every offer of our law chair has been declined, and a late renewal of pressure on Mr. Gilmer has proved him inflexibly decided against undertaking it. What are we to do? The clamor is high for some appointment. We are informed, too, of many students who do not come because that school is not opened, and some now with us think of leaving us for the same reason. You may remember that among those who were the subjects of conversation at our last meeting, Judge Dade was one; but the minds of the Board were so much turned to two particular characters, that little was said of any others. An idea has got abroad, I know not from what source, that we have appointed Judge Dade, and that he has accepted. This has spread extensively, perhaps from a general sense of his fitness, and I learn that it has been received with much favor, and particularly among the students of the University. I know no more myself of Judge Dade than what I saw of him at our Rockfish meeting, and a short visit he made me in returning from that place. As far as that opportunity enabled me to form an opinion, I certainly thought very highly of the strength of his mind, and the soundness of his judgment. I happened to receive Mr. Gilmer's ultimate and peremptory refusal while Judge Stuart and Mr. Howe Peyton of Staunton were with me. The former, you know, is his colleague on the bench of the General Court; the latter has been more particularly intimate with him, as having been brought up with him at the same school. I asked from them information respecting Mr. Dade; and they spoke of him in terms of high commendation. They state him to be an excellent Latin and Greek scholar, of clear and sound ideas, lucid in communicating them, equal as a lawyer to any one of the judiciary corps, and superior to all as a writer; and that his character is perfectly correct, his mind liberal and accommodating, yet firm and of sound republican principles. . . . This is the substance, and these, I may say, the terms in which they spoke of him; and when I considered the character of these two gentlemen, and their opportunities of knowing what they attested, I could not but be strongly impressed. It happened, very much to my gratification, that Gen. Cocke was here at the same time, received the same information and impression, and authorizes me to add his concurrence in proposing the appointment to our colleagues; and to say, moreover, that if on such further enquiry as they may make, they should approve the choice, and express it by letter, in preference to a meeting for a conference on this subject, I might write to Judge Dade; and, on his acceptance, issue his commission. I should add that the gentlemen above named, were confident he would accept, as well from other circumstances, as from his having three sons to educate. Of course, this would put an end to the anxieties we have all had on this subject. The public impatience for some appointment to this school, renders desirable as early an answer as your convenience admits. Accept the assurance of my great esteem and respect.

TH: JEFFERSON.

Mr. Cabell

APPENDIX P

THE TEACHING OF HISTORY

On October 25, 1825, Jefferson wrote a long letter to an unnamed member of the faculty, recommending the works to be read by students of history. (*Library Ed.*, XVI, 124–128, *Ms., L. C.*, Vol. 230.)

Dear Sir,—I do not know whether the professors to whom ancient and modern history are assigned in the University, have yet decided on the course of historical reading which they will recommend to their schools. If they have, I wish this letter to be considered as not written, as their course, the result of mature consideration, will be preferable to anything I could recommend. Under this uncertainty, and the rather as you are of neither of these schools, I may hazard some general ideas, to be corrected by what they may recommend hereafter.

In all cases I prefer original authors to compilers. For a course of ancient history, therefore, of Greece and Rome especially, I should advise the usual suite of Herodotus, Thucydides, Xenophon, Diodorus, Livy, Caesar, Suetonios, Tacitus, and Dion, in their originals if understood, and in translations if not. For its continuation to the final destruction of the empire we must then be content with Gibbons, a compiler, and with Segur, for a judicious recapitulation of the whole. After this general course, there are a number of particular histories, filling up the chasms, which may be read at leisure in the progress of life. Such is Arrian, Q. Curtius, Polybius, Sallust, Plutarch, Dionysius, Halicarnassus, Micasi, etc. The ancient universal history should be on our shelves as a book of general reference, the most learned and most faithful perhaps that ever was written. Its style is very plain but perspicuous.

In modern history, there are but two nations with whose course it is interesting to us to be intimately acquainted, to wit: France and England. For the former, Millot's General History of France may be sufficient to the period when 1 Davila commences. He should be followed by Perefixe, Sully, Voltaire's Louis XIV and XV, la Cretelle's XVIIIme siecle, Marmontel's Regence, Foulongion's French Revolution, and Madame de Stael's, making up by a succession of particular history, the general one which they want.

Of England there is as yet no general history so faithful as Rapin's. He may be followed by Ludlow, Fox, Belsham, Hume, and Brodie. Hume's, were it faithful, would be the finest piece of history which has ever been written by man. Its unfortunate bias may be partly ascribed to the accident of his having written backwards. His maiden work was the History of the

Stuarts. It was a first essay to try his strength before the public. And whether as a Scotchman he had really a partiality for that family, or thought that the lower their degradation, the more fame he should acquire by raising them up to some favor, the object of his work was an apology for them. He spared nothing, therefore, to wash them white, and to palliate their misgovernment. For this purpose he suppressed truths, advanced falsehoods, forged authorities, and falsified records. All this is proved on him unanswerably by Brodie. But so bewitching was his style and manner, that his readers were unwilling to doubt anything, swallowed everything, and all England became Tories by the magic of his art. His pen revolutionized the public sentiment of that country more completely than the standing armies could ever have done, which were so much dreaded and deprecated by the patriots of that day.

Having succeeded so eminently in the acquisition of fortune and fame by this work, he undertook the history of the two preceding dynasties, the Plantagenets and Tudors. It was all-important in this second work, to maintain the thesis of the first, that "it was the people who encroached on the sovereign, not the sovereign who usurped on the rights of the people." And, again, chapter 53d, "the grievances under which the English labored [to wit: whipping, pillorying, cropping, imprisoning, fining, etc.,] when considered in themselves, without regard to the Constitution, scarcely deserve the name nor were they either burdensome on the people's properties, or anywise shocking to the natural humanity of mankind." During the constant wars, civil and foreign, which prevailed while these two families occupied the throne, it was not difficult to find abundant instances of practices the most despotic, as we are wont to find occurring in times of violence. To make this second epoch support the third, therefore, required but a little garbling of authorities. And it then remained, by a third work, to make of the whole a complete history of England, on the principles on which he had advocated that of the Stuarts. This would comprehend the Saxon and Norman conquests, the former exhibiting the genuine form and political principles of the people constituting the nation, and founded in the rights of man, the latter built on conquest and physical force, not at all affecting moral rights, nor ever assented to by the free will of the vanquished. The battle of Hastings, indeed, was lost, but the natural rights of the nation were not staked on the event of a single battle. Their will to recover the Saxon constitution continued unabated, and was at the bottom of all the unsuccessful insurrections which succeeded in subsequent times. The victors and vanquished continued in a state of living hostility, and the nation may still say, after losing the battle of Hastings,

> What though the field is lost?
> All is not lost; the unconquerable will
> And study of revenge, immortal hate
> And courage never to submit or yield.

The government of a nation may be usurped by the forcible intrusion of an individual into the throne. But to conquer its will, so as to rest the right on that, the only legitimate basis, requires long acquiescence and cessation of all opposition.   The Whig historians of England, therefore, have always gone back to the Saxon period for the true principles of their constitution, while the Tories and Hume, their Coryphaeus, date it from the Norman conquest, and hence conclude that the continual claim by the nation of the good old Saxon laws, and the struggles to recover them, were "encroachments of the people on the crown, and not usurpations of the crown on the people."   Hume, with Brodie, should be the last histories of England to be read.   If first read, Hume makes an English Tory, from whence it is an easy step to American Toryism.   But there is a history, by Baxter, in which, abridging somewhat by leaving out some entire incidents as less interesting now than when Hume wrote, he has given the rest in the identical words of Hume, except that when he comes to a fact falsified, he states it truly, and when to a suppression of truth, he supplies it, never otherwise changing a word.   It is, in fact, an editic expurgation of Hume.   Those who shrink from the volume of Rapin, may read this first and from this lay a first foundation in a basis of truth.

For a modern continental history, a very general idea may be first aimed at, leaving for future and occasional reading the particular histories of such countries as may excite curiosity at the time.   This may be obtained from Mollet's Northern Antiquities, Vol. Esprit et Moeurs des Nations, Millot's Modern History, Russel's Modern Europe, Hallam's Middle Ages, and Robertson's Charles V.

APPENDIX Q

JEFFERSON'S MOTIVES

The sincerity of Jefferson's motives has frequently been attacked. The following extracts from letters to Cabell, written as an octogenarian in the intimacy of friendly correspondence are significant.

(*Cabell*, 331–2; 365–7.)

Monticello, January 11, 1825.

* * * * * * * * *

In your letter of December 31, you say my hand-writing and my letters have great effect there, i.e., at Richmond. I am sensible, my dear sir, of the kindness with which this encouragement is held up to me; but my views of their effect are very different. When I retired from the administration of public affairs, I thought I saw some evidence that I retired with a good degree of public favor, and that my conduct in office had been considered, by the one party at least, with approbation, and with acquiescence by the other. But the attempt in which I have embarked so earnestly to procure an improvement in the moral condition of my native State, although perhaps in other States it may have strengthened good dispositions, it has assuredly weakened them within our own. The attempt ran foul of so many local interests, of so many personal views, and so much ignorance, and I have been considered as so particularly its promoter, that I see evidently a great change of sentiment towards myself. I cannot doubt its having dissatisfied with myself a respectable minority, if not a majority of the House of Delegates. I feel it deeply and very discouragingly, yet I shall not give way. I have ever found in my progress through life, that, acting for the public, if we do always what is right, the approbation denied in the beginning will surely follow us in the end. It is from posterity, we are to expect remuneration for the sacrifice we are making for their service, of time, quiet, and good will. And I fear not the appeal. The multitude of fine young men whom we shall redeem from ignorance, who will feel that they owe to us the elevation of mind, of character, and station, they shall be able to attain from the result of our efforts, will ensure us their remembering us with gratitude. We will not then "be weary in well doing." *Usque ad aras amicus tuus.*

TH: JEFFERSON.

Mr. Cabell.

287

Monticello, February 7, 1826.

*   *   *   *   *   *   *   *   *

I have been very much mortified by the publication, in the Enquirer of the 4th, of two letters from some person called an "American Citizen," who seems to have visited Mr. Madison and myself, and has undertaken to state private conversations with us.   In one of these he makes me declare that I had intentionally proceeded in a course of dupery of our Legislature, teasing them, as he makes me say, for six or seven sessions, for successive aids to the University, and asking a part only at a time, and intentionally concealing the ultimate cost, and gives an inexact statement of a story of Obrian.   Now, our annual reports will shew that we constantly gave full and candid accounts of the money expended, and statements of what might still be wanting, founded on the Proctor's estimates.   No man ever heard me speak of the grants of the Legislature, but with acknowledgments of their liberality, which I have always declared had gone far beyond what I could have expected in the beginning.   Yet the letter-writer has given to my expressions an aspect disrespectful of the Legislature, and calculated to give them offence, which I do absolutely disavow.   The writer is called an American Citizen.   It is evident, if he be so, that he is an adopted one only, who, after calling on us in his travels through the country, as a stranger, may have obtained naturalization and settled in Philadelphia, where he is enjoying the society of the Bonapartes, &c.   The familiar style of his letter to his friend in England, and the communication of it to the Literary Gazette there, indicate sufficiently his foreign birth and connections.   I can not express to you the pain which this unfaithful version and betrayment of private conversation has given me.   I feel that it will add to the disfavor I had incurred with a large portion of the Legislature by my strenuous labors for the establishment of the University, to which they were opposed, insomuch as to let it overweigh whatever of satisfaction former services had given them.   I have been long sensible that while I was endeavoring to render our country the greatest of all services, that of regenerating the public education, and placing our rising generation on the level of our sister States (which they have proudly held heretofore), I was discharging the odious function of a physician pouring medicine down the throat of a patient insensible of needing it.   I am so sure of the future approbation of posterity, and of the inestimable effect we shall have produced in the elevation of our country by what we have done, as that I cannot repent of the part I have borne in co-operation with my colleagues.   I disclaim the honors which this writer (among the other errors he has interlarded with the truths of his letters) has ascribed to me, of having made liberal donations of timber and stone from my own estate, and of having paid all the contracts for materials myself, and I restore them to their true source, the liberal legislators of our country.   My pain at these false praises and representations should merit with them an acquittal of any supposed approbation of them by myself.

Ever and affectionately yours,

TH: JEFFERSON.

BIBLIOGRAPHY

JEFFERSON'S WRITINGS

Adams, James Truslow, Ed.—*Jeffersonian Principles: Extracts from the Writings of Thomas Jefferson,* Boston, Little, Brown, and Co., 1928.

Cabell, Nathaniel Francis, Ed.—*Early History of the University of Virginia as contained in the letters of Thomas Jefferson and Joseph C. Cabell,* Richmond, J. W. Randolph, 1856. (This book does not give the name of the editor, but his identity is well known. It is cited as *Cabell.*)

Chinard, Gilbert, Ed.—*The Commonplace Book of Thomas Jefferson, A Repertory of his Ideas on Government,* Baltimore, The Johns Hopkins Press, 1926.

Chinard, Gilbert—*The Literary Bible of Thomas Jefferson, His Commonplace Book of Philosophers and Poets,* Baltimore, The John Hopkins Press, 1928.

Catalog, Manuscript, Coolidge Collection, Massachusetts Historical Society, dated March 6, 1783. (This book lists a part of the works in Jefferson's second library as well as many that he intended to procure.)

Catalogue of President Jefferson's Library, copied from the manuscript in his handwriting, Washington, Gales and Seaton, 1829. (This book lists the works in Jefferson's third library which were offered for sale after his death.)

Foley, John P., Ed.—*The Jeffersonian Cyclopedia,* New York, Funk & Wagnalls Co., 1900.

Ford, Paul L., Ed.—*The Writings of Thomas Jefferson,* 10 volumes, New York, G. P. Putnam's Sons, 1892–99 (cited as *Ford Ed.*).

Ford, Paul L., Ed.—*The Works of Thomas Jefferson,* Federal Edition, 12 volumes, New York, G. P. Putnam's Sons, 1904 (cited as *Federal Ed.*).

Ford, Paul L., Ed.—*The Autobiography of Thomas Jefferson,* New York, G. P. Putnam's Sons, 1914.

Ford, Worthington, C., Ed.—*Thomas Jefferson Correspondence, printed from the originals in the collection of William K. Bixby,* Boston, 1916.

Lipscomb, Andrew A., Ed.—*The Writings of Thomas Jefferson,* Library Edition, 20 volumes, Washington. The Thomas Jefferson Memorial Association, 1903 (cited as *Library Ed.*).

Malone, Dumas—*Correspondence between Thomas Jefferson and Pierre Samuel du Pont de Nemours,* 1798–1817, Boston, Houghton Mifflin Co., 1930.

Notes on the State of Virginia; Paris, 1784–85.

Randolph, Thomas J., Ed.—*Memoirs, Correspondence, and Miscellanies, from the papers of Thomas Jefferson,* 4 volumes, New York, G. & C. & H. Carvill, 1830 (cited as *Randolph Ed.*).

Richardson, James D., Ed.—*Messages and Papers of the Presidents,* 10 volumes, Washington, Government Printing Office, 1896–99.

University of Virginia, Enactments of the Rector and Visitors, 1825.

Washington, H. A., Ed.—*The Writings of Thomas Jefferson,* 9 volumes, Washington, Taylor & Maury, 1853–54 (cited as *Washington Ed.*).

WORKS LARGELY ABOUT JEFFERSON AND HIS EDUCATIONAL WORK

Adams, Herbert—*Thomas Jefferson and the University of Virginia,* Washington, Government Printing Office, 1888.

Arrowood, Charles F.—*Thomas Jefferson and Education in a Republic,* New York, McGraw-Hill Co., 1930.

Banks, Louis A.—*The Youth of Famous Americans,* 1902.

Barneaud, Charles—*Origines et Progrès de L'Education en Amérique— Jefferson et L'Education en Virginie,* Paris, 1895.

Boutell, Lewis H.—*Thomas Jefferson, Man of Letters,* Chicago, private print, 1891.

Bowers, Claude G.—*Jefferson and Hamilton,* Boston, Houghton Mifflin Co., 1925.

Bruce, Philip A.—*History of the University of Virginia, 1818–1919,* 5 volumes, New York, The Macmillan Co., 1920–21.

Calendar of the Correspondence of Thomas Jefferson, United States Department of State, Bulletin of the Bureau of Rolls and Library, 1894–1903, 2 volumes.

Carter, James C.—*The University of Virginia,* Charlottesville, 1898.

Catchings, Benjamin S.—*Master Thoughts of Thomas Jefferson,* New York, The Nation Press, 1907.

Chinard, Gilbert—*Jefferson et les idéologues d'après sa correspondence inédite avec Destutt de Tracy, Cabanis, J.-B. Say, et Auguste Comte,* Baltimore, The Johns Hopkins Press, 1925.

Chinard, Gilbert—*Thomas Jefferson, the Apostle of Americanism,* Boston, Little, Brown, & Co., 1929.

Culbreth, David M. R.—*The University of Virginia, Memories of Her Student Life and Professors,* New York & Washington, The Neale Publishing Co., 1908.

Curtis, William E.—*The True Thomas Jefferson,* Philadelphia, J. B. Lippincott Co., 1901.

Dabney, Charles W.—*Jefferson the Seer,* 1903.

Fitzhugh, Thomas—*The University of Virginia in Texas and the Southwest.*

Forman, Samuel E.—*The Life and Writings of Thomas Jefferson,* Indianapolis, The Bowen-Merrill Co., 1900.

Griggs, Edward H.—*American Statesmen,* Orchard Hill Press, 1927.

Henderson, John C.—*Thomas Jefferson's Views on Public Education,* New York, G. P. Putnam's Sons, 1890.

Hirst, Francis W.—*Life and Letters of Thomas Jefferson*, New York. The Macmillan Co., 1926.

Johnston, Richard H.—*A Contribution to a Bibliography of Thomas Jefferson, Washington*, 1905. (Published in the Library Edition of Jeferson's Writings, Vol. 20.)

Kimball, Fiske—*Thomas Jefferson, Architect*, Boston, The Riverside Press, 1916.

Lambeth, William A.—*Thomas Jefferson as an Architect*, Boston, Houghton Mifflin Co., 1913.

Linn, William—*The Life of Thomas Jefferson*, Ithaca, Mack & Andrus, 1834.

Manning, Warren H.—*Thomas Jefferson as a Designer of Landscapes*, Boston, Houghton Mifflin Co., 1913.

McKee, George H.—*Th. Jefferson Ami de la Revolution Française*, Lorient, 1928.

Merwin, Henry C.—*Thomas Jefferson*, Boston, Houghton Mifflin Co., 1901.

Minnigerode, Meade—*Jefferson, Friend of France*, New York, G. P. Putnam's Sons, 1928.

Morse, John F., Jr.—*Thomas Jefferson*, Boston, Houghton Mifflin Co., 1883.

Muzzey, David S.—*Thomas Jefferson*, New York, C. Scribner's Sons, 1918.

Nock, Albert J.—*Jefferson*, New York, Harcourt, Brace & Co., 1926.

Patton, John S.—*Jefferson, Cabell and the University of Virginia*, New York & Washington, The Neale Publishing Co., 1906.

Parton, James—*Life of Thomas Jefferson*, Boston, J. R. Osgood & Co., 1874.

Randall, Henry S.—*The Life of Thomas Jefferson*, 3 volumes, New York, Derby & Jackson, 1858.

Reid, Whitelaw—*One Welshman, a Glance at a Great Career*, London, Macmillan & Co., 1912.

Schmucker, Samuel M.—*The Life and Times of Thomas Jefferson*, New York, J. A. Fletcher & Co., 1890.

Schouler, James—*Thomas Jefferson*, New York, Dodd, Mead & Co., 1893.

Tompkins, Hamilton B.—*Bibliotheca Jeffersoniana*, New York, G. P. Putnam's Sons, 1887.

Trent, William P.—*English Culture in Virginia*, Baltimore, The Johns Hopkins Press, 1889.

Trent, William P.—*The Influence of the University of Virginia upon Southern Life and Thought* (Chapter XI in Adams—*Thomas Jefferson and the University of Virginia*) 1888.

Tucker, George—*Life of Thomas Jefferson*, 2 volumes, Philadelphia, Carey, Lea & Blanchard, 1837.

Wayland, John W.—*The Political Opinions of Thomas Jefferson*, New York & Washington, The Neale Publishing Co., 1907.

Watson, Thomas E.—*The Life and Times of Thomas Jefferson*, New York, D. Appleton & Co., 1903.

Wilstach, Paul—*Jefferson and Monticello*, Garden City, Doubleday, Page & Co., 1925.

Woodward, Frank E.—*Reference List of Works Relating to Thomas Jefferson*, Malden, Mass., 1906.

GENERAL WORKS

Adamson, John William, Ed.—*The Educational Writings of John Locke*, London, Edward Arnold, 1912.

American Philosophical Society, Early Proceedings of the, 1744–1838, Philadelphia, 1884.

Barlow, Joel—*Prospectus of a National Institution to be Established in the United States*, 1806.

Bronson, W. C.—*The History of Brown University, 1764-1914.*

Brown University, *Historical Catalogue, 1764–1914.*

Cubberley, Ellwood P.—*Public Education in the United States*, Boston, Houghton Mifflin Co., 1919.

Destutt de Tracy, M. le Comte—*Observations sur Le Système Actuel D'instruction Publique.* Contained in *Élemens D'Idéologie*, Troisième partie, Tome deuxième, De La Logique, Paris, 1825.

Dexter, Edwin G.—*A History of Education in the United States*, New York, The Macmillan Co., 1906.

Dexter, Franklin B.—*Yale Biographies and Annals, 1778–1792.*

DuPont de Nemours—*National Education in the United States of America*, Translated by Bessie Gardner DuPont, Newark, Delaware, University of Delaware Press, 1923.

Eckenrode, H. J.—*The Revolution in Virginia*, Boston, Houghton Mifflin Co., 1916.

Everett, Edward—*Address at Charlestown, August 1, 1826*, Boston, W. L. Lewis.

Frothingham, Paul Revere—*Edward Everett, Orator and Statesman*, Boston, Houghton Mifflin Co., 1925.

Green, Edwin L.—*A History of the University of South Carolina*, Columbia, S. C., The State Co., 1916.

Guild, Reuben A.—*Early History of Brown University*, Providence, Snow & Farnham, 1897.

Hampden-Sidney College, *Board Minutes, 1776–1876.*

Hansen, Allen O.—*Liberalism and American Education in the Eighteenth Century*, New York, The Macmillan Co., 1926.

Harvard College, Laws of, 1820.

Harvard University, *Quinquennial Catalogue, 1636–1925.*

Heatwole, Cornelius J.—*A History of Education in Virginia*, New York, The Macmillan Co., 1926.

Johnston, William Dawson—*History of the Library of Congress*—Washington, Government Printing Office, 1904.

Jullien, M. A.—*Essai Général D'Education Physique, Morale et Intellectuelle*, Seconde edition, Paris, 1835.

Kennedy, John P.—*Memoirs of the Life of William Wirt, Attorney General of the United States*, 2 volumes, Philadelphia, Lea & Blanchard, 1849.

Knox, Samuel—*An Essay on the Best System of Liberal Education, Adapted to the genius of the Government of the United States,* Baltimore, 1799.

La Borde, M.—*History of the South Carolina College*—Columbia, S. C., Peter B. Glass, 1859.

Maddox, William A.—*The Free School Idea in Virginia before the Civil War,* New York, Teachers College, Columbia University, 1918.

Madison, James—*The Writings of James Madison,* edited by Gaillard Hunt, 9 volumes, New York, G. P. Putnam's Sons, 1900–10.

Malone, Dumas—*The Public Life of Thomas Cooper, 1783–1839,* New Haven, Yale University Press, 1926.

Maury, Dabney H.—*Young People's History of Virginia and Virginians,* Richmond, 1904.

Monroe, Paul,—*Cyclopedia of Education,* 3 volumes, New York, The Macmillan Co., 1925.

Morrison, Alfred J.—*The Beginnings of Public Education in Virginia, 1776–1860,* Richmond, D. Bottom, 1917.

Ogilvie, James,—*Cursory Reflexions on Government, Philosophy, and Education,* Alexandria, J. & J. D. Westcott, 1802.

Page, Thomas Nelson—*The Old Dominion: Her Making and Her Manners,* New York, C. Scribner's Sons, 1914.

Priestley, Joseph—*Lectures on History and General Policy, to which is prefixed An Essay on a course of Liberal Education for civil and active Life,* 2 volumes, London, 1793.

Priestley, Joseph—*Miscellaneous Observations relating to education, more especially as it respects the conduct of the Mind. To which is added, an Essay on a Course of Liberal Education for Civil and Active Life,* Cork, 1780.

Priestley, Joseph—*The Proper Objects of Education in the present State of the World,* second edition, London, 1791.

Reisner, Edward H.—*Nationalism and Education since 1789,* New York. The Macmillan Co., 1922.

Robinson, Morgan P.—*Virginia Counties,* Bulletin of the Virginia State Library, 1916.

Rollin, Charles—*The Methods of Teaching and Studying the Belles Lettres,* 4 volumes. London, second edition, 1737.

Russel, Michael—*View of the System of Education at present pursued in the Schools and Universities of Scotland,* Edinburgh, J. Moir, 1813.

Smith, Francis H.—*Schools and School Masters of Virginia in Olden Times,* 1878.

Smith, Samuel Harrison—*Remarks on Education, Illustrating the close connection between Virtue and Wisdom. To which is annexed a system of Liberal Education,* Philadelphia, John Ormrod, 1798.

Steiner, Bernard C.—*Rev. Samuel Knox,* from the Report of the Commissioner of Education for the year 1898–99, volume I, Washington, Government Printing Office, 1909.

Ticknor, George, Life, Letters, and Journals of, 2 volumes, Boston, Houghton Mifflin Co., 1909.

Todd, Charles Burr—*Life and Letters of Joel Barlow,* New York, G. P. Putnam's Sons, 1886.

Tyler, Lyon G.—*A Few Facts from the Records of William and Mary College,* American Historical Association Papers, 1890.

Washington, George—*The Writings of George Washington,* edited by Worthington C. Ford, 14 volumes, New York, G. P. Putnam's Sons, 1889–93.

William and Mary, A History of the College of, 1660–1874, Richmond, J. W. Randolph & English, 1874.

PERIODICALS

Allen, E. A.—"Thomas Jefferson and the Study of English," *Academy* (Syracuse), IV, 1–10, 1889.

Arnett, Frank S.—"College Days of the Presidents," *Munsey,* XXVI, 670–671, 1902.

Baird, William—"The University of Virginia," *Educational Review,* December, 1896, 417–434.

Barnard, Henry, Ed.—*The American Journal of Education*—
Jefferson:
"Intellectual Capabilities of the Negro," XIX, 297.
"Memoir and Educational Views," XXVII, 513.
"Proposes a National University," XXII, 45.
Virginia:
"Constitutional and Statutory Provision for Education," XVII, 94; XXIV, 324, 722.
"Early Educational Movements," XXVII, 33.
"Field Schools," 1800, XIII, 748.
"Condition of Educational Institutions," 1796, XXIV, 152, 1806, 162.
"University of Virginia," XXVII, 332, 539.

Barnard, Henry, Ed.—*The American Journal of Education, International Series*—
Jefferson:
"Educational Views," XVII, 23; XIX, 900.
Virginia:
"Schools as they Were," XIII, 872.
"Early Free Schools and Colleges," XXIV, 843.
"Elementary Schools," XVII, 31; XXIV, 843.

Education—"Virginia a Leader in Southern Education," XX, 372.

Educational Review—"The University of Virginia and Thomas Jefferson its Founder," XII, 417–419.

Garnett, James M.—"The Elective System of the University of Virginia," *Andover Review,* April, 1886.

Jefferson, Thomas—"Letter on Education," *Niles Register,* XIV, 173; "Life and Character of," *Edinburgh Review,* LI, 496, LXVI, 156.

Kean, R. G.—"Thomas Jefferson as a Legislator," *Virginia Law Journal,* December, 1887.

Kent, C. W.—"Thomas Jefferson's University," *Review of Reviews,* XXXI, 452–459, April, 1905.

Kimball, F.—"Thomas Jefferson and the Origins of the Classical Revival in America," *Art and Archaeology,* I, 219–227, May, 1915.

Knight, Edgard W.—"The Evolution of Education in Virginia," *Sewanee Review,* January, 1916.

Mabie, Hamilton W.—"Some Famous Schools," *Outlook,* LXV, 785, 1900.

MacDonald, W.—"Thomas Jefferson and the Tax on Knowledge," *Nation,* LXIV, 298.

Magoun, George A.—"The Sources of American Education," *The New Englander,* XXXVI, 445.

Mellon, George F.—"Thomas Jefferson and Higher Education," *New England Magazine,* July, 1902.

Nason, Charles W.—"Jefferson and Washington on National Education," *Education,* XIX, 159.

Old Dominion Magazine—"Historical Sketches of Virginia, Literary Institutions of the State," March 15, 1870, June 15, 1871.

Page, Thomas N.—"Jefferson and the University of Virginia," 198–234.

Parton, James—"College Days of Thomas Jefferson," *Atlantic,* XXIX, 16.

Parton, James—"Thomas Jefferson, a Reformer of old Virginia," *Atlantic,* July, 1872.

Powell, E. P.—"Thomas Jefferson on our Education," *New England Magazine,* XIV, 699.

Robinson, Morgan P.—"The Burning of the Rotunda," *University of Virginia Magazine,* October, 1905.

Shepherd, Henry E.—"Thomas Jefferson as a Philologist," *American Journal of Philology,* III, 213–214.

Southern Literary Messenger—
  "On Public Education in Virginia," XIII, 685–689.
  "Free Schools and the University of Virginia, Education a Nation's Defense," XX, 65–75.
  "The Late J. C. Cabell," XXII, 394.

University of Virginia Record, March 15, 1927.

Virginia Magazine of History and Biography, April, 1921.

William and Mary College Quarterly Historical Magazine—
  "Free Schools in Virginia," XVII, 35, 244.